Great American FIGHTER ACES

Dan Bauer

Motorbooks International
Publishers & Wholesalers ®

First published in 1992 by Motorbooks International Publishers & Wholesalers, PO Box 2, 729 Prospect Avenue, Osceola, WI 54020 USA

Motorbooks International is a certified trademark, registered with the United States Patent Office

The information in this book is true and complete to the best of our knowledge. All recommendations are made without any guarantee on the part of the author or Publisher, who also disclaim any liability incurred in connection with the use of this data or specific details

We recognize that some words, model names and designations, for example, mentioned herein are the property of the trademark holder. We use them for identification purposes only. This is not an official publication

Excerpts from *Joe Foss, Flying Marine* by Walter A. Simmons as told by Joseph Foss copyright 1943 by E.P. Dutton; used by permission of the publisher, Dutton, an imprint of New American Library, a division of Penguin Books USA, Inc.

Motorbooks International books are also available at discounts in bulk quantity for industrial or sales-promotional use. For details write to Special Sales Manager at the Publisher's address

Library of Congress Cataloging-in-Publication Data
Bauer, Dan.
    Great American fighter aces / Dan Bauer.
       p.   cm.
    Includes index.
    ISBN 0-87938-585-5
    1. World War, 1939-1945—Aerial operations, American. 2. World War, 1939-1945—Aerial operations, American—Pictorial works. 3. Fighter pilots—United States—Biography. 4. Fighter pilots—United States—Biography—Pictorial works. I. Title.
D790.B37   1992
940.54'4973'0922—dc20   91-48241

On the front cover: *The painting "Lightning Over Leyte" by noted aviation artist Mike Machat, which depicts Col. Charles MacDonald's victory over a Mitsubishi J2M3 Raiden on December 7, 1944. Illustration copyright 1985 Mike Machat.*

On the back cover: *Tom McGuire in front of his P-38 Pudgy. Dennis Glen Cooper*

Printed and bound in the United States of America

Contents

To Charlie "Smokey" Cook,
P-40 pilot,
74th Fighter Squadron,
23rd Fighter Group,
Fourteenth Air Force,
China,
World War II

Acknowledgments

Any book, like a marriage, is a team effort. So it was with this book. I would like to thank the following for help in its completion. First the great aces themselves who submitted to interviews and frequent requests for pictures: John Alison, 23rd Fighter Group and 1st Air Commandos; Tom Blackburn, VF-17, for a letter and advice which helped me through a personally trying time; Jerry Collinsworth, 31st Fighter Group; Marion Carl, USMC; Perry Dahl, 475th Fighter Group; James Goodson, Eagle Squadron and 4th Fighter Group; David "Tex" Hill, American Volunteer Group and 23rd Fighter Group; James Howard, American Volunteer Group and 354th Fighter Group; Joe Foss, USMC; and Charles MacDonald, 475th Fighter Group.

Also I would like to thank the following World War II veterans who offered taped accounts, pictures and other materials: Bob Scott, 23rd Fighter Group; Dennis Glen Cooper, 475th Fighter Group; John Stewart, 23rd Fighter Group; Sam Palmer, 23rd Fighter Group; Luke Lissick, 23rd Fighter Group; Buster Keeton, American Volunteer Group; Bill Johnson, 1st Air Commandos; Bill "Wilson" Edwards, 4th Fighter Group; Glen Berwin, Fifth Air Force; Wiltz Segura, 23rd Fighter Group; Skip Stanfield, 23rd Fighter Group; R. T. Smith, American Volunteer Group and 1st Air Commandos; John Fawcett, 31st Fighter Group; Pete Madison, 475th Fighter Group; Vermont Garrison, 4th Fighter Group; Walter Eason, 1st Air Commandos; and Dixie Alexander, Eagle Squadron and 4th Fighter Group.

Many thanks to: Michael O'Leary, editor of *Air Classics,* magazine for the inspiration to get started; Roy Thomas, colleague, friend and fellow aviation enthusiast; Jeff and Irv Ethell, for a delightful afternoon in Myrtle Beach, South Carolina, talking about airplanes; Marcelia Helmus, typist extraordinaire; Stan Piet, Baltimore, Maryland, come and visit me again sometime Stan; John Campbell; Herb Steffen, good father and Ninth Air Force veteran; and Mary Cook, of Myrtle Beach, South Carolina.

I would also like to thank Doug Thropp Jr. of the 475th Fighter Group for answering many questions about the last flight of Tom McGuire.

Lastly thanks to Lindsay Bauer, at the time of this writing a freshman at Monroe Senior High School, and Kirby Bauer, a fourth grader at Northside Elementary School. Someone once said to me, "Those children need you!" But like most single parents I found I need them more than they need me.

Chapter 1

The Odyssey of John Alison

John Alison's wartime duty assignments included stops in England, Russia, Iraq, India, Burma, China, New Guinea, the Philippines, Okinawa and Japan. Alison served in China as squadron commander of the 75th Fighter Squadron, 23rd Fighter Group. He is credited with destroying seven Japanese planes in aerial combat. He also served as deputy commander of the 1st Air Commando force, which landed British general Orde Wingate's troops behind Japanese lines in Burma. After the war he followed business interests and also served as assistant secretary of commerce in the Truman administration. Retired with the rank of major general, he settle in Washington, D.C. Unless attributed to another source, all quotes are from an October 1991 interview with General Alison.

It was the winter of 1941 and 2d Lt. John Alison was on duty at Mitchell Field, New York, when the telephone rang and he was ordered to take a P-40 Tomahawk fighter and fly down to Bolling Field in Washington, D.C.

Alison thought the request was a rather strange one, but he promptly obeyed and flew down to Bolling Field, where he reported to the office of the commander.

After entering the office, Alison was introduced to Gen. Claire Chennault and several high-ranking officers of the Chinese Air Force and Army. Also present were two representatives of the Curtiss-Wright Aircraft Company: a salesman and a test pilot.

The commander of the base told Alison that he wanted him to demonstrate the capabilities of the P-40 to General Chennault and the Chinese. Alison—still unsure of what he was supposed to do—asked for further instructions.

I said, "Well, what do you want me to do?"

The base commander answered, "Well, demonstrate the airplane."

I said, "You know we have some pretty severe restrictions on aerobatics and flying low."

The base commander then said, "Well, don't break any of the regulations!"

At this point Alison was thoroughly confused. He knew it would be impossible to properly demonstrate the P-40 without breaking the regulation that forbade low aerobatic flying.

A solution to the dilemma was finally worked out, remembered Alison: The commander at Bolling finally said, "Well, you go out and do the best you can."

Chennault and the rest of the party walked out onto the airfield, and Alison climbed up into the P-40 and taxied out to the end of the runway.

Alison, sitting in the P-40 at the end of the runway, was facing into a bitterly cold 20 mph wind. He was soon given the signal to take off and begin his aerial demonstration.

I hadn't had the P-40 refueled so it was light. It had no armored plate or bulletproof tanks. Also, at that time they limited the engine to 980 hp; you weren't supposed to go above a certain redline. I had already found out that the engine would go above that redline and run almost a minute before it would start shaking.

So I headed down into the wind and held the airplane just on the runway and started the gear up. I had it right on 980 hp and then when I got just to the intersection I pushed it up to full power. The Curtiss people told me I was going up between 1,200 and 1,400 hp. I just pulled the airplane up and I did a half-loop right off the runway. Then because the airplane was light I cut back on the throttle and came right down over Chennault and his party and did about three 360s under 100 feet right around them on the ground, pulled the airplane up into a split-S and put it back on the runway. I taxied in and I was out of the airplane and standing in the middle of the hangar as they were walking in. I could see by the smiles of the Curtiss-Wright people that they were happy.

As Chennault approached Alison one of the Chinese generals turned to Chennault and said, "What we need is 100 of these airplanes!"

Chennault looked the general right in the eye, stuck out his chin and said, "No! What you need is 100 of these," as he came over and tapped Alison on the shoulder.

General Chennault was so impressed by Alison's demonstration of the P-40's capabilities that he recorded the incident in his book *Way of a Fighter*, which was published after the war. "Johnny Alison," wrote Chennault, "got more out of that P-40 in his five minute demonstration than anybody I saw before or after."

John Alison was born and educated in Gainesville, Florida. The flying bug struck him at an early age.

Since the time I was in grade school I wanted to be an Army flyer. I remember there was a pilot by the name of Ralph Rudy, a pursuit pilot. He had a brother who lived in Gainesville and he came to visit and he brought a P-1. He put it into a power dive over the city and that airplane just made a beautiful racket, it was shaking the windowpanes. I was in study hall in high school at the time and I heard that wonderful noise and I thought, *One of these days I'm going to do that myself.*

I met Lieutenant Rudy and he said, "Yes, it was a great life." I never saw the P-1, but I decided that was what I wanted to do.

After graduation from high school Alison entered the University of Florida, majoring in engineering. Although he liked the academic life, the lure of flying was strong.

At the end of my second year I wanted to leave college and go to the Army flying school. All you needed at that time was two years of college and they would accept you. My mother insisted I stay in school and get my degree, and I'm grateful to her for that.

John Alison, Tex Hill, Ajax Baumler and Mark Mitchell, left to right. Alison and Baumler were participants in the famous July 30, 1942, night interception of Japanese bombers over Hengyang.

After shooting down two bombers Alison had to make a forced landing at night in the Siang Kiang River. Smithsonian Institution

Alison received his bachelor of science degree in engineering from the University of Florida in 1936. He joined the US Army Air Corps (USAAC) the same year and was assigned to Kelly Field, Texas. He recalled with fondness his early days at Kelly:

I spent one of the most delightful and exciting years of my life; going through flying school was just a great experience.

When we went through flying school at that time I was one of the fortunate ones. I had excellent instruction. I had over 300 hours in the flying school and we flew all types of airplanes: bombers, attack airplanes, observation airplanes.

I think I had over 20 hours in the B-2 or B-3 bomber—it was the old Keystone. It was an amazing flying machine, a bamboo giant. It was a great big biplane with twin engines suspended between the wings and a cockpit bigger than a couple of bathtubs. We took one or two flights with an instructor and then we flew them by ourselves. It was a great thrill to be up there, all by myself.

After receiving his commission at Kelly Field in 1937, Alison was assigned to the 8th Pursuit Group, Langley, Virginia. Alison found the peacetime army very restricted. Budgets were tight and units often had little time for flying or money for new equipment.

As war clouds began to gather on the horizon the USAAC began to expand and Alison found himself in a fortunate position.

I was there ahead of the wave of pilots that came in. All of a sudden I was given responsibilities far beyond my capabilities in training other people.

It was an exciting time. We really started to do some flying. One of the things I loved to do was dogfight. I loved to dogfight in a fighter plane. I've spent a large part of my career going around in circles. I learned how to make the airplane turn as short as possible. You pull it into its maximum and you don't let it skid or slip, because if you do the guy is going to creep up on you from behind.

I learned how to get the maximum performance out of an airplane. I got fairly good at it and there are some people who thought I got quite good at it. I was never quite as good as I'd [have] liked to be.

In the spring of 1941 Alison suddenly found himself assigned to London as assistant military

Lt. Joe Griffin, Lt. Mark Mitchell, Capt. John Hampshire and Capt. Hollis Blackstone, left to right on ground. Maj. Edmund Goss, Lt. Col. John Alison and Lt. Mark Pryor, left to right on plane. This was *the last picture made of Hampshire before his death. At the time Hampshire was the leading ace of the CBI. Fourteenth Air Force Association*

attaché for training with the Royal Air Force (RAF). "I was fortunate," recalled Alison; "I got sent on a great adventure along with Hub Zemke to help the British with lend-lease P-40s."

Alison and Zemke were being sent to Britain to help the RAF operate the P-40. The British had purchased 1,180 P-40s from the United States and had originally intended to use them as fighters against the suspected German invasion of Britain. However, with the increased production and use of the famous Spitfire, they changed their plans and decided to use the P-40 as a ground-support airplane.

At the request of the British, several American specialists were sent to England to advise on aircraft types supplied or purchased under the lend-lease arrangement between the two countries. These specialists, including Alison and Zemke, were known as observers. A secondary purpose of their visit was to acquaint themselves with RAF equipment and procedures and to learn as much as they could about German planes and operations.

Alison and Zemke were first sent to Washington for a briefing by Lt. Col. Pete Quesada. While in the capital they were advised that although they could take any opportunities offered to fly British aircraft, they must not participate in any combat missions against the Germans, as the United States was still a neutral nation.

Upon arrival in England Alison and Zemke were soon aware that a war was on. Zemke recalled their first night in London in his book, coauthored by Roger Freeman, *Zemke's Wolf Pack*:

On reaching London we were picked up by an embassy car, and on our journey through the streets to the Dorchester Hotel we saw plenty of evidence of the blitz: buildings reduced to rubble by the bombing. That night we were made well aware that we were in a combat area. In contrast to the lights of New York and Lisbon, London was blacker than black after dark. During the evening, the sirens began to wail. Innocents that we were, Johnny and I went up to the roof of the hotel to see what we could of any action. Searchlights were sweeping back and forth, and as the German bombers arrived . . . the antiaircraft batteries in Hyde Park, opposite the hotel, began to fire. We were excitedly taking in our first view of a war when there was a sudden "clunk" on the roof beside us, then another. It didn't take many seconds to realize that shell fragments were falling around about and here we were chancing our

The famous shark-nosed P-40, the workhorse of the air war in China. "We had a steady airplane in the P-40," remarked John Alison. "We had better arma- *ment and we had an instructor in General Chennault who knew how to take advantage of the P-40's strength." Fourteenth Air Force Association*

bare heads. A hasty retreat was made back into the hotel.

Once beginning his job in England, Alison had many opportunities to fly British combat aircraft, including both the Hurricane and the Spitfire. On one occasion, while visiting a British air base, he was challenged to a dogfight by an RAF ace. Alison was quick to accept the challenge.

He had a Hurricane; fortunately it was one of the eight-gun Hurricanes. The eight-gun Hurricane and the P-40 were just about equal. I not only held my own against this British ace (I think he had twenty-one victories), I was able to get on his tail and he was quite surprised. But I was fighting where he was at a disadvantage, at 3,000 feet. We fought at this altitude so the group below could see us.

The P-40 was a low-altitude airplane. The Hurricane was a high-altitude airplane to get the German bombers, so it did not perform well at low altitudes. At a higher altitude I'm sure he would have been able to take me easily.

He landed and came up to me and said, "I thought you Yanks were just all mouth." Then he added, "You did very well."

One day in July 1941 Alison was visiting one of the Eagle squadrons and was suddenly called to the phone. He was told to report immediately to the American Embassy in London and that he would find out what was going on when he got there.

Upon arriving at the lobby of the US Embassy Alison found Zemke also waiting. Eventually they were ushered in to see the US ambassador, John Wyant. Waiting with Wyant were President Franklin D. Roosevelt's roving ambassador-at-large, Harry Hopkins, Averill Harriman and Brig. Gen. Joe McNarney. Alison and Zemke learned, to their astonishment, that they were being sent to Russia.

In 1941 the British had offered 200 P-40s to the Russians, who were reeling under the impact of the German invasion. Alison and Zemke were to oversee the planes' reassembly, test fly them and instruct Soviet pilots in their use. Alison was to accompany Hopkins and Harriman's party, which was flying to Moscow immediately; Zemke was to follow by sea.

That night Alison, Hopkins, McNarney and others of the party boarded a five-car passenger train that was proceeding nonstop to northern

Gun camera film showing hits on a parked Japanese plane at an air base in China. On one strafing mission John Alison was fortunate to come home, *when five Zeros flying above his strafing P-40 for some reason failed to attack. Luke Kissick*

11

Scotland. Hopkins was known as a man who liked to have a drink on occasion, recalled Alison:

When we got on the train before 11:00 P.M., Hopkins said, "Let's have a nightcap." We were in the lounge car and the bartender came up and said, "What will it be?" Both General McNarney and Hopkins ordered a nightcap. Hopkins drank bourbon and he said, "Alison, what will you have?" I said, "Thank you, sir, but I don't drink."

He smiled and the bartender brought me a lemon squash. We had one drink and went to bed. Then the next day before dinner he said, "Come on, let's have an appetizer." I once again said, "I don't drink."

Hopkins looked over at me and said laughingly, "I don't care whether you do or not. Please just don't look so damn superior!"

From Invergordon, Scotland, the party flew by PBY Catalina to Archangel where they were met by representatives of the Soviet armed forces and American and British embassies.

That night Alison, Hopkins and others of the party were invited to dinner aboard the yacht of a Russian admiral. This was Alison's first experience with the hospitality shown by Soviet officials to visiting dignitaries.

They had placed five glasses at each place setting. They had a short glass for vodka and right up the line to a tulip glass for champagne.

They started with vodka. They toasted Stalin, Roosevelt, Churchill. Finally I think they were toasting the sea gulls.

Then this big Russian general who was sitting across the table stood up and said, "I want to propose a toast to the young American flyer who has come so far from his home to help in our struggle against a common enemy."

He stood up, he was a big man, and he picked up a short glass of vodka and downed it in one gulp. I stood up and drank my vodka in one gulp. It was the first drink of hard liquor ever in my life.

It didn't go down quite so easy, [but] fortunately it was good vodka, and I sat down, but for just a moment I had to put my napkin over my face to regain my composure. When I looked out from under the napkin, Mr. Hopkins was sitting across from me and he looked me right in the eye with a twinkle and said, "Oh, Alison, that shows a definite lack of character."

After going to Moscow with Hopkins, Alison returned to Archangel, where he met Zemke. There the two men helped the Russians assemble and test the newly arrived P-40s. They test flew all forty-eight of the P-40s before turning them over to the Russians. They were disappointed that the Russians would not let them test fly any of their combat aircraft.

In December Alison and Zemke were called to the US Embassy in Moscow. The Germans were at the gates of Moscow and the two flyers could hear the rumble of heavy artillery fire in the distance. Rather at loose ends, with little now to do, they were in Kuybyshev when they learned early on the morning of December 7 that the Japanese had attacked Pearl Harbor. "The United States was at war," recalled Zemke in *Zemke's Wolf Pack*, "and here were two fighter pilots far away from the action. Both of us immediately put in requests for transfer."

Zemke was soon ordered to report to the 56th Field Group at Charlotte, North Carolina. After a long delay fighting red tape Alison found himself in Tehran, Iran.

From Tehran Alison proceeded to Basra, Iraq, to join an American engineering detachment that was helping to build a railroad into Russia that would carry lend-lease supplies to the Russians. While he was in Basra lend-lease B-25 Mitchell and A-20 Havoc bombers started arriving from the United States. Alison talked a retired Pan Am captain who was flying one of the B-25s into giving him a check ride in the twin-engine bomber. "He made three landings, I made three, and he said, 'Now you know all about the airplane.'"

Col. Philip Cochran, left, and Col. John Alison, right, at Hailakandi, India, in February 1944. As no table of organization existed for the air commando units, Cochran and Alison developed their own. 1st Air Commando Association

Alison stayed in Basra for five months delivering B-25s and A-20s to the Russians. Eager to get into combat, he applied repeatedly for a transfer to a fighter group. He was beginning to give up hope of ever leaving Iraq when one day he received a wire from Gen. Henry Harley "Hap" Arnold, chief of the US Army Air Forces (USAAF), ordering him to report to China.

After arriving in India Alison flew a P-40 across the Burma Hump into China with two flights of the 16th Fighter Squadron. For several weeks after his arrival in China he stayed with the 16th Fighter Squadron, until General Chennault attached him to the 75th FS to serve as David "Tex" Hill's deputy.

Hill recalled his first meeting with Alison:

The first time I met him was at a little base called Lingling. He had a little musette bag and I said, "What are you doing here?"
He said, "I came to fight!"
I said, "Boy you came to the right place."

The 23rd Fighter Group historian, in *A Brief History of the 23rd Fighter Group, 1941-1955*, of-fered this capsule description of Alison at the time of his arrival in China:

Major Alison towers every bit of 5 feet 5½ inches into the air, looking more like an office boy than one of the finest pilots in the China theater. Continually in need of a haircut despite the thin [spot] on the top of his head, he is a quiet, easygoing, efficient man, who carries in his mind an absolute dislike for any man who prevents his squadron from fighting.

One of Alison's first encounters with the Japanese in China took place on August 5, 1942. During this engagement, eight P-40s of the 75th FS encountered a force of Japanese fighters over Hengyang at 0645 hours.

"The Japs," wrote the group historian, "came back over Hengyang using their celebrated 'flying circus tactics.'" In this rather unorthodox arrangement the Japanese fighters used a circling and weaving formation that moved slowly forward looking for combat. "Each plane in the formation rolls, spins, loops, does Immelmann turns and other man[eu]vers. It is a very difficult formation to

A group of C-47 pilots of the original 1st Air Commando Group at Lalaghat, India, in March 1944. The wartime career of Bill Johnson—middle row, third from right—was probably typical of this group. Johnson served as a C-47 pilot and flew 1,700 *hours and 184 combat missions over Burma and China in support of Gen. Orde Wingate's forces and the British Fourteenth Army. 1st Air Commando Association*

Orde Wingate, left, and Phil Cochran, right. "Wingate," wrote Shelford Bidwell, "was one of those nonconformists and Mavericks, who occasionally appears in the ranks of the highly authoritarian British Army." 1st Air Commando Association

attack, but the flexibility necessary for offensive tactics is limited."

To counter this circling strategy Alison led his formation above the Japanese and made two attacks from above, five planes in the first wave and three planes in the second. The group historian described the attack:

Diving out of the sun, the first attack passed through the enemy top cover at 17,000 feet and came out at the bottom, 5,000 feet lower down.

Each of the planes in this attack was followed by each Jap fighter for a short distance. In fact, our planes were running a gauntlet of fire from the Jap planes from all sides.

While attacking the Japanese formation the P-40 flown by Lt. Lee Minor was shot down from directly astern by a Japanese fighter. Minor's P-40 caught fire and exploded in the air.

Alison and Lt. Lauren Barneby each shot down one Japanese fighter during the attack. Two other American P-40s were forced down, but ground crews were able to repair both planes.

During the air battle, several Japanese planes broke through to strafe the airfield. One was hit and exploded in flames only 100 yards from the gun crew that brought it down.

Later in the day John Alison, Col. Robert Lee Scott, Ajax Baumler and Jack Belden, of *Life* magazine, drove out along a Chinese highway, hoping by some fluke that Lieutenant Minor had been able to bail out. Several miles down the road they observed four Chinese coolies walking toward a village carrying an object lashed to poles. "The thing they were carrying," wrote Colonel Scott in *God Is My Co-Pilot*, "was wrapped in grass matting but I saw the bare feet sticking out." Stopping the jeep and calling to the coolies, they took the cover from the face. "It was Lt. Minor and of course he was dead. He had definitely not crashed with the ship for there was hardly a mark on his body."

They took Minor's body to the Catholic mission across the river and made a coffin out of wood about 6 inches thick. "Then we filled the casket with quicklime," wrote Scott, "sealed it upon our brother officer, covered it with ten layers of heavy bricks to protect it from robbers and rats and left it there."

When each new pilot reported for duty with the 75th FS, Alison personally took him up and tested his skill in formation flying and individual combat. On one such training flight Alison was scheduled to fly with the newly arrived Dallas Clinger from Wyoming. Scott, in his wartime book *God Is My Co-Pilot*, wrote about the resulting training flight:

[Alison] took Clinger up and they practiced attacking one another. . . . Up there at nearly 20,000 feet they came at one another head-on, time after time, until the moment when, as Johnny told me later, he was sure Clinger was going to run into him. Alison, who usually forced others to give way, had to dive under Clinger's P-40. They circled it and tried again, and again Clinger kept right on coming until as the ships drew together at well over 600 miles an hour relative speed, once more Johnny had to dodge, and the wild man from Wyoming went on over his head.

They landed then, and by the time Johnny had climbed out of his ship he had calmed down. Clinger came nonchalantly over. Just in passing Alison said, "That was pretty good flying, Clinger; you fly formation well and you look around okay. But you want to watch those head on runs, you nearly hit me up there. Did you know that?"

Clinger shifted the weight of his body back to both feet. With his chin out, he answered: "Yes, sir, Major—I tried to. You see, you've been flying longer than I have and I know I'm not as good a pilot as you are. But, sir, I knew I'd come closer to you than you would to me."

14

On November 27, 1942, the largest American aerial formation ever assembled in China attacked Japanese targets in the Canton area. Fourteen bombers and twenty-two P-40s made up the American attack force.

The Japanese sent up more than forty-five fighters to resist the attack and as a result a series of vicious dogfights occurred all over the Canton area. During one of these battles, a Japanese fighter positioned itself on Alison's tail. John Hampshire, one of the 75th FS's best pilots, came to Alison's rescue, shooting the Japanese fighter down in flames with a brief burst.

It was an extremely successful mission for the Americans, as they shot down twenty-two enemy planes without suffering any losses. Alison flew back over Canton Harbor after the attack and was able to confirm that the bombers had been able to sink two Japanese freighters carrying replacement Zeros.

In May 1943 Capt. John Hampshire was shot down and killed during an engagement near Hankow. Alison wrote about Hampshire's last mission in a 1964 article in *Air Force* magazine:

> About 100 miles north of our airfield we encountered a thunderstorm and let down to about 500 feet to pass underneath it. I saw three Zeros hugging the earth ahead and making for home. As we bored in, Hampshire went underneath and pulled up in front of one while I was firing, and we both missed the enemy leader. But his two wingmen, who were tucked in tight, hit the ground simultaneously. It was a spectacular start, and I'd been so intent on the three sitting ducks that I'd missed seeing a larger formation of Japanese above us. They attacked, and there was adequate confusion until it was over a few short minutes later—six Zeros were down, and we formed up again to return to base.
>
> When we counted noses Hampshire was missing.

When Alison landed, he received a wire that Hampshire was hit in the stomach and needed medical help quickly. Ray Spritzler, a flight surgeon, volunteered to go to Hampshire's aid. Dr. Spritzer was stuffed in the baggage compartment of a P-40 piloted by Lt. Joe Griffin. The plan was for the good doctor to parachute out near where Hampshire went down.

Only after Griffin and Spritzler took off did Alison have second thoughts about the plan. He spent many anxious hours waiting for them to return.

Griffin and Spritzler were caught in a chain of vast electrical storms and their radio went dead. Lost and almost out of gas in the furious storm, Griffin luckily saw a dim light below that looked as if someone had set fire to a field. Flying lower, Spritzler was able to set down the P-40, aided by thoughtful Chinese peasants who had heard the plane, opened a drum of gasoline and rolled it down the field, and then set fire to the fuel spilled from it.

Phil Cochran, an excellent fighter pilot and inspirational leader, served as the model for the character of Flip Corkin in Milton Caniff's Terry and the Pirates *comic strip.* 1st Air Commando Association

Next morning they managed to make it back to base, where they found that Hampshire had died of his wounds on the way to the hospital in Changsha.

In a 1964 *Air Force* magazine article, Alison wrote:

> Looking back I can distinguish between the foolish and the brave. . . . I remember John Hampshire for the brave and wonderful man he was. I remember the doctor who was perhaps even braver in a different way, and how Joe Griffin and the doctor made futile plans to help a good friend who was beyond help.

One day in 1943 Chennault sent Alison to a base near Chungking accompanied by Lt. Charlie Tucker and Lt. Don Brookfield to help newly trained Chinese pilots who had just returned from pilot training in the United States. Alison's mission was to acquaint the Chinese with the P-40 and tactics that could be used against the Japanese in combat.

The day after the Americans arrived, they were prepared to escort nine B-24 Liberator bombers from the 300th Bomb Group to attack a Japanese air base near Hankow. Since the three Americans spoke little or no Chinese and the Chinese pilots spoke little English, the Chinese agreed to watch Alison and stay with the bombers until he dove to the attack.

Brookfield had to abort the mission, so Alison and Tucker flew the lead for seven of the Chinese pilots accompanying them. The fighters managed to rendezvous with the B-24s and then flew toward the target at 15,000 feet.

Arriving over the target, Alison found cloud cover at 9,000 feet obscuring the view. He radioed the bomber commander, Maj. Bruce Beat, and told him to stay up high while he dove down to see if the formation could fly underneath the clouds.

Alison put his P-40 into a dive, looked back and was startled to see nine B-24s and eight P-40s behind him. He quickly radioed back the command to stay high while he dove alone to look the situation over.

Alison and his wingman dove down toward the clouds at 9,000 feet. Suddenly through the clouds numerous Japanese fighters began to appear. "It looked," recalled Alison, as if "somebody had thrown pepper in the air as the Japanese fighters began to break through the overcast and climb toward the bombers."

As Alison put his P-40 into a climbing turn he observed at least a dozen Zeros ahead of him and more behind and below. Maneuvering behind one of

Bob Fiske, an L-5 pilot, in Burma. The L-5 sentinel was used to evacuate wounded and provide liaison and transport of light supplies between India and the forward lines. 1st Air Commando Association

the Zeros, he fired a burst, his incendiaries raking the Japanese fighter in the cockpit. The badly damaged Zero plunged straight down into the clouds.

As Alison drew close to the bombers he knew he would have to act quickly to divert the incoming Japanese fighter attack.

I saw three Japanese fighters flying in a V-formation coming in toward the bombers. I knew I probably couldn't hit them, but I threw my airplane up into a stall and fired my guns at them, hoping to divert the attack.

I had seen another Japanese plane below me and off to one side. I could see he was climbing toward me, but I thought he'd never get to me in time. However, he was either a very good shot or lucky. He fired a burst, hitting me in the main hinge of my rudder, and the rudder came off and I had to quickly reduce speed because the airplane was shaking— shaking itself to pieces and I had to fly straight.

The Japanese pilot maneuvered behind Alison at almost pointblank range and began firing. Alison was, needless to say, in a bad tactical situation.

He was 100 to 200 feet behind me, just eating me up!

My wingman had lost me and I'm screaming for help and the Chinese didn't speak much English and I couldn't speak Chinese.

My wingman, Charlie Tucker, kept radioing, "Where are you?"

I said, "Charlie, I'm going down! There's a Japanese on my tail and he's shooting the hell out of me."

Suddenly a stream of tracer fire flashed past Alison's P-40. "Oh, Lord," he thought, "one of the Chinese pilots is behind the Japanese pilot and he is going to kill us both." The Zero, hit and smoking, dropped straight down. Alison's rescuer was Captain Tsang, one of the new Chinese pilots. With Tsang flying above him Alison was able to pilot his badly damaged plane into the clouds and safety.

Flying was difficult but Alison was able to nurse the P-40 back to a little grass strip in Chinese territory. The landing wasn't picture perfect, but Alison somehow managed it.

All three of my gas tanks were punctured, and one armored piercing bullet was in the armored plate between my shoulder blades.

I got it on the ground and I think I would have been able to land except my tires were shot out. So the airplane skidded along on the rims and finally ended up on its nose.

When I got out of my plane, standing on the ground looking at me was Capt. Eddie Rickenbacker, who was on an inspection trip.

I looked at him and recognizing him went over and said, "Captain Eddie, you're very experienced at this and of course you recognized immediately that that's not the way to do it." He laughed and shook my hand.

I never saw the airplane again. There were four machine gun holes right down the rudder post. The airplane was riddled.

Even though his plane was a total loss, Alison knew he owed his life to the rugged construction of the P-40. Also, the firepower of the Japanese planes was rather weak compared with that supplied by the armament carried in the P-40 and other Allied fighters, which often made the difference in air-to-air combat, recalled Alison:

Our big advantage was our guns. The six .50 caliber machine guns we had in American aircraft in World War II were probably the best aerial guns in the entire war.

The Zero had only one 20 mm cannon, so the chances of getting hit were reduced. Also the 20 mm cannon would shoot far enough, but the rate of fire was slower.

Our guns in comparison to the Japanese guns had higher muzzle velocity and a higher rate of fire.

When the Japanese hit us they had a hard time bringing us down. When we hit them they usually disintegrated.

Receiving orders to return to the United States, in 1943 Alison boarded a C-47 and flew back to Kunming, China. There he would await a transport flight back to India.

While waiting, Alison had little to do but lounge around the air operations office listening to the Chinese warning net track the Japanese air traffic over China. One day the warning net reported a possible Japanese attack on Kunming. The attack never materialized, and Alison said to a pilot standing next to him, "I don't think the Japanese will attack; they're going to go back and land at Lashio, Burma." This was the Japanese air base closest to China.

Alison took a jeep and drove out to the airfield. Upon arrival he found a P-40 that was gassed up, armed and ready to go. Climbing in, he taxied the P-40 out onto the runway and took off.

Heading west, Alison ran into a flight of four P-40s patroling the Kunming area. Pressing his mike button, he radioed to the flight leader, "I think the Japanese are returning to Lashio, and that's where I'm headed; come and join me."

The flight leader replied, "They couldn't; they were almost out of fuel."

Alison decided to continue toward Lashio on his own, but he soon noticed a P-40 breaking away from the patrol flight and joining up on his wing. Alison tried to contact his new wingman, but his radio was dead. He looked at the pilot of the P-40 but couldn't recognize him because he was a new replacement.

Approaching Lashio at 18,000 feet, Alison saw two Japanese planes preparing to make a landing at the air base far below. Eager to attack so tempting a target, he put his P-40 into a steep dive.

I put the nose of the P-40 over just as hard as I could and came down just as fast as I could. I did a very steep spiral, but I wasn't able to get down before they hit the runway. As I approached firing range I noticed the Japanese planes had turned off the runway onto a clay path.

I picked one out and pulled the trigger at about 3,000 feet in a very steep dive and the Japanese plane just exploded. It was a very beautiful explosion.

My wingman, who was following me, began to fire also, and he started short and he walked his rounds right through the other Japanese plane, but he didn't set it on fire.

Flashing over the target, the two P-40s were now surrounded by a hail of antiaircraft fire. Alison realized he was headed in the wrong direction to return home. Diving to only 50 feet above the ground, he made a sharp 180 degree turn right over the middle of the Japanese air base. Looking back, he was reassured to see his wingman turning to follow although surrounded by antiaircraft fire.

Alison's wingman pulled into formation with him and kept motioning back with his hand. Alison kept shaking his head. "I knew he had missed his airplane and wanted to go back and get it, but the antiaircraft fire was too heavy."

Heading for home, Alison once again observed his wingman excitedly pointing back, but Alison knew they had barely enough fuel to return to Kunming let alone make another attack.

Because of low fuel, Alison was forced to land at an auxiliary base. Taxiing to a stop, he jumped out of his P-40 and walked over to his wingman's plane.

Phil Cochran, pointer in hand, lectures on the Broadway landing strip, in the final briefing. 1st Air Commando Association

17

As I approached his plane, I thought it would be a good opportunity to pass on some of my experience to this new young pilot.

I said, "I'm sorry; I knew you wanted to go back and get that airplane, but it was just too dangerous. There was just too much antiaircraft fire. One of us would have been killed and I certainly didn't want to lose you on this mission."

He looked at me and said, "No, I didn't want to go back."

Puzzled, I asked, "Then what was all the fuss about, why did you keep pointing back?"

He said, "I was pointing at those five Zeros right above us!"

The rather embarrassed Alison withdrew quickly to his quarters and reflected further upon the incident. After some thought he arrived at an explanation of what had probably happened.

The five Zeros above us were waiting to land and in my eagerness to attack I never saw them.

Of course we were right down on the deck and they had every advantage, but I think I know why they didn't attack. Because there they are in the landing pattern at their own base thinking they are secure and here come two P-40s right through them and probably blew up their squadron commander. I'm sure they started looking up, thinking, *Where are the rest of them?*

Alison ended his tour of duty with the Fourteenth Air Force in China with eight aerial victories. Only six Fourteenth Air Force pilots would shoot down more Japanese planes in World War II. For heroic air action one night in initiating a pioneer bomber interception, he was awarded the Distinguished Service Cross.

The 75th FS, which Alison commanded after December 1, 1942, was heavily involved in combat throughout the war in China. During one seven-month period in 1944, pilots of the 75th suffered a seventy-two percent casualty rate. The squadron was also fortunate to have some of the best pilots in the USAAF on duty. Four percent of the 116 officers who served in the 75th went on to become generals. It was a magnificent squadron that was skillfully and bravely led.

After leaving China Alison returned to the United States and found he was assigned to organize and command the 367th Fighter Group at Hamilton Air Force Base (AFB). He was told he would have six months to organize and train the group before it wuld leave for combat duty in England.

Alison threw himself into the myriad duties required of a group commander and felt he had been given a great assignment. After about a month he received a wire from the War Department ordering him to report to General Arnold in Washington, D.C., immediately.

Glider pilots of the 1st Air Commando Group. During the air assault on Burma, the glider pilots had to struggle with bad haze conditions and aircraft *overloaded to 9,000 pounds (technical data limited gross weight with cargo to 7,500 pounds). 1st Air Commando Association*

Rather perplexed, he boarded a plane and flew to Washington. He recalled his first trip to Arnold's office:

> The next morning I went to see Arnold and there in the outer office sat Phil Cochran. I said, "Phil, what are you doing here?" He said, "I don't know. I haven't the slightest idea."

During the interview with Arnold, Alison and Cochran learned that one of the two would be named to head an elite air unit that would help Gen. Orde Wingate of Britain in his campaign to take Burma back from the Japanese. Arnold explained that Wingate wanted the unit to airlift his troops into Burma and help evacuate the wounded. Recalled Alison:

> Arnold told us that we had L-5s with stretchers and we were going to airlift out Wingate's wounded and one of [you] boys have got to do it. Which one will it be?
>
> I said, "General, if all you're going to do is airlift wounded with little airplanes, you don't need me. I've just come from a year of active fighting in China. I'm at the peak of my fighting ability and you have given me a fighter group.
>
> "I'm going to England and I can do a lot more for you there. Besides, I don't want to go to Burma."
>
> Phil, who was seldom thoughtful, said, "General, he doesn't mean it."
>
> Arnold then said, "I wasn't going to tell you this at this time but let me tell you what I really intend to do."
>
> He said, "Wingate has four brigades and to infiltrate them takes six weeks to get into position where they can fight. By that time, many have been killed, wounded or are sick with malaria.
>
> "You know we can move his whole force in just a few hours. I don't want him to walk into Burma. I want to set up an operation that will airlift him over the Japanese and behind their lines.
>
> "I'm going to give you all the equipment necessary to do it."
>
> Arnold then asked, "Now which one of you want to go?"
>
> Phil and I looked at each other and asked, "Can both of us go?"

Arnold quickly agreed and named Cochran and Alison cocommanders. Arnold then ended the interview by saying, "To hell with paper work, go out and fight."

Cochran's fame in the USAAF began even before he went to war, when the cartoonist Milton Caniff, creator of the *Terry and the Pirates* comic strip, modeled one of his characters, Flip Corkin, on him. One advantage that he and Alison would have in their working relationship was that they were personal friends. At one time they had rented a house along with another pilot, John Aiken. People who visited frequently called it the John-Phil-John house. According to Lowell Thomas in his book *Road to Mandalay*, Cochran recalled their days together at Mitchell Field:

> Little John, Crazy John and I ran competitions, each trying to make his squadron the best. We'd have air fights, squadron against squadron, and would fight our heads off all morning. Then, sitting at lunch, we'd fight the battles all over again.

Alison, a teetotaler whose close friends often jokingly called Father Alison, was in many ways almost the opposite of the intense, extroverted, fun-loving Cochran.

The two former P-40 pilots were now faced with a monumental task. Almost from scratch they had to develop a specially trained air commando unit to fly Wingate's jungle troops and their heavy equipment behind the Japanese lines in Burma. No table of organization existed for a unit of this kind, so Cochran and Alison used their imagination to determine structure and personnel requirements. Fortunately, General Arnold had given them the highest-priority orders to gather the necessary people and material.

For the transportation requirements Cochran and Alison decided to use C-47s, gliders and light

Logs and ditches block the clearing at the Piccadilly landing site. After a hasty conference it was decided to land Gen. Orde Wingate's force at the Broadway site. 1st Air Commando Association

cargo airplanes. Later the unit was given fighter planes because Cochran and Alison, being fighter pilots, couldn't visualize a campaign without them. Their biggest problem was selecting the right personnel. "You can't have many men," General Arnold told them, "so you'll have to pick flyers who can do at least four other jobs."

A 1944 *Collier's* magazine article detailed the process Alison and Cochran used to pick their people:

Cochran and Alison sat down in a hotel room in Washington and thought of all the top-notch flyers and mechanics they personally knew. . . .

"I know a hot radioman from the Aleutians. I hear he's back [in] the States, or there's a new chief who used to be in my outfit in Africa that would give his right arm to go on a deal like this."

Someone told them about Jackie Sartz, for instance: On the retreat from Burma in 1942, he had been flying out a cargo plane with a load of bombs, and the fighter cover got separated from him over Lashio, so Jackie, all alone in his undefended plane, flew down Lashio's Main Street, kicking bombs out the door every now and then—practically burned the town out, they said.

Cochran said, "That guy's nuts, that's the kind we [want]. . . ."

They got veterans who had thought they were all through with foreign service, and they got men out of squadrons fighting overseas, and once Cochran sent M.P.'s aboard a train to get a bridegroom who was just setting out on his honeymoon.

Cochran said to them all, "It's going to be a tough deal and there won't be any promotions, but there'll be a lot of fun. What do you say?"

And they all said, "What in the hell are we waiting for?"

The troops that the air commandos would be airlifting behind the enemy lines were known as Wingate's Chindits. These were tough, battle-hardened soldiers who had been extensively trained for jungle warfare. The composition of Wingate's brigade was most unusual. It included Gurkhas; a battalion of Burma Rifles, who were quite familiar with the Burmese jungle; and a battalion of officers and men from the King's Liverpool Regiment, who were intended for less daunting military tasks but by the happenstance of war found themselves in Burma.

Whatever their nationality or background, Wingate's troops were put through rigorous training to prepare them for the hardships of campaigning in the jungle. Christopher Sykes, in *Orde Wingate*, described this training:

The rule was merciless severity throughout: To make men able to bear privation and fatigue up to the very limit of human endurance, and far beyond what men thought they could endure. Wingate followed the wise rule . . . that the best way to learn to combat a human enemy is to take arms against natural forces, and accounts of life in the jungle camp record almost every ordeal under nature except ice and snow. The men had to outdo our earliest ancestors in power of survival; if they collapsed under the stress of heat in long marches they were revived . . . [and] when the monsoon broke they were forced to continue the exercises in mud and incessant rain with no allowance for rising rivers. . . . They had to carry out heavy tasks on light rations; they had to ignore thirst, they had to bear midges and mosquitoes and leeches by will rather than protection; and they were virtually forbidden to go sick.

On Christmas Eve, 1943, Alison arrived in India and flew with Cochran to the Assam region of Northeast India to inspect the two airfields recommended for use, Lalaghat and Hailakandi. Although the airfields needed work, Alison and Cochran decided they were suitable.

Having found a permanent home, the 1st Air Commando Unit, as Alison and Cochran's force was now called, began training for its mission. Joint training drills involving gliders and Wingate's Chindits helped cement the bond between the two units.

In early February 1944 the unit received twelve B-25H Mitchell medium bombers. The B-25H was ideal for close air support, as it was equipped with six .50 caliber machine guns and a 75 mm cannon in the nose. To head the bomber section Cochran acquired Maj. Robert T. Smith, who had shot down eleven Japanese planes while flying with the American Volunteer Group (AVG) in China. "Smith," wrote Cochran, "was so competent that he could plunge into bombardment aviation . . . in a hurry."

A mule balks at his first plane ride. Mules, water and radios were vital to Gen. Orde Wingate's men in the jungle. Because mules tended to bray, a disadvantage in the tropical forest where secrecy and surprise were vital, their vocal cords were severed by surgery. 1st Air Commando Association

As a former fighter pilot, Smith brought a fighter pilot spirit into bombing. "He would handle those B-25s as if they were fighters."

On February 3 the P-51 Mustang fighters and B-25 bombers of the 1st Air Commando Unit began an offensive against Japanese air bases as a prelude to the invasion. On February 12, during a B-25 mission, Major Smith demonstrated how effective the 75 mm cannon in the nose of the B-25 could be when he blew the roof off a huge building. Smith later "sheepishly admitted he was aiming at a railway switch 200 yards in front of the warehouse."

From early February to March 4 the air commandos flew fifty-four fighter-bomber missions against the Japanese. Smith described one of the bomber attacks:

Our cannon and [machine guns] were bore sighted for 1,000 yards, and a typical pass would consist of three cannon rounds at approx[imately] 1,500, 1,000 and 500 yards, interspersed with bursts of [machine gun] fire. . . . Most attacks were made at between 200 and 250 mph air speeds. Now, assuming the air was reasonably calm or only moderately turbulent, most of us could hit a target the size of a one-car garage fifty percent of the time or better with the 75 mm cannon. I know that I, and others in my squadron, scored many direct hits on targets as small as trucks and barracks-type buildings, and accuracy went up accordingly.

The date for Wingate's invasion of Burma was set for March 5, during the first full moon after the monsoon rains. The glider trains were to take off at sundown and make their landings under cover of darkness. The invasion plan called for the landing of eighty gliders loaded with assault troops and equipment on the first night.

Alison and Cochran had planned to fly gliders in the invasion. Alison related the reasoning behind this decision:

Phil and I both had the philosophy that a commander had to lead. I'd never flown a glider. The day before the mission I got them to pull me up two times with an empty glider. I got above the field, cut loose and landed. "Well," I said, "this isn't difficult, this will be easy." Well, I was flying an unloaded glider in the daytime.

Wingate, hearing that both Alison and Cochran were going to fly into Burma in the first wave, considered it military folly to let both of his air commanders lead. He demanded that one stay behind. Cochran tried to convince Alison to stay behind, but Alison convinced Cochran to stay.

The landings were scheduled to take place in two openings deep in the Burmese jungle, evidently old paddy fields now deserted and overgrown with rank elephant grass. Aerial photographs of the sites convinced Alison and Cochran that the landings could be made there. The openings were given the code names Piccadilly and Broadway.

As takeoff time neared, preparations intensified. Bulldozers and machinery were loaded on the blunt-nosed gliders, and gas tanks topped off. Every man of the two combat teams had been briefed to the last detail. All they could do now was wait for the signal to go and sweep out over the 160 miles of jungle into Burma.

Cochrane concluded a last-minute mission briefing by saying, "Nothing you've ever done, nothing you're ever going to do counts now. Only the next few hours. Tonight you are going to find your souls." Unfortunately, in the drama-filled night that lay ahead, many would also be required to lose their life.

Shortly before takeoff Lt. Charles L. Russhon handed Cochran some recently developed photographs he had taken on an aerial recon mission. The photographs showed that Broadway was clear but that Piccadilly was scattered with logs in a somewhat regular pattern. Two days before, Piccadilly had been clear. These logs made the clearing a potential deathtrap for gliders and raised the potential of a Japanese ambush at Broadway.

Cochran and Alison studied the photographs and then went to Wingate. Wingate studied the pictures and wondered whether the Japanese had blocked off one clearing to lure the glider force into the other. Cochran, aware that seven months of

A troop-filled glider is towed into Burma. Ropes, each 300 feet long and ¹¹/₁₅ inch in diameter, with enough nylon for 30,000 pair of hose, were used to tow the gliders. 1st Air Commando Association

planning and hard work would be wasted if the mission was called off, responded to the crisis in typical fashion: "Look, sports," he said jauntily, "some of us were going to Piccadilly, but I've found a better place. We're all going to Broadway."

Lt. Col. James Bellah flew to Broadway in the glider piloted by Alison. In a wartime article in *Reader's Digest* he related his experiences of that memorable flight:

> John Alison came over on the run. . . . He got in; co-pilot [Derek] Tulloch and I climbed aboard and the detachment filed in behind us. Everyone was in full field kit and armed to the teeth with carbines, tommy guns, knives and grenades—a pirate crew, Wingate's army and Cochran's air commandos, in mottled camouflage suits, with broad-brimmed, rakish, paint-dabbed jungle hats, most of them with a growth of rank beard. . . .
>
> The gliders are towed in pairs on long ropes. . . . We came up over the trees fighting for altitude and presently settled into the long, slow grind of wide circling to get height for the mountains ahead. . . .
>
> Soon all we could see was the blue blob of the exhaust from the tow ship's starboard motor. All we could feel was the breathing of tightly packed men and the animal shudder of the glider as it swung into the prop wash and out again, weaving on its long tow rope. . . .
>
> Target in 20 minutes. . . . Bolts clicked sharply as cartridges snapped into chambers. Men got their packs adjusted.
>
> Ahead, the tow ship banked lazily and suddenly John Alison called out, "They've got the smudges lit!" . . . Halfway around in the bank, Alison hit the cut-off at a thousand feet and we were gliding free. Here we go—in complete darkness into a blind clearing at 100 miles an hour, howling down the night wind, deep in enemy territory—with little

Two gliders are towed by a C-47. John Alison, with only one glider flight to his credit, made a successful landing at Broadway during the air attack on Burma. Thirty-four gliders were damaged during the landing and twenty-four men were killed. 1st Air Commando Association

> John Alison fighting the controls and Doc Tulloch calling out altitude and flying speed to him.
>
> . . . We strike the ground and bounce. The skids tear into the dust and suddenly we have stopped. The doors fly open; the security party is off on the run, fanning out toward the jungle that may burst into shattering enemy fire at the next breath.

Other gliders coming in made crash landings, and the invaders suffered more wrecks than had been anticipated. The ground, they later found, was full of deep furrows where teak logs had been dragged in by the natives. As the main wave came in, gliders hit the ruts and crashed. Wrecked gliders littered Broadway. Others gliders coming in crashed into the wrecks.

In the August 26, 1944, issue of *Collier's* magazine, Alison wrote of the hellish scene:

> Before the crews could get out, another would be coming in. We would be trying to get boys out of a glider when another was landing. Getting the wounded out of the wrecks was a terrible job, it was so dark. I saw people nearly run down. If a glider hit a man it would kill him. You'd hear a glider come in whistling in the wind. When you finally saw it, it would be 200 feet away, and you'd start to run.

Swooping down like great silent bats, the gliders continued to pour into Broadway. Every now and then one would crash,

> and you'd hear screams of pain in the night, and the rescue party [would rush] across the field, and the screams [would] choke and cease. It is not a pretty sight, wrote Corey Ford, to watch the surgeons amputate the arm of a sergeant with a Gurkha Kukri [knife] by moonlight.

One of the late-arriving gliders was carrying a bulldozer that was to be used for laying out the flying field. It whistled overhead and hit the ground with a tremendous crash. By some miracle of fate no one aboard was killed when it crashed. The crash was described by Lowell Thomas in *Road to Mandalay.*

> The glider . . . flew too far down the field, cleared the wrecks and hit the trees. . . . The wings had been ripped off, and under the impact the bulldozer had been hurled forward. It pulled the straps that raised the nose of the glider, and up went the nose, cockpit, pilot, co-pilot and all. The two were hoisted suddenly out of the way of the plunging bulldozer, which ran out of the front of the glider and stopped among the trees, little damaged.

Lt. Col. Mike Calvert, one of Wingate's officers, had come to the conclusion that the landing was a failure. He approached Alison and told him that he thought the best thing the landing party could do would be to bring in light planes and evacuate the wounded. The rest of the landing force could walk out. Calvert assured Alison they could get through the jungle on foot and return safely to India.

Alison thought a bit and said, "Let's wait until daylight and see how badly off we really are."

Alison recalled the situation at Broadway at that time:

We had a horrible night, but the next morning the sun was shining, and enough of us were alive.

The commander of the engineering company had been killed in the landing.

I said, "Who is in command now?"

A lieutenant came up and said he'd go out and survey the landing area, which looked terrible, because there were gliders piled up everywhere.

I said, "Can you make an airfield out of this?" He said, "We'll have one ready this afternoon. Will that be all right?"

I said, "Yes, indeed!"

Working hard, the engineers began to construct a long landing strip for big transport planes across the lines of the teak-log furrows. By nightfall they had finished grading and filling a crude runway.

In the afternoon light planes swooped down onto Broadway to evacuate the casualties. One of those killed was a glider pilot named William Ritzinger. Just before takeoff, perhaps sensing his fate, he had thrust a note into the pocket of Taylor, who now found it—a bit of verse that Ritzinger had adapted from Kipling:

We're the prophets of the utterly absurd
Of the patently impossible and vain,
But when the thing that couldn't has occurred
Give us time to catch our breaths
                        AND GO AGAIN.

That night a large force of Chindits and tons of armament, munitions and supplies were flown in by cargo planes of the Air Transport Command. Twelve C-47s landed and disgorged soldiers to defend the landing strip against any Japanese attack. Then night after night the transports flew in, operating on a regular schedule and pouring in troops, armament and ammunition. Overjoyed with the steady stream of reinforcements, Alison remarked, "La Guardia has nothing on us."

On March 24 the Chindit operation suffered a major setback from which it never recovered when General Wingate was killed in a plane crash. Wingate had flown to the front line on March 23 in an L-5 liaison plane to observe operations and discuss strategy with his brigade commander. After the conference he boarded a B-25 at Broadway and headed for his headquarters, at Shylet. On the last leg of the journey the B-25 inexplicably exploded into the side of a hill, killing all aboard.

For Alison, Wingate's death came as a severe shock. He and the British general had become close friends during the operation. A superb pilot, Alison always regretted the circumstances surrounding Wingate's death.

John Alison relaxes after a day's work in the Burma jungle. Alison and Phil Cochran made an effective team. Their leadership did much to ensure the success of the air commando concept. 1st Air Commando Association

On several occasions I went back and picked up Wingate and flew him in, then out again.

When he flew in at night he went in on C-47s; usually in the daytime I flew him in because there were Japanese airplanes around. I usually flew in a B-25; I would then fly him to the battle sites in an L-5.

On this day I was so busy I couldn't fly. So we assigned a very experienced bomber pilot, and he flew him in and flew him out again. Somehow or other the airplane went out of control and dove into a mountain range, about 15 minutes short of home.

We lost Wingate and I have always wondered if I had been flying the airplane if the story would have been different, but I wasn't flying.

After Wingate's death Alison received a call from Cochran advising him to return to India, as he had just received a message from General Arnold. Alison returned promptly and later recalled his meeting with Cochran:

Phil said, "Well now, you have two messages; both are very short."

I opened one and it read, "Report to me without delay—Arnold."

I opened the other and it read, "Report to me without delay—Eisenhower."

Receiving permission from General Arnold to delay two days to visit with General Eisenhower, Alison flew from Burma to London. Once there he met with Eisenhower, who told him, "Alison, we want to talk to you! We're going to invade Europe and we're going to use gliders, and you're going to tell us all you know about them."

Alison then spent the next couple of days conferring with Ninth Air Force officers and others who were interested in glider operations. "I told people the problems we had encountered," remembered Alison, "and what we could have done better."

Returning to the United States, Alison met with Arnold in the Pentagon to discuss the Burma Air Operation.

> Arnold was very enthusiastic. The air commando concept was his idea and we had been a success. We had put Wingate in position behind enemy lines, and everything considered, we had done it very well.

To Alison's surprise Arnold had visions of expanding the air commando concept even further.

> Arnold said to me, "I'm going to organize four more air commando groups and I'm going to give you four combat cargo groups with 100 C-46s each, and we're going to retake Burma from the air."
> I said, "General, but whose troops are you going to use?"
> He said, "We will use British troops."
> I said, "I don't think the British will fight for Burma, but I can't be sure."
> I then told Arnold, "I got this from talking to Wingate, but Phil Cochran is the one closest to the British and he can confirm this."
> Arnold then called Phil back to the United States and had us both in his office.
> Arnold then said to Phil, "Alison tells me the British won't fight."
> Phil said, "John's right, the British are not going to fight."
> Arnold then got us both in his car and drove over to Combined Headquarters to see Sir John Dill, the British representative. Arnold and he were close friends.
> Once there Arnold said to Sir John, "You know, Sir John, I've committed these resources and we can retake Burma from the air, but these boys tell me the British have no plans to fight to retake Burma."
> Sir John looked at Arnold and said, "That's correct."

To Alison, aided by the hindsight of the years, the British decision was the correct one. "The British, I think, were right. Why waste the resources in India and Burma when the war was going to be decided in the Pacific."

After his return to the United States Alison was sent to the Pacific, where he served with the Fifth Air Force during the last year of the war. While with the Fifth Air Force he served as deputy commander of the 300th Bombardment Wing and deputy chief of staff operations in the Philippines, Okinawa and Japan.

After the war Alison left active duty in the USAAF in 1946 to enter the business world. "I liked the Air Force, but because of family reasons I got out."

With Cochran, Alison then spent some time attempting to organize an air cargo line. "We got our airplanes," he remembered, "and then decided not to do it and I then joined the Truman administration as assistant secretary of commerce."

After his service with the Truman administration Alison became president of Transit Van Corporation in Redwood City, California. This, he recalled,

> was a development company which developed an integrated container system to coordinate shipments between railroads, trucks, ships and airplanes. We ran vans on the Southern Pacific and made vans for airplanes and we were maybe twenty years ahead of our time.

During his long and distinguished military and civilian career, Alison, who retired as a major general from the Air Force Reserve in 1971, has ventured over the globe. In 1991 he had the opportunity to reflect on his travels and military service:

> We have an obligation to defend our country and we do it kind of stupidly at times. But World War II was the best from the point of having the country united behind the war effort.
> The thing I regret was that when I went into World [War] II I was a fighter pilot with an engineering education and I really had no understanding of history or of different cultures, the things that would have made this odyssey that I went on far more meaningful.
> When I arrived in Russia I didn't know what nazism or communism were or even why they were fighting.
> There was a lot of naiveté in the young people we sent overseas to fight, but we also had a lot of naive leaders who didn't really understand the problems we were going to face.
> The problem is not really winning a war but what are you going to do after you win it.
> Americans say, "Let's go out and win it and come home!" But the job is not done when you win it.

Alison and Cochran were part of a unique generation. Unlike the Korean and Vietnam wars, World War II saw few exemptions from military service. Everybody who was physically able entered the service.

Young and confident of their abilities, these representatives of America's democratic army were flung to the far corners of the earth, there to perform tasks and labors undreamt of in their youth. "They were," wrote William Manchester in his book *Glory and the Dream,* "perhaps the best prepared generation ever to go to war willingly." They could erect Bailey bridges overnight, build mile-long airstrips on mountainous islands, fly thousand-plane formations and airlift an army into the Burma jungle. America may never see a generation like theirs again.

Chapter 2

Tom Blackburn and the Magnificent Men of Fighting 17

John Thomas Blackburn was born with the Navy in his blood. The son of a US Naval Academy graduate, he graduated from the Naval Academy, Annapolis, Maryland, in 1933. His prewar career focused on learning to fly a Navy fighter in combat. In 1943 he assumed command of Fighting Squadron 17. He molded this squadron into one that in seventy-six days of combat downed 156 Japanese planes. Flying his F4U Corsair, Big Hog, he led VF-17 into a daily battle of attrition during the Allied siege of Fortress Rabaul. After the war he commanded the supercarrier Midway and then retired from the Navy in 1962. A long battle with alcoholism followed. Finally, in 1981 Blackburn overcame his addiction. A successful author, he settled in Florida. Unless attributed to another source all quotes are from an October 1990 interview with Tom Blackburn.

Late in 1942 an American naval force of four aircraft carriers and a small escorting screen of destroyers sortied from Bermuda. Heading east, the carrier force joined with the rest of the North African invasion armada on October 27. Operation Torch, the first major American amphibious assault of World War II in the European theater of operations, was underway.

The Allies were not yet strong enough to attempt an invasion of Europe, but if they could win control of North Africa, they would be in an excellent position to attack the soft underbelly of Europe. The German Afrika Korps under the legendary Gen. Erwin Rommel had driven British forces back across the desert toward Egypt earlier in 1942, but Gen. Bernard Montgomery of Britain had rallied the Eighth Army. If Operation Torch—as the joint British-American invasion was code-named—was successful, the Germans might be crushed between two powerful Allied armies.

The Navy carriers were to furnish air support for the landings at the Moroccan cities of Casablanca and Mehdia to the north and Safi to the south.

The carrier *Santee* was to help guard the southern flank of the invasion force. Aboard the *Santee* were fourteen Wildcats of VGF-29. The commanding officer of Fighting 29 was Lt. Comdr. John Thomas Blackburn.

Blackburn's command was briefed to attack the French Vichy air forces at Safi and destroy any planes found there. They were then to provide air cover for the amphibious task force charged with landing the invasion troops.

Blackburn was unsure how much enemy opposition his command would encounter once the attack began. In his memoir of World War II, *The Jolly Rogers,* he related the sad state of preinvasion intelligence:

> We had zero data on the Vichy French Air Forces in the target area, and no clue as to how many, if any, Germans were positioned there or nearby. I do not believe any of us had enough experience or sense to be alarmed by how little we knew.

For Blackburn's command Operation Torch began with a dangerous night takeoff from the *Santee.* After lifting off from the carrier each pilot turned on his running lights to facilitate a rendezvous at 10,000 feet. Blackburn soon observed that only four other planes had joined up with him.

"We were at 10,000 feet and ten miles north of Safi when the clear dawn broke," wrote Blackburn. From this height Blackburn's flight could easily observe the landings taking place as well as the heavy covering fire from the Allied warships. Flying inland, Blackburn soon found out that the airfield his command had been sent to neutralize did not exist. Finding little to shoot at, Blackburn led his pilots back toward the coast and placed a voice-radio call to the task force flagship, but he received no response.

With fuel running low Blackburn headed his command back toward the *Santee*. It soon became apparent, however, that getting home would be difficult.

I had not kept notes of courses and times on the way out to our orbiting station [recalled Blackburn] because I anticipated no strain in spotting the ship and getting back aboard quickly and safely. However, by the time we quit our station, the weather had deteriorated from perfect to low overcast and numerous rain squalls.

After several unsuccessful attempts to locate the *Santee* by radio, Blackburn called for a radar steer. The controller told him to take several identifying turns and then instructed the formation to fly in a northwesterly direction.

Flying in a northwesterly direction, Blackburn radioed once more. "According to the radar man, the F4Fs were circling the ship. Blackburn realized the *Santee* had plotted another flight."

Blackburn's engine coughed and it was obvious he was out of fuel. Signaling by hand to the other pilots to continue on course, he made hasty preparations to ditch in the frigid Atlantic.

As soon as Blackburn felt the tail hook drag in the water he let the plane's nose drop slightly and entered the water. He recalled his departure from the plane:

Before the spray subsided, I tripped the seatbelt [and] shoulder harness release, stood up and dived straight over the windshield. My Wildcat 29-6F-1 rapidly reared her tail up and sank. By then I had already set the unconfirmed world's record for the 10 yard dash, freestyle, to avoid getting bashed in the head or taken down by the vertical fin as the fighter flipped over. I shucked off my chute, pulled the raft in front of me and pulled the toggle hooked to the carbon dioxide bottle. As soon as it inflated, I climbed aboard. My watch said it was 1030 November 8, 1942. My first thought was that I had racked up a brief, ignominious war record.

As he floated alone in the cold Atlantic Blackburn's thoughts quickly turned sour. Depressed and

Coming from a family with a strong naval tradition, Tom Blackburn, right, graduated from the US Naval Academy in 1933. His father, center, and his brother, left, also graduated from the academy. His brother was also a naval aviator and retired as a vice admiral. National Archives

frightened, he knew his chances of rescue were slim.

> As I plumbed the underside of self-pity I conducted an internal conversation: why go through an agonizing, futile effort to survive; why not just stick the pistol in my mouth; no one will ever know. But I lacked the courage.

After floating in his rubber raft for almost 60 hours Blackburn was finally rescued by a destroyer of the southern task force. Upon his return to the carrier *Santee* he learned that the four pilots in his flight had crash-landed ashore and had been briefly interned.

After this near disastrous beginning Blackburn would learn his lessons well. He would go on to become the commander of Navy Squadron VF-17, which would distinguish itself in Pacific fighting by shooting down eight Japanese planes for each plane it lost. VF-17 would fly 8,577 combat hours over the Solomon Islands and shoot down 156 Japanese planes. This magnificently led squadron would boast of twelve aces—more than any other Navy unit would claim. It would accomplish this in only seventy-six days of combat.

John Thomas Blackburn grew up and attended schools in Washington, D.C. He graduated from Western High School in 1928. "Most of the students" he recalled, "were from armed forces families and the diplomatic corps." It was, in his opinion, a most enjoyable school.

Graduating when he was fifteen years old, Blackburn attended Severn School in Maryland for a year.

Blackburn's family had a long Navy tradition. His father graduated from the US Naval Academy, Annapolis, Maryland, in 1904 and an uncle graduated in the class of 1916. His brother was in the class of 1930 and became a naval aviator, retiring after a long and distinguished career as a vice admiral.

Since he was indoctrinated from youth with Navy tradition and history, it was only natural that Blackburn would enter the Naval Academy in 1929. Always somewhat of an iconoclast, he gave this description of life at the academy in the thirties:

> It was very formal and very black shoe and we called it, with a certain amount of justice, Sing Sing on the Severn. I was in hot water frequently. I tend to be a nonconformist and somehow that didn't fit the pattern of being a midshipman in the 1930s.

Blackburn had been exposed to aviation while attending functions at the Naval Academy with his family when he was a small boy. He had witnessed "quite a few of the catapult experiments and some of the early naval aviators were friends of [his] parents." His interest in aviation was enhanced when his brother went into naval aviation and received his wings in 1931.

Blackburn was an able student and in 1933 graduated in the top quarter of his class. He was

then required to serve in the fleet for two years before entering the flight training program and earning his wings. He and his fellow midshipmen would soon be called upon to serve as the professional nucleus around which the Navy's prodigious wartime expansion took place.

After graduation from the academy Blackburn's entire prewar naval career was focused on just one thing: preparing himself to fly a Navy fighter in combat. If his disappointment in his flying and command performances during the North African invasion lingered, it was soon dissipated when he received orders to form and commission VF-17 as the commanding officer.

Tom Blackburn in front of a VF-17 scoreboard of squadron victories. "My time in VF-17 was one of the most exciting and rewarding times of my life," recalled Blackburn. "It was very stressful and there was a lot of grief mixed in with joy and pride. At times I was sorely pressed to keep ahead of these guys and turn in a good enough performance so I was leading them, instead of them leading me." National Archives

By assuming command of VF-17 Blackburn would control the destiny of many people. He considered it a terrific assignment.

As his executive officer, Blackburn was able to snag Lt. Comdr. Roger Hedrick. This was a fortunate choice, as Blackburn and Hedrick made a good team, and Blackburn had nothing but admiration for Hedrick.

"When the dust settled," wrote Blackburn in *The Jolly Rogers,* "VF-17 totaled forty-two pilots and no fighters." What made Blackburn and Hedrick optimistic was that the squadron was slated to receive and evaluate a hot new fighter, the Vought F4U-1 Corsair.

Blackburn's first impression of the Corsair was that it was "huge, far bigger than any fighter [he] had ever seen. Most of it seemed to be engine." With a 2,000 hp engine and a long nose stretching 12 feet in front of the windshield the aircraft would allow poor ground visibility, Blackburn realized. Once in flight, however, the big fighter had a maximum speed of 415 mph and a rate of climb of 3,120 feet per minute.

During combat trials in early January 1943, a captured Japanese Zero was set in air-to-air combat against a Corsair. The F4U-1 proved more than a match for the Japanese plane.

"The hardest thing for me to do as a combat pilot," related Tom Blackburn, *"was to not let my self-confidence get shaken when I saw people going down in flames or getting shot up. You can have a lot of faith in yourself, yet when you see people get knocked off with chance shots or accidents it can undermine you. You must face up to the fact that the dice may roll against you and if they do you have to learn to accept that."* National Archives

At another time a pair of Corsairs were teamed against two Grumman F6F Hellcats. Navy ace and Medal of Honor winner Edward Henry "Butch" O'Hare flew one of the Hellcats. "Observers said the Hellcat was no match for the F4U-1."

At one point, while rehearsing takeoffs, landings, and group and squadron tactics from the aircraft carrier the *Bunker Hill,* the Corsair began giving VF-17 and the *Bunker Hill* fits. Many problems arose, but perhaps the one that caused the most trouble was the stiffness of the landing gear oleo. Upon landing, the Corsair tended to bounce too high, resulting in missed arrestings, barrier crashes and nose-ups. This led to a decision not to deploy the plane on carriers until the problem was corrected. After a series of accidents Blackburn had to make a tough decision: to keep the Corsair or reequip the squadron with Hellcats. According to Barrett Tillman in his book *Corsair Aces,* when asked pointblank by the captain of the *Bunker Hill* what his preference was, Blackburn replied in no uncertain terms:

> Skipper, I'm so convinced, and so are my pilots, that I recommend in the strongest terms that we go forward with the Corsairs. Fighting 17 could make the switch to the F6Fs without even breathing hard. But we believe that would be a cop-out and a serious mistake. The F4U is the better combat airplane.

It was a decision that neither Blackburn nor the Navy would ever regret. "VF-17 exerted a major influence on future Corsair design, [and its] engineering and maintenance department experimented with field modifications at East Coast bases which eventually became production line standards," wrote Blackburn in his book, *The Jolly Rogers.*

It remained Blackburn's staunch opinion that the Corsair "was the best fighter aircraft of the war, of any service, of any country." Blackburn felt the Corsair was superior to the Mustang and the Spitfire and way ahead of the German Me 109 and FW 190. The only combat aircraft he saw superior to the Corsair was the German Me 262 jet fighter.

As VF-17 began training, Blackburn instituted a rigorous training schedule. The squadron's job was to become skilled in air-to-air combat and to defend against Japanese attacks on Allied shipping and airfields. The pilots also practiced escorting American bombers and torpedo planes and protecting them from enemy attack.

After leaving the United States, late October 1943 found VF-17 staging north through Espiritu Santo and Henderson Field on Guadalcanal to Ondonga, New Georgia, of the Solomon Islands. The squadron had been detached from the *Bunker Hill* and would enter combat as a land-based unit.

On the eve of combat the pilots of VF-17 were ready for battle. For the previous six months they had flown under all types of conditions, training to meet any combat emergency.

In surprise moments in formation flying the skipper would turn tightly into his wingman to test his nerve as well as his technique. They never let up on the deflection shooting drills until one day Blackburn bragged that the enemy didn't have a chance. I've got some guys who can cream them.

On November 1 the Allied invasion of Bougainville, the largest island in the Solomons chain, began. . . VF-17 was ordered to provide overlapping high-cover support over Empress Augusta Bay. It was expected that the Japanese would attempt to attack the invasion forces with their air power.

At 0800 hours eight Corsairs of VF-17 were flying a 10 by 3 mile racetrack orbit pattern at 25,000 feet, 10 miles north of the landing area. Even after almost fifty years Blackburn remembered the setting well:

The scene was so magnificent and even with my preoccupation with doing my job I couldn't help but he impressed by the magnificence of the scenic area we were fighting in. To say I was hyped up is an understatement because of the fact that it was the first time I was leading my own squadron against the Japanese.

Alerted by radio, Blackburn sighted a formation of Japanese planes about 15 miles to the east and 10,000 feet below. "What a moment," he wrote in *The Jolly Rogers*. "First combat! The tension and concentration were almost corporeal."

The Japanese formation of eighteen Val dive-bombers at 14,000 feet escorted by a dozen Zeros at 16,000 feet was flying toward the thin-skinned Allied transport ships far below.

Eager to be at the Japanese before they could peel off to the attack, the Corsairs dove into the formation at 350 knots. Blackburn focused on the flight leader. When he was 1,000 feet away he watched the Zekes drop their belly tanks. "Instantly," Blackburn wrote in *The Jolly Rogers*, "the leader, followed in quick succession by his three wingmen, honked his Zeke around in a tight, tight right climbing turn."

Blackburn opened fire at 500 yards and held the trigger down until he had to raise the Corsair's nose to clear the Japanese plane as it flashed past.

Recovering, Blackburn climbed to 20,000 feet. Spotting another Zeke below, he went into a shallow dive and came up fast on the tail of the Japanese fighter. Holding his fire until the Zeke filled his wind screen, he pressed the trigger and sent a barrage of .50 caliber bullets into the enemy plane. "The next thing I knew," wrote Blackburn in *The Jolly Rogers*, "I was flying through a fireball, emerging with a coating of his oil and hydraulic fluid. Wow! What a sensation!"

Looking around, Blackburn realized he had lost his wingman. He was finally able to join up with

a Corsair piloted by Don Malone and fly a steady orbit at 15,000 feet while trying to calm down from the excitement of his first combat victory.

When it was time to turn for home Blackburn and Malone flew south and eased down to 8,000 feet. Sweaty and tired from the grinding tension of air combat, they cracked their canopies for some cooling air. Far below, at 1,000 feet, Blackburn observed a P-40 from the New Zealand Air Force being pursued by a Zeke. The Japanese plane was about a mile behind the P-40 and closing fast. Rolling over in a steep dive to help the beleaguered New Zealander, Blackburn fired a long burst "in the dim hope [his] tracers would spook the [Japanese plane]." By some miracle the Japanese pilot broke off the chase and made a 180 degree turn to reach home. The two Corsairs closed in on the Zeke from the rear, fully expecting the Japanese pilot to take evasive action. "The Zeke just flew on," wrote Blackburn in *The Jolly Rogers*, "straight and level. It was unbelievable; he had to know we were there. I

VF-17 was known as Blackburn's Irregulars and had a reputation as a maverick outfit. "I did encourage people to use their own ways rather than just following the party line," recalled Tom Blackburn, "and I didn't discourage too much guys who were very aggressive and exhibitionist, if you like. So the charge that we were nonconformist is valid. To say that we were undisciplined is complete nonsense. There was, shall we say, organized chaos." National Archives

put out a brief burst from 200 yards and sent him flaming into the Solomon Sea."

It was a busy initiation to combat for VF-17. That same afternoon Hedrick was leading a high-altitude patrol when he spotted a group of Japanese planes at 20,000 feet. Hedrick recalls the action that followed:

> I swung out west to get up-sun from them, and as I got up close I saw that red meatball on the wings of those babies and I thought, "My God, this is it!"
>
> I opened fire using as the point of aim the inter-section of the wing root and fuselage, and when his wingspan filled 50 mils in my gunsight I pressed the trigger for about 2 seconds and whoosh, he went up in a ball of fire.

In the resulting dogfight the Japanese planes worked effectively in pairs. It was obvious that the Japanese pilots were of a superior caliber, and the battle ended in a standoff with no further casualties on either side.

Jim Halford's division returned for a second mission over Empress Augusta Bay later in the day. After a fruitless 2 hour patrol Halford led his men down to strafe Ballale on the way home. Ens. William Landreth lost his best friend, Johnny Keith, when Keith's plane was hit by shrapnel, went down and sank 2 miles off the beach of a Japanese-occupied island.

Despite the loss of Keith the squadron acquit-ted itself well in its first taste of combat. It shot down six Japanese planes and effectively protected the invasion force below. For the Japanese November 1 was a disaster. They had sent 120 planes from Rabaul to stop the Allied forces on the beaches of

Tom Blackburn, center, and two fellow pilots in front of a Corsair. When he assumed command of VF-17 Blackburn clearly stated the mission of the squad-ron. "I left nothing to chance in getting across to my men that VF-17 was a fighter outfit, charged with engaging the enemy and blowing him out of the sky."
National Archives

Empress Augusta Bay and lost twenty-two in the futile attempt.

On November 8 bad weather prevented a rendezvous with a group of B-25 bombers VF-17 was supposed to escort on a low-level bombing and strafing attack on Matchia Bay. Free of the duty of protecting the bombers, Blackburn and four other pilots of the squadron set a course to the north. Halfway to the Japanese air base at Buka the Corsairs broke into clear skies. Flying low toward the target, the pilots set up for a strafing run on Bonis and Buka.

As they approached Buka they spied a Japanese transport plane on its final landing approach. Closing to within 200 yards, Tom Blackburn and Eddie March opened fire at the same time. The transport immediately caught fire and went down in flames. Flying low over the flaming wreckage, the Corsairs concentrated on a parked Zeke and a "fifty-man reception committee still in parade formation for the newly deceased dignitary aboard the flamed transport," Blackburn wrote in *The Jolly Rogers*. As they scurried for home a single antiaircraft shell burst in their direction, the lone resistance offered to the raid by the surprised Japanese.

Later in the day Blackburn was ordered to fly down to Munda to confer with the commander of Fighter Command. After landing his Corsair, *Big Hog,* on the Munda strip he had a lengthy discussion with high-ranking Marine and Army officers.

After the meeting Blackburn taxied out to return to his base on Ondongo. Over his radio he learned that a B-25 with a full load of gas and bombs on board was approaching the airfield with one propeller feathered. Blackburn described the approach of the bomber in his book *The Jolly Rogers:*

> Less than a quarter-mile short of the strip the B-25 ran out of airspeed and dropped into the rough ground. He bounced once, landing gear sheared off, and he slid on his belly in a great cloud of dust onto the end of the runway. The wreckage stopped less than 50 feet from me and torched off into a ball of flames. I got close enough to feel intense heat and, with the Big Hog's tail toward him, revved up full blast in a desperate hope I could blow the flames clear enough for at least some of the five man crew to get out. As the crash trucks and meat wagon screeched to a halt 200 yards from the inferno, I got the message and had just rolled rapidly to a safe distance when the Mitchell's bombs started cooking off. There were only small bits and pieces to be seen when the smoke finally cleared.

This tragic accident illustrated, all too well, the dangers faced by air crews in World War II. Murderous flak and deadly fighters were only two of the hazards of a mission. Planes loaded with highly volatile bombs and aviation fuel could ignite instantly and engulf the crew in a blazing inferno.

The war fought by the infantry may have been grim but the one fought by the air crews was no less deadly.

Before VF-17 deployed to the combat zone the Japanese stronghold of Kahili was defended by large numbers of fighters and accurate antiaircraft defenses. Over a period of time Kahili was made untenable for Japanese fighters but the antiaircraft defenses were still formidable.

Kahili Knock, as the pilots came to call it, was a phenomenon of the mind brought on by an overactive imagination. Pilots bound for a tough mission to Kahili often aborted for mechanical reasons. A strange knock in the engine or some other unusual vibration could lead any pilot to question the wisdom of continuing with the mission. Plane malfunctions could occur but a pilot would become suspect when he routinely aborted for mechanical reasons too often. After the war moved beyond Kahili the Kahili Knock was still imagined by many pilots on their way to heavily defended targets.

Blackburn had to deal with Kahili Knock in his role as squadron commander. He understood the occurrence well.

Going across the 100 miles of open water from New Georgia to the south end of Bougainville, you

Roger Hedrick, VF-17's executive officer and Tom Blackburn's alter ego. Hedrick returned from the Navy in 1958 with the rank of rear admiral. Blackburn said Hedrick was "the top fighter pilot [he] flew with in World War II." Tom Blackburn

could be chunking along and you knew action was coming up. You also knew it was going to be rough, and one could imagine all sorts of weird noises coming out of the engine.

There were people that turned back; the ones that did it were generally accused of hearing the Kahili Knock. Everybody heard it, but not everybody turned back.

Blackburn felt that no squadron commander could tell who would perform well in combat and who wouldn't. Intense and realistic training could, in some instances, give those in leadership positions an idea of which men would perform in combat and which would have to be watched closely.

Any and all squadron commanders, in getting ready to go into combat, endeavored to put their people under as much pressure as they could, without unduly exposing their lives, to find out who

was going to be around when the bullets started flying.

There are indicators you get in the training phase. Yet there are times when people seem perfectly sound and aggressive and you want to take them into combat. However, when it comes down to the nitty-gritty, the guys just don't have it and you have to put them on the bench.

During this period, many enormous air battles took place over Bougainville. When the Japanese, to reinforce their depleted air arm, diverted a portion of their Central Pacific fleet to the Rabaul area, the US Navy countered by sending the aircraft carriers *Essex, Independence* and *Bunker Hill* to join forces with the carriers *Saratoga* and *Princeton.*

On November 5 an air strike by planes from the *Saratoga* and *Princeton* had severely damaged units of the Imperial Navy's Second Fleet.

Tom Blackburn, sixth from left in front row, and the men of VF-17. In 76 days of combat the squadron destroyed 154 Japanese planes in the air and two on the ground. At the end of their combat tour 13 men of VF-17 *were aces. They accomplished this while losing only 20 planes and 12 pilots to enemy action. Four of these losses were from antiaircraft fire.* National Archives

Despite the success of the November 5 attack, it was felt that Bougainville was still in danger of attack from Japanese surface ships. Accordingly, it was determined to launch a second attack on the Japanese forces at Rabaul.

The second attack on Rabaul was to be a one-two punch. Planes from the *Essex, Bunker Hill* and *Independence* were to attack from the Solomon Sea while planes from the *Saratoga* and *Princeton* were attacking from due east of the objective. This assault against Japanese warships and the estimated 270 planes defending Rabaul was to be launched on November 11.

On Armistice Day twenty-four Corsairs of VF-17 took off into a pitch-black night. Their mission was to provide air cover for the carriers *Essex, Bunker Hill* and *Independence* while their own fighter squadrons escorted the carrier-based bombers to Rabaul.

By 0600 VF-17 was flying cover over the carriers with a dozen Hellcats of VF-33 from Segi Point. After flying overhead for almost an hour Blackburn received a radio report from the *Essex* that an unknown aircraft was approaching at 15,000 feet.

Climbing to 18,000 feet, Blackburn spotted a plane that looked remarkably similar to the P-51 Mustang. The huge red ball on its wing, however, identified it as a Japanese Imperial Army Ki-61 Tony fighter.

Approaching unseen from above, Blackburn dove to intercept the Tony. The Japanese pilot saw the Corsair dive and frantically started for a nearby cumulus cloud. Blackburn's .50 caliber machine guns spat a stream of bullets into the Japanese plane, which caught fire and fell flaming into the ocean.

Two and a half hours after starting their air patrol over the carriers, Blackburn led three divisions onto the *Bunker Hill's* 800 foot flight deck. The Corsairs with their macabre skull and crossbones insignia landed on board to refuel and give the pilots a chance to rest.

Blackburn's pilots received a royal welcome. As they taxied to park their Corsairs the deck crew "gave ebullient thumb-up signs or clasped their hands over their heads," wrote Blackburn in *The Jolly Rogers.*

While their planes were being refueled, the pilots availed themselves of the hospitality of the *Bunker Hill.* Served hot coffee, steak, eggs and toast, they realized just how good life had been aboard the carrier.

After a brief rest the pilots were ordered to the fighter ready room. As they arrived, a teletype clanked out the message "Welcome Home Fighting 17." After the briefing the flight deck coordinator arrived with the announcement that all planes were reserviced, rearmed and ready for takeoff.

Beginning at 1030 hours, the twenty-three Corsairs of VF-17 and twelve Hellcats of VF-23 were launched off the carriers to resume the air patrol as the task force strike planes returned from Rabaul.

The strike force fighters and bombers began returning well after noon. A second attack was to have been made on Rabaul but it was canceled so that the fighters could be used to oppose any Japanese counterattack.

Adm. Alfred Montgomery, the commander of the task force, employed a circular cruising formation that kept his three carriers close together and massed the antiaircraft fire. It was well he did this, for the carriers were soon under the heaviest air attack ever experienced by a US carrier force.

The first word of the attack came from a Navy Corsair pilot patrolling between the fleet and Rabaul, according to Barrett Tillman's book *Corsair: The F4U in WWII and Korea:*

"Jesus Christ, boys, there's a million of them!"
"Let's go to work!"

The Japanese strike force was from Rabaul and consisted of thirty-five Zeros, twenty Vals, and fourteen torpedo-carrying Kates. The Japanese pilots knew where the American fleet was located because a reconnaissance plane had spotted it at 1055 hours. The pilots and crews were Japan's best; all the Val and Kate personnel were from the Navy carrier squadrons.

The weather, which had been clear in the morning, turned sour toward noon. Heavy clouds formed to the north and west. Some topped 35,000 feet with bases as low as 1,000 feet. The clouds did not form a solid front, however; the gaps were wide-open over one third of the sky.

It appears that interference from the thunderstorms allowed the Japanese to approach the fleet undetected. By the time VF-17 was aware of their presence the Japanese were only 30 miles out and closing fast. With the enemy so close Blackburn had no time to deploy his fighters to optimum advantage.

From 25,000 feet VF-17 pushed their throttles to the fire wall and turned north to intercept the incoming Japanese. Spotting the lead Zero formation, Blackburn deployed his flight to gain position over the lead enemy planes. He half-rolled into a dive and headed for the lead Zero. Spotting the diving Corsair, the Zero pilot snapped into a split-S and dove. As the lead Zero dove, his wingman made a tight, level right turn to be in position to nail Blackburn. It was a beautifully executed vertical scissors by the Japanese pilots. Blackburn's only thought was, *These guys are good!*

The Japanese dive-bombers broke through the fighter screen and bore in on the fleet. In his book *Breaking the* Bismarck's *Barrier,* Samuel Eliot Morison described the action that followed:

A Japanese bomber in flames over the Pacific. VF-17 was so skillful and courageous that no ship for which the squadron provided air cover was ever hit by a bomb or torpedo. US Navy

Yeoman John Mroski's far-sighted eyes picked up the "Vals" at 20,000 yards, 22,000 feet up, flying in a beautiful flat V unopposed by fighters. At 1354 we opened fire at the bat-wings before they'd gone into their dives. Two fell smoking. Others pushed over.

Thereafter, the sky rained airplanes and bombs. Near-misses hammered alongside each carrier.

Blackburn followed a Zero down to 2,500 feet before losing him into a cloud. With his windshield and canopy fogged over by condensation, he flew into the nearest cloud and opened his canopy, and waited for the moisture to evaporate.

Coming out of the cloud, Blackburn noticed a flight of six Ki-61 Tonys, 5,000 feet above him. The leader of the Japanese formation rolled to his left, diving toward Blackburn. Turning back toward the cloud, Blackburn began a hasty retreat, his head and shoulders pressed hard into the seatback, expecting at any moment to hear and feel the impact of machine gun bullets.

Escaping into the cloud, Blackburn circled in the mist, his heart pounding and his shirt soaked with sweat from the narrow escape.

Easing the Corsair back up to 200 knots, he flew out of the cloud, expecting to find the Japanese had gone. Instead, off to his right, about 300 yards out, were two Corsairs. Surprised by a plane abruptly appearing in front of them, one of the F4Us opened fire. Blackburn saw the gun flashes erupt on the leading edges of the Corsair's wings.

As quickly as it started, the machine gun fire stopped, and Blackburn was relieved to see Hedrick

pull up to his left, concern written all over his face. Luckily Hedrick had stopped firing the moment he realized his target was a friendly Corsair. Blackburn escaped with only three .50 caliber bullet holes behind his seat and three through the engine accessory section.

Recovering after his narrow escape, Blackburn was able to get a bird's-eye view of the battle taking place before him and described it in *The Jolly Rogers*.

The whole hemisphere of the sky was polka-dotted with black 5 inch shell bursts interlaced with colorful 20 mm and 40 mm tracers. Here and there, dark-tailed orange comets marked the passage of burning airplanes as they arched toward the cobalt surface. Around the twisting shapes, bomb and shell spouts heaved up spectacular white geysers. Through it all, planes rolled and turned with sunlight glinting off their flat surfaces and contrails streaming off their wing tips. . . . The scream of overrevving engines and props was punctuated with the whomps of bombs, guns, shells, plus the staccato rat-a-tat of machine guns. It was technicolor bedlam.

The battle lasted 46 harrowing minutes. It was so intense that the three carriers fired over 33,000 antiaircraft shells during that period.

The battle over and low on fuel, VF-17 flew back to the base at Ondongo. Some of the planes landed with only a few gallons of gasoline left.

In all, VF-17 was credited with shooting down 18.5 Japanese planes and damaging seven others. Ike Kepford led the way with four bombers shot down, and ten other pilots were also given credit for kills.

The Battle of the Solomon Sea—as the November 11 clash came to be called—was a significant setback for the Japanese. It tore up their carrier air strength just before the invasion of Tarawa, bled their air strength from Bougainville and caused them to withdraw the rest of their carrier planes from Rabaul. Once withdrawn to Truk the Japanese found their "carriers had lost fifty percent of their 'Zekes,' eighty-five percent of their 'Vals' and ninety percent of their 'Kates' in less than a fortnight at Rabaul," according to Eliot Morison's book *Breaking the* Bismark's *Barrier.*

VF-17's first combat tour lasted from October 27 to December 1, with the squadron averaging 140 combat flying hours per week. The Navy, impressed with the way the pilots had covered the Marine landings on Bougainville, awarded a unit citation to the squadron. In addition, Blackburn was awarded the Distinguished Flying Cross.

When the squadron was rotated out of combat it tallied forty-five confirmed victories. Three pilots had been killed and five Corsairs lost to enemy action, including two in air-to-air combat.

After a fun-filled period of rest and relaxation in Australia, VF-17 was to return on January 24, 1944, to a new air base on Bougainville. All hands were eager to make the move. They had just one slight problem: what to do with the 148 cases of beer the squadron had amassed in a giant Quonset hut. A puzzled Blackburn, in his best leadership style, put the question directly to the men: "How in the world [are] we going to get the cache from Espiritu to Bougainville?"

It was a time of great crisis for the men of VF-17. Would they have to leave their alcoholic treasure behind to some unappreciative rear-echelon outfit? Sending it aboard a ship to Bougainville was out of the question. Some eagle-eyed sailor would soon discover the precious booze and alert the ship's company to their good fortune. Knowing the great medicinal value of the liquid, the sailors would undoubtedly consume the beer, leaving VF-17 high and dry.

Blackburn wrote in *The Jolly Rogers* that when it began to look as if all was lost, Lt. Hal Jackson arrived on his doorstep with an idea worthy of Thomas Edison:

"Skipper! Rog! I got it! I got it!" yelled Jackson.

"Got what?" answered Blackburn and Hedrick.

"How to get the beer to Bougainville!"

Blackburn and Hedrick were now all ears as Jackson began to unfold his master plan.

"Well," stated Jackson, "the most planes we've ever had in one flight in the forward area was twenty-four. And we did all right. Right?"

Blackburn and Hedrick couldn't dispute this statement of fact.

The cunning Jackson now gave the details of his ploy: "The flight going up to Bougainville will be the whole squadron. We'll never in God's world get jumped. But if we do, wouldn't four guns per plane and 200 rounds per gun be plenty?"

Like a sinner who has received salvation, Blackburn saw the light.

"Jackson," he shouted, "you're a bloody genius! I'll have Duke write you up for the Legion of Merit."

It wasn't long before members of the squadron were out on the flight line experimenting with the best way to stow the beer in the huge ammunition cans. It was soon apparent that they had room for all 148 cases.

Buoyed by the knowledge that their cache of beer could be transported to Bougainville in the wings of their Corsairs, VF-17 began the flight to their new base on January 24. They flew the last hour of the flight at 25,000 feet. Landing at their new base and taxiing to a stop, "each pilot solemnly handed a new church key to his Marine plane captain and bade him fetch and open two ice cold cans of beer from one of the ammo cans in the wings." VF-17, with its morale high and beer cold, had arrived for its second tour of combat.

A Japanese torpedo bomber going down in flames. The rear gunner can be seen standing in the after part of the cockpit as though preparing to bail out. As the plane neared the water the gunner suddenly sat down and failed to get out of the plane, which exploded upon hitting the water. US Navy

The conquest of Bougainville had given command of the entire Solomon Sea to the Navy and would serve as a final springboard to the assault of the Japanese bastion of Rabaul, on the island of New Britain.

Rabaul had five airstrips ringing Simpson Harbor and Karavia. Four of the fields had concrete runways and revetments for 430 aircraft—265 fighters and 165 bombers. Almost 300 Japanese planes had been on Rabaul in December 1943. The pilots of these aircraft were some of Japan's best. Lt. Tetouzo Iwamoto of the Imperial Navy's 204th Fighter Group had shot down fourteen enemy planes in China. During his tenure at Rabaul, he would claim forty more victories, including eleven Corsairs. Iwamoto and other veteran Japanese pilots would offer stiff resistance to any Allied attempt to neutralize Rabaul.

In the sixty-one days it took to defeat Japanese air power at Rabaul, the Allies developed a highly efficient method of attack. A typical day's work was two missions of light bombers and one of medium or heavy bombers—B-25s or B-24s. Each bomber formation was assigned separate fighter cover, but all fighters combined for mutual support in the 30 to 90 minute period they were over Rabaul. The B-24s usually bombed at from 19,000 to 21,000 feet; the B-25s approached at 11,000 to 14,000 feet, dove to pinpoint antiaircraft gun positions once they were over the target, released their bombs at 2,500 feet, and then retired at between sea level and 300 feet.

Fighter cover for the bombers was carefully calculated to provide maximum protection. A typical formation of bombers would have the escorting P-40s stacked in close, with Hellcats and Corsairs low, medium and high. As the B-25s pushed over, the two lower levels of fighters dove down slightly in front, scissoring violently to stay near the bombers so that they could provide protection during the low-level attacks. The low-level fighters would then level off above the bombers and sweep the route to the rallying area about 15 miles away from the target. At the same time the high-level fighters would make a circular sweep to brush off any passing Zekes, being careful not to be averted by any of the acrobatic stunts the Japanese pilots put on to distract them. After clearing the area they would dive down behind the bombers, offering protection for the rear of the formation.

Fighting 17 flew its first mission to Rabaul on January 26. The Americans expected to meet stiff opposition and the Japanese didn't disappoint them, putting up fifty to sixty fighters to defend the area.

During the mission, VF-17 provided medium and high cover for the bombers. After following the bombers over the target Blackburn encountered a lone Japanese plane north of Rapopo airfield. The Zeke came straight-on at him. As the two planes approached, Blackburn fired a long burst that hit the Zeke's engine and then the wing root. The Japanese plane passed under the Corsair with smoke pouring from the engine and crashed into the ocean off Matupi Island. It was Blackburn's fifth victory and made him VF-17's first ace.

VF-17's first mission to Rabaul was hardly a one-sided affair, however, as two Corsairs were shot down and four damaged. One of the pilots, Ens. Robert H. Hill, ended up in the hospital with head

A Japanese torpedo bomber under fire as it makes a low-level attack. During the Battle of the Solomon Sea on November 11, 1943, Ike Kepford caught a Japanese torpedo bomber off the bow of the Bunker Hill *just as the pilot was preparing to launch his torpedo. Kepford downed the Japanese plane, one of his four kills that day, to save the carrier. National Archives*

injuries sustained while crash-landing his badly shot up Corsair, *Lonesome Polecat*.

The loss of the two pilots deeply affected the men of VF-17, wrote Blackburn in *The Jolly Rogers:*

> Our rather gloomy happy hour conversation revolved around variations on the same theme: We faced six weeks in the forward area, and most of our flight time would be spent on missions to Rabaul; if we continued to lose two a day, we would all be dead in only nineteen more days; if we averaged "only" one loss per day, one of us would survive to tell the tale.

If the heavy resistance encountered over Rabaul increased the tension and anxiety of the pilots, it also brought the emotion of fear into their life. This fear could manifest itself in many ways: a knot in the stomach, a constant tightness of the shoulder and neck muscles, a nervous tic. For the combat pilot fear was always present; it was the silent voice in the subconscious that constantly told the pilot that no matter how well trained or skilled he was, a terrible accident or skillful enemy tactic could send him to sudden death or injury. Pilots dealt with fear in various ways: for some the anesthesia of alcohol offered relief; others turned to religion or hard work. Whatever technique a pilot used to deal with fear, it was still always there, like a dull toothache slowly wearing away at his physical and mental resources.

Blackburn was no stranger to fear, but he also felt he knew how to deal with it.

> There's fear, but once the action is joined things are just a rapidly whirling kaleidoscope of reflexes and reactions and there isn't any reasoning involved.
>
> When you can see the action is about to begin there is an anxiety time, a time when you think you may go haywire, get buck fever or similar things. Once you start being shot at and tangling with people there isn't any portion of your mind that's available to be afraid.

January 27 found VF-17 once again in the skies over Rabaul. With Marine F4Us and Army P-40s it covered B-25s attacking Lakunai Airfield. Sixty to seventy Japanese planes took to the sky with a pressing aggressiveness that found the pilots of VF-17 continually having to knock them off the tail of a fellow pilot. The Japanese employed a new tactic, waiting until the bombers were retiring before diving to the attack.

Despite the forceful Japanese maneuvers, VF-17 shot down sixteen enemy fighters and probably downed five more. All the B-25s returned safely from the mission. The only damper on the day was the death of fighter pilot Tad Bell, who was shot down early in the mission.

In the first two days over Rabaul VF-17 had shot down twenty-four Japanese planes and lost three of its own. As favorable as these numbers were, Blackburn was concerned and called a meeting to discuss possible tactical changes. Out of this brainstorming session came the concept of roving high cover, which Blackburn felt was their single best tactical contribution to the Allied cause.

During the raids on Rabaul, the Japanese, forewarned of the attacks, would pounce on the Allies from a higher altitude and out of the sun. These tactics permitted the Japanese to inflict heavy losses with a diminished risk.

To counter them Blackburn proposed to send in four to six fighters at an altitude of 32,000 feet almost 10 minutes ahead of the strike force. This would enable the Allies to surprise and attack the Japanese while they were climbing to altitude and before they could attack the incoming formation.

The concept of roving high cover soon became so successful that the pilots of the VF-17 quickly began calling it the gravy train. The Japanese were taken completely by surprise and their top ace, Lieutenant Iwamoto, wrote of the Corsairs as "wolves who pounce on the unsuspecting Zeros," according to *The Jolly Rogers*.

Roving high cover worked so successfully on January 28 and 29 that twenty-four Japanese planes were shot down. Squadron morale soared after these successful attacks and Fighter Command was elated. Blackburn, however, was less than pleased.

Although Ike Kepford and Howard Burriss each shot down four Japanese planes on January 29, Blackburn felt they had taken unnecessary risks in order to run up a high individual score. At a debriefing after the mission he told the assembled pilots he would ground any pilot who he thought was getting Zero happy.

Ike Kepford would become one of the leading Navy aces of World War II. Blackburn felt that Kepford was a superb shot and excellent pilot but lacked the experience to be rated as highly as a Roger Hedrick. "Hedrick," recalled Blackburn, "came into combat with 2000 hours in fighters under his belt, whereas Kepford, when he joined Fighting 17, had never been in a fighter, much less had any flying time in one."

Blackburn felt strongly that the squadron should operate as a team, that what really counted was getting the bombers to the target and back safely.

> I have a great deal of respect and admiration for Kepford [explained Blackburn]. I was very happy he was our top gun. However, he was beginning to show signs of hubris, which was generally called getting Zero happy.
>
> I told Kepford that if he didn't restrain himself and use a little more discretion he might find himself grounded for a while. He was much too valuable a man to expose himself unnecessarily by running up his score with a couple of victories. I let it be known in the squadron that I had cautioned

Ike Kepford in the cockpit of his Corsair. Kepford was the leading ace of VF-17 with 17 victories. After the war Kepford answered a newspaper ad placed by the Rexall Drug Company, wanting young men to learn retail selling. Fourteen years later he was president of the Liggett Drug Company with over 150 company-owned stores. National Archives

Kepford in this manner and that I had requested Hedrick to lay it on me if I started getting Zero happy. I saw a number of people get themselves shot down unnecessarily because they were taking needless risks in order to try to run up their score.

The battle over Rabaul went on day after pulverizing day. Often emotions were on edge and pilots made decisions based on their feelings instead of critically analyzing the situation. These hasty decisions, made in the heat of battle, frequently had dangerous consequences. Roger Hedrick relates one such incident:

> We had had a big melee and I was split up and lost my wingman. Normally the Japs would chase us twenty miles or so off shore toward Bougainville, and they would pull back and turn away, and we could look back and see them doing their victory rolls.
>
> Well, this time, I saw one character doing that and I was so incensed, and I thought, I'm not going to let him get away with that. So by myself I went back after him.
>
> I bounced him and shot him down, the plane burned and he parachuted out. I came around and he was coming down in his chute and I thought to myself, well there's one rascal that isn't going to be back up there tomorrow, shooting at us.

Approaching the slowly descending Japanese pilot Hedrick squeezed off a short burst. He had misjudged his rapid closing speed, however, and missed the Japanese pilot with his machine gun fire, while almost flying right into the parachute's canopy. As he passed by Hedrick turned to look at his foe and watched the Japanese pilot bravely raise his arm in defiance.

Realizing his fuel was running low Hedrick turned for home only to find his path blocked by three Japanese Zeros. His tactical position, to say the least, was poor:

> Here I had them on both sides of me, and behind me, and I had to go over 225 miles of water to go home. That was the one time I experienced real terror.
>
> They were making runs on me and I am not doing much dodging, because I knew I had to get more acceleration to get far enough ahead to get out of range. We had a slight speed advantage over them, so I kept going. This couldn't have lasted very long but it seemed like an eternity. They finally pulled off and went back and landed. I opened my canopy and took out my canteen of water and lit a cigarette and I never tasted anything so good in my life.

Heavy combat took place on January 30. The squadron escorted bombers on two separate missions. Four pilots flew both missions, including Tom Blackburn, Ike Kepford and Doug Gutenkunst.

In the afternoon Blackburn, leading the high cover, observed Japanese planes forming up over Simpson Harbor. As he and Gutenkunst flew toward the harbor they viewed the sky around them. He describes the battle in *The Jolly Rogers*.

> The scene over Rabaul was spectacular. The heavy AA was laying a thick carpet around the TBFs, which were approaching at 14,000 feet. Just slightly lower down was an equally lethal array of tracers from lighter AA. [Allied] fighters were all over the sky, sending down burning Japanese fighters. Here and there, one or another of our fighters plummeted earthward trailing long plumes of thick black smoke.

The two Corsairs came flashing out of the sun to surprise a group of Zeros in loose formation. The Japanese, unaware of the presence of the Navy fighters, flew through a gentle turn. Coming down in a steep dive, Blackburn let out a burst that clobbered the lead Zero. The Japanese plane staggered under the impact of the rain of .50 caliber bullets and blew up.

Recovering, Blackburn spotted another pair of Zeros trying to set up on a high-cover Corsair. As he turned toward one of the Zeros the Japanese pilot dove away in a spiral. Following the enemy plane down, Blackburn fired short bursts, which set the Zero afire and forced the pilot to bail out. A hard right turn pulled more g's than expected and pushed Blackburn to the edge of blacking out. Pulling out of the turn, he spotted the enemy pilot's opened parachute off in the distance. Flying toward the parachute, Blackburn decided to finish the flier off, reasoning he wouldn't have to face him over Rabaul in the future. As he neared shooting range he noticed the chute was empty; a close look as he flew by told him that the straps had burned through and the pilot had fallen 18,000 feet to his death.

Blackburn and his wingman eased down to 10,000 feet to provide cover for the bombers, when they were jumped by a bevy of Zekes and Hamps. Taking violent evasive action, they lost the attacking Japanese and rejoined the bombers.

As Blackburn and Gutenkunst once again joined up with the bombers they observed a Zero beginning a firing pass from far astern. In desperation Blackburn fired a long full-deflection shot that rocked the Japanese plane and started a fire in the cockpit. Just as he stopped firing the flames died out and the Zeke dove away.

In the wild melee above Rabaul the rest of VF-17 had fared well, scoring ten confirmed kills. The victory was costly, however, as Tom Kropf was lost and Ray Beachim's Corsair badly riddled.

Blackburn and Gutenkunst were among the last fighters home. As they returned, darkness had begun to set in and Piva Yoke, the fighter runway, was closed. They were diverted to Piva Uncle, the bomber strip, which was a madhouse with F4Us, TBFs and SBDs trying to land.

Seeing a temporary lag in the number of planes trying to land, Blackburn eased down, Gutenkunst following behind. Blackburn made a successful landing and checked his rearview mirror to see if it was safe to leave the runway. As he looked back in the mirror he observed, in horror, a huge ball of orange flame at the other end of the runway.

Gutenkunst and a badly shot-up Corsair flown by a Marine major flying almost blind because of a head wound had collided at the edge of the runway. It was a tragic accident, as neither pilot was at fault. The red-hot inferno rising brightly against the night sky marked the end for two brave but unfortunate men.

In the six days of January combat VF-17 shot down 60.5 Japanese planes against a loss of five pilots shot down and killed and one pilot killed in a midair collision. It was an admirable record that said much about the skill of VF-17's pilots and the leadership of Blackburn.

A February 24 mission to Tobera illustrated the emotional and physical price a leader must pay during wartime. On two different occasions during this mission Blackburn ordered the fighters under his command not to leave the bombers and help fellow squadron members who had to leave the formation. Both times Blackburn made the "brutal decision" to withhold cover for these men. The impact of this responsibility never left him.

These were the toughest decisions I ever had to make. They were basically both the same—to keep

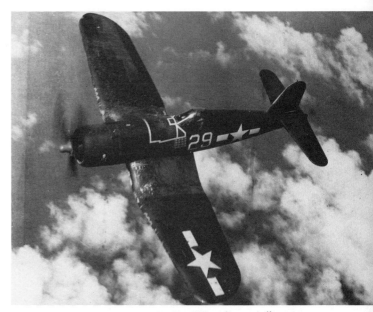

Ike Kepford's Corsair in flight. "The Corsair," wrote Tom Blackburn, "was completely the equal to any plane I know of in World War II. The plane had its weaknesses to be sure; it was a very unforgiving airplane. The saying was, in a Corsair, a little carelessness wouldn't hurt you, it would kill you!" National Archives

the airplanes under my command on their mission, which was protecting bombers—with the realization that two guys we might have been able to bring home were going to get killed.

It was tough as hell to do and tough as hell to live with afterwards.

Blackburn gained a measure of revenge on February 6 as he shot down four Japanese planes during 15 minutes of violent air combat.

During the approach to Rabaul, forty Japanese fighters were observed forming up over the target. Diving from 25,000 feet, Blackburn bore in on the first Zeke he saw and fired a short burst, causing the Zeke to explode. Recovering in a right chandelle, he flew up through the expanding ball of debris and leveled off at 23,000 feet.

He downed his second Japanese plane over Lakunai. The Zeke started burning after only a short burst and fell flaming to the earth below.

Before he had completed his recovery from the firing pass, another Zeke flew straight into his sights. Seeing the Japanese plane only a short distance ahead, he instinctively opened fire. The Zeke dove and Blackburn followed in a tight diving turn, firing short bursts at the enemy plane. At about 4,000 feet and on the verge of blacking out, Blackburn watched the Zeke explode into a huge ball of fire.

After several unsuccessful firing passes Blackburn and his wingman turned for home with fuel running low. As they neared Cape St. George they were surprised to see a lone Hamp flying straight and level. In *The Jolly Rogers*, Blackburn described the attack that followed:

Talk about a death wish; this guy had clearly secured from General Quarters a mite too soon. We closed up his tail to about 50 yards and never got a glimmer of reaction. The Hamp blew into a million pieces as soon as I began squirting rounds at him. My wingman's windshield was doused with oil and fuel, and he heard chunking debris hitting his [plane] as I led him through a fireball for the second time that morning.

On February 19 VF-17 shot down sixteen enemy planes over Rabaul. This marked the last great air battle over the Japanese base. From that date on the enemy was seen infrequently and never in formations larger than six.

The eight-week Allied offensive had proven costly to the Japanese, as they lost over 400 aircraft. Allied airmen were now able to fly almost without opposition in the sky over the Solomon Islands.

At the end of its tour of duty VF-17 was the highest-scoring squadron in the Solomons. From November 1943 through February 1944 it was given credit for 152 Japanese planes. Nearly 100 of these kills were recorded by the aces of the squadron, with Kepford leading the way with seventeen and Blackburn following with eleven. The squadron lost twenty Corsairs and twelve pilots to enemy action, and four Corsairs and one pilot fell victim to operational accidents.

Although these numbers were impressive, Blackburn recalled the squadron record that gave him the most satisfaction:

The fact that we had the record in the Solomons for the highest number of enemy kills makes good reading and better publicity. But the fact that we always brought all of our bombers home and provided cover for the ships that we were assigned to protect, and that none were ever hit by bombs or torpedos, is the thing I'm proudest of.

Even though the pilots of VF-17 decimated the Japanese air opposition over Rabaul, they never underestimated their opponents. The Japanese, facing superior Allied planes and better-trained pilots, battled valiantly against long odds. Blackburn later reflected on the quality of the Japanese he faced over Rabaul:

The ability of the pilots we saw was very uneven. There were some who were expert and very formidable opponents and there were others who flew in combat as if they were still in flight training.

There was no lack of courage at any time with these guys. You have to admire the courage of the people we were tangling with over Rabaul in 1944 because they were seeing every day their fellow pilots getting shot down by vastly superior performing aircraft. It must have been tough for them to [get] back in and give it the old college try when they knew the deck was stacked against them. There could be no doubt the odds were against them; you can't be in combat and watch your comrades go down in flame and not know this.

The Kawasaki Ki-61 Hien, or Tony, was a Japanese fighter that entered service in 1942. It looked much like the smaller P-51 Mustang. Tom Blackburn shot *down a Tony after a brief combat in November 1943.*
National Archives

It was Tom Blackburn's belief that the media campaign emphasizing Irregulars, Castoffs and other nicknames earned VF-17 the enmity of many of the Navy brass. One wartime *Saga* magazine story's lead ran: "They made training-field commanders wake up screaming. Squadron leaders damned them. When the Admiral saw them, his thoughts became unprintable. So one man took them and whipped them into the finest aerial team in the US Navy." National Archives

After his last tour of duty with VF-17 ended, Blackburn was summoned back to Washington, D.C. There he met with officials from the aircraft companies and high-ranking Navy officers to discuss the performance of the Corsair in combat and the tactics that had proven successful.

He wound up at the end of the war as the air group commander of a thirty-six-plane fighter-bomber squadron on the carrier *Midway*. The pilots had finished training and were ready to go to war when V-J Day ended any further chance at combat.

Blackburn stayed on the *Midway* for eight months after the war ended, until he was detached and sent to shore duty. He then served with the Bureau of Aeronautics at the Fighter Design Desk for several years.

He returned to sea duty as the executive officer for the light carrier *Saipan* for a year and a half and was then ordered to command Composite Squadron 5. "The title was a screen for the fact that it was an atomic weapons delivery squadron," recalled Blackburn; "all the atomic weapons business in the late forties was of course hush-hush."

Following a variety of other challenging assignments, Blackburn was given command of the big carrier *Midway* in the spring of 1958. It was a challenging assignment and one that would tax any person to the maximum, recalled Blackburn:

The stress was ferocious, particularly during any type of air operation—refueling, reprovisioning, restocking ammunition—and doing this while at sea, in all kinds of weather.

I recall we were in the western Pacific in the fall of 1958, when Quemoy and Matsu were hitting the headlines, and we thought we might be getting into a shooting war with Communist China. We had some dirty weather and we had to operate anyway and I know I was on the bridge for 65 hours straight. I was practically a basket case when we got into port after that. It was a fascinating job, but it was . . . enormously demanding, wearing.

Vice Adm. James Stockdale won the Medal of Honor for his heroism in Vietnam. As a young pilot, he served aboard the *Midway* when Blackburn was the captain. In his introduction to Blackburn's book *The Jolly Rogers*, he offered a vivid description of the *Midway*'s captain:

John Thomas Blackburn was forty-five or forty-six years old during the time I spent with him on the aircraft carrier *Midway* in the late fifties. He was, to be sure, that great ship's commanding officer, but to her four thousand officers and sailors, and particularly to her pilots he was The Immediate Presence, the mentor, the guide—the man we all knew could do anything better than anybody aboard without half trying. He could turn the ship around on a dime in a narrow channel, take over from a boat coxswain in high winds and choppy seas . . . or outfly the hottest fighter pilots with aplomb. He "had it" upstairs, at the tips of his fingers, in the seat of his pants. If ever a man was tailor-made to be an across the board role model and leader of men flying and fighting from ships at sea, it was Tommy Blackburn.

Blackburn retired from the Navy in 1962 at the age of fifty. Although a seemingly logical choice to make admiral, he retired with the rank of captain. As he frankly acknowledged in *The Jolly Rogers,*

"By mid-1962, the navy sensibly decided that it didn't need an Admiral who could not handle his booze."

Blackburn spent years battling an opponent more vicious and deadly than any Japanese pilot he faced over the Solomon Islands. His fight against alcoholism was marked by endless recoveries followed by shameful relapses. It was a grim struggle, one that Blackburn courageously related:

I never did drink while I was aboard ship. My abuse of alcohol was confined to my activities on the beach and was carefully separated from any professional activities ashore, for that matter. When I retired from the Navy I still had that albatross hanging around my neck and it made getting into a new life more difficult.

A good friend got me into AA [Alcoholics Anonymous]. Unfortunately that wasn't enough for me. I would sober up and get squared away, but I couldn't stay sober. There was a period of two and a half years when I was dry and happily so. Other times I would get squared away and last just a few days until I would start drinking again.

I finally went voluntarily to a hospital in Berkeley, California, that had a core unit. The counsellors there found I am destroying myself because I lacked self-esteem. I am a case of an overachiever who was hypercritical of myself when I didn't achieve what I thought I should or could.

Once that finally got resolved, I was able to hold onto my sobriety and regain my sanity and keep it.

In 1981 Blackburn "was fully reprieved from [the] hideous squirrel cage" of alcoholism and free to regain control of his life. At the age of seventy-eight, living in Jacksonville, Florida, he was happy in retirement: "My life is very full and my health is good. I see friends that I cherish and my cup runneth over!"

A successful author—*The Jolly Rogers* was published in 1989—Blackburn has been working on a book that will detail the story of the Navy B-24 squadrons in World War II.

Blackburn has lived life to the hilt. An introspective man, he has been able to look back on his fabled Navy career and try to put it in perspective.

I'm very much aware that I was very fortunate in the assignments I received and the people I had under me. I was in the right place at the right time and had a chance to get into combat, and was one of the people who was blessed enough to be a fighter pilot in the final times when a fighter pilot was doing it on his own. Then it was a matter of one's own abilities and intelligence for the most part. It was jousting, pretty much, one-on-one without a lot of assistance from a great deal of sophisticated equipment and other people being in on the act. I am truly thankful I did have a shot at it and was able to perform adequately.

The men of VF-17 get together for a reunion every two years. Twenty of the pilots were still surviving and in touch in the early nineties. Usually fifteen or sixteen attend each reunion. They gather to laugh and to reminisce, to celebrate the living and to honor the dead. They are a rare breed of men, brought together by bonds that run deep. In a video tape called *The Jolly Rogers,* Blackburn said:

The feeling we have for each other goes beyond ordinary friendship [remarked Robert Hill]. It's a special relationship. It's a camaraderie enjoyed by men whose lives have often depended on the actions of their comrades. It's a feeling that will never be lessened by distance apart or the passage of time. It will always be that way until Father Time accomplishes what the Japanese could not do.

Chapter 3

Marion Carl, the Ultimate Fighter Pilot

To paraphrase Will Rogers, Marion Carl never met a plane he didn't like. During his storied career, Carl flew more than 250 different types of aircraft. He became the first Marine Corps ace and ended World War II with 18.5 Japanese planes to his credit. He also at one time held both the world altitude and world speed records. Carl retired from the Marine Corps a major general and settled in Oregon. Unless attributed to another source, all quotes are from a 1991 interview with Marion Carl.

On December 25, 1941, Capt. Marion Carl of the US Marine Corps put full power to his Brewster Buffalo and flew off the carrier *Saratoga* toward Midway Island. Carl and other pilots of Marine Fighter Squadron 221 were originally intended to bolster US defenses at Wake Island, but the squadron was still 400 miles from Wake when it was captured by the Japanese, so they were diverted to Midway.

Occupying a strategic area in the central Pacific, Midway Atoll lies about 1,150 miles northwest of Hawaii and 2,250 miles from Japan. The two major islets, Sand and Eastern, are extremely small land masses; Sand Island, the largest, is barely 2 miles long.

While stationed on Midway, Carl's squadron went through a difficult transition period. He recalled the many personnel changes:

> I stayed on Midway until after the battle but most of the squadron was transferred. They took out all of the old-timers. Also in that period of about five months we went through four squadron commanders and four executive officers, and got a lot of second lieutenants out of training command who didn't have much time in fighters period, let alone in the Brewster.

In late May 1942 tension on Midway heightened, as a Japanese invasion force was expected at any time. On May 26 reinforcements arrived in the form of sixteen SBD-2s for the scout-bomber squadron and seven F4F Wildcats. With these additions Marine air strength numbered no fewer than sixty-four planes, including thirty-six dive-bombers, twenty-one Brewster Buffalos and seven Wildcats.

Few of the Marine pilots were familiar with the Wildcat. Carl was assigned to one of the F4Fs because, as he explained, "I had some previous flight experience in it, even though it was only 6 hours. I got in another 6 hours before the battle." Even though relatively new to the Wildcat, Carl was a qualified fighter pilot, having logged more than 1,400 hours in fighters in his previous assignments.

For six months before the battle the Marine pilots had been warming up their engines a half-hour before dawn and then sitting at readiness for an hour in case of a surprise Japanese attack. Shortly before 0600 on June 4 the Midway radar station detected a large formation of airplanes heading toward the island.

The Japanese formation approaching Midway consisted of 108 planes launched from four Japanese carriers. Thirty-six Zero fighters served as escort for the thirty-six Vals and thirty-six Kates. As the first wave approached Midway the Vals and Kates flew in V-shaped echelons and the faster Zeros hovered protectively near the bombers.

Adm. Chester Nimitz had ordered the Marines on Midway to adopt offensive rather than defensive tactics. He wanted them to strike the Japanese aircraft carriers as well as defend the airfield on Eastern Island. However, in war the best laid plans often go awry. Carl described the confusion that attended the initial scramble of the Marine planes:

> On the scramble we had six Wildcats in the air and nineteen Brewsters. A total of twenty-five airplanes scrambled when we were warned the Japanese were coming.

We had radar, but it was rather primitive, but in this case they were pretty accurate in letting us know where the Japanese were.

Unfortunately the group commander decided to keep about half the squadron over the field. He vectored the Wildcats out first, but he didn't realize (because we were under radio silence, we could receive but not talk) that we only had three Wildcats. Two had been up on patrol and they had to land to refuel.

So there were only three of us (Wildcats) when we ran into the Japanese and operations didn't realize there were only three—they assumed there were six Wildcats. Things were kind of chaotic, as you might imagine.

As Carl climbed toward the Japanese planes 2d Lt. Clayton M. Canfield was flying on his wing. As they continued to climb Carl noticed that he was not gaining altitude as rapidly as he should and motioned Canfield to move up on the wing of John Carey. This left Carl in the tail-end Charlie position.

Carey—flying the lead—made the initial contact with the incoming Japanese formation. At precisely 0612 he radioed: "Tally ho! Hawks at

Marion Carl received his wings on December 1, 1939. After being assigned to a fighter squadron he flew the Grumman 3F2 biplane. After six months Carl, a superior pilot, was transferred back to the Training Command for duty as an instructor. National Archives

angels twelve!" These radio transmissions informed Midway and the following American pilots that he had observed Japanese bombers at 12,000 feet.

Gordon Prange, in his book *Miracle at Midway,* recorded the initial attack by Carey and Canfield on the Japanese bombers:

Carey saw that the fighters were not preceding the [Val dive bombers] in the formation, as might be expected, but were slightly above and behind them. This gave Carey the opportunity for a quick chance at the bombers before the Zero[s] could catch up with him.

Turning his Wildcat in a smooth roll and screaming down to gain speed, Carey caught a lead plane squarely in his gunsight. A bullet cracked his windshield, but he pressed the attack and saw his quarry explode in front of him.

Carey swept through the Vee, headed upward and sent his fighter into a tight, skidding turn toward the end of the formation. As he sped back, a rear gunner in one of the bombers raked the Wildcat and smashed steel into both of Carey's legs.

Canfield was with Carey all the way, concentrating on the Number Three plane "until it exploded and went down in flames." In the middle of his run he saw a column of Japanese Zeros diving down from the left. To lose the Zeros, Canfield headed for a large cloud about five miles away, flew around the cloud and looked back. A large trail of smoke led his eyes to the Japanese bomber bur[n]ing on the ocean, but no enemy fighters were in sight, so he rejoined Carey who was now flying in the general direction of Midway "on an unsteady course."

Carl, flying behind Canfield and Carey, had watched them peel off to the attack. As he began his pass at the bombers below him, he paused an instant to size up the tactical situation. The following passage is from *Wildcat: The F4F in World War II* by Barrett Tillman:

I was tail-end Charlie . . . and both Canfield and Carey pulled through going the same direction as the dive-bombers—that's the natural thing to do—but I saw all those Zeros coming down on me and thought, *Boy, I'm going to be easy meat!* So I reversed course and pulled away from the island. I figured in my own mind these Zeros were there to escort the bombers and they wouldn't follow me, and I was correct.

Knowing that altitude was his best protection, Carl climbed to about 20,000, "wondering what one lone Wildcat was doing out there all by himself." Leveling out, Carl was surprised by a Zero that had latched onto his tail and was pumping bullets into the Wildcat. Carl was in a desperate situation and he reacted instantly.

I tried the most violent maneuvers I could and it didn't do any good, he was still on my tail. That Zero made it look easy. They could just turn sharper, outclimb us and outgun us; they couldn't outdive us, though. I headed for the nearest cloud and in the meantime took a few bullet holes. When I got in the cloud I chopped the throttle, threw the airplane into a skid, and when I came out the other side of the cloud the Zero was down below and ahead of me. Without thinking, I shoved over, and when I was still on negative g's I pulled the trigger and all four of my guns jammed, because of the negative g's.

While Carl was fighting for his life the Zeros had swarmed all over the attacking Marine fighters, shooting down fifteen of the twenty-five engaged. During the clash, the Japanese almost destroyed the Marine squadron in 20 minutes of combat.

The Japanese attack force pressed on toward Midway and at 0630 the first bombs began to fall.

Canfield and Carey had the misfortune to return to Midway while the Japanese attack was still in progress. Walter Lord recorded the reception they received from the waiting Japanese Zeros in his book *Incredible Victory*.

Shot in both legs, Captain Carey "proved the hard way you could fly an F4F with just the stick and no rudder." Lieutenant Canfield's flaps were gone, and when he touched the ground his landing gear collapsed. Sliding in a stop, he dived into a trench while a Zero slashed away at the abandoned plane.

Carl returned to Midway at 20,000 feet to look the situation over. Unable to land because the Japanese attack was still in progress, he circled over the island. In the meantime he had managed to manually clear three of his jammed machine guns.

As the battle ended, Carl seized an opportunity to attack one of the remaining Zeros.

Finally there were only three Zeros left and they were pretty well spread out. When they started leaving, I dove on the tail-end one and got behind him and shot him down just off the reef. That was the end of the battle.

Only Carl's plane and one other F4F were fit to fly after the battle. "Of the ten fighters that returned," recalled Carl, "all had bullet holes in them except one Wildcat, and we all wondered if he had gone into a cloud and hid." Carl's Wildcat had eight bullet holes, whereas other fighters counted more than 200. Neither of the Wildcats that Carey and Canfield took into battle ever flew again.

Carl, Canfield and Carey were fortunate to survive the battle. "Rather strangely, despite all that happened," Carl said years later, "Carey, Canfield and Carl are still alive." Many of the Brewster pilots were not so lucky; thirteen of the outclassed planes were shot down. The Brewster was so inadequate as a fighter that Midway marked the last time American pilots would fly the plane against enemy opposition.

For Carl the Zero shot down off Midway Atoll would be the first of a long string of victories. During bitter air fighting over the island of Guadalcanal on August 26, 1942, he would shoot down

Capt. Marion Carl shot down his first Japanese plane during the Battle of Midway. He felt his survival during the battle was due to his experience as a fighter pilot. "Generally speaking," Carl stated, "pilots were put into combat squadrons too soon before they had enough experience. I was one of the lucky ones because at the Battle of Midway I had 1,400 hours. Some of those guys who showed up at Midway came right out of flight training." National Archives

his fifth Japanese plane to become the first Marine Corps ace. This event would mark the beginning of a long series of firsts for this remarkable man and pilot. Among the other firsts were first Marine to be designated a helicopter pilot, first Marine to land a jet aboard an aircraft carrier and commander of the first Marine jet squadron. Carl would also set the world speed record on August 25, 1947, at 650.6 mph, flying the Douglas Skystreak, and on August 23, 1953, he would set the world altitude record, flying to a height of 83,235 feet in the Douglas Skyrocket.

The foundation for Marion Carl's success as a soldier and pilot was laid during his youth in Oregon. His father went to Oregon in 1915 and bought 200 acres of land with borrowed money. Carl detailed the early family struggles to make a living:

Most of the land my father bought was in virgin timber, so he had to clear the area in order to develop farmland. The first thing he built was the barn, which housed forty-five cows, and we lived in a tent for three years. The tent had a wooden floor and wooden sides up to about 4 feet, but the roof was canvas. Both my brother and I were born in that tent.

My father once said that he never got up later than four o'clock from the time he was twenty-one years old. My mother usually got up at five o'clock and did all the bottle washing and cleaning besides keeping the house and feeding three hired men in addition to the whole family.

Carl went to elementary and high school in the little town of Hubbard, Oregon. Hubbard, with all of 350 people, had one school, which housed all twelve grades. When Carl graduated, his class of eight students was the largest in many years.

Carl's father wanted him to attend college, get a degree in agriculture and return to the farm. Carl had no intention of returning to the farm and enrolled in Oregon State University, majoring in mechanical engineering with an aeronautical option. While at Oregon State he took four years of ROTC and upon graduation in 1938 he was commissioned a second lieutenant in the Corps of Engineers.

Before graduation Carl had journeyed to Fort Lewis in Washington to take the physical exam for Army flight training, but he was turned down. Later he found out he was rejected because the quota for pilots was filled.

Carl then went to the Navy Training Center at Sand Point, Seattle, and was accepted. Once at Sand Point he had the option of going to flight training as a Navy cadet or a Marine cadet. Carl—at a crossroads in his life—had to make a decision.

A Marine captain got ahold of me and said, "Look, you're the only one of these eight people here who qualifies for the Marines." It just so happened that I had a degree and the other seven did not. The Navy was accepting cadets with two years or more of college, and he said, "Joining the Marines, you'll get to Pensacola a month ahead of the rest of them"— which turned out to be true.

I wasn't all that eager about flying off carriers or living the sea type of life, so I went with the Marines, which turned out to be a fortunate thing.

After completing flight training at Pensacola, Florida, Carl received his wings and commission on December 1, 1939. Shortly before accepting his wings he had gotten a letter from a friend who had graduated from flight training several months ahead of him. The friend, writing from Quantico Marine Corps base in Virginia, informed Carl that

Marion Carl—third from right, front row—about to receive the Navy Cross on Guadalcanal. National Archives

one of the fighter squadrons had a vacancy and advised him to hurry to Quantico if he wanted the position. Carl had leave coming but decided this was too good an opportunity to let pass.

> I had thirty days leave and five days travel time coming, but I didn't take any leave. It took me just two days to get to Quantico and report in.
>
> I walked in and the first thing the group adjutant said was, "Where in the hell did you come from? You're not supposed to be here for another five weeks." I said, "I heard there was a vacancy in a fighter squadron and I want it."
>
> A guy who had graduated a month ahead of me showed up three or four days later, interested in the vacancy. I don't know where in the hell he ended up.

After serving in the fighter squadron for six months Carl was transferred back to the Training Command to serve as an instructor. This gave him a chance to do a lot of flying and to become proficient in aerobatics, a form of flying he enjoyed a great deal.

While serving as an instructor Carl on one occasion took student pilot Joe Foss up for a flight. It was a trip Carl would never forget.

> I had a Stearman, which was a nice plane for aerobatics. I guess I really wrung it out, because Joe Foss never lets me forget what happened. When you don't have the controls even an experienced pilot can get airsick. When we landed, Foss promptly upchucked and was very glad to see the ground again.

After a year as a flight instructor Carl was assigned to Marine Fighting Squadron 221. It was while serving with this squadron that he participated in the battle of Midway in June of 1942.

After service at Midway Carl was sent back to Hawaii to join VMF-223. The commander of 223 was John L. Smith, who promptly made Carl the number 3 man in the squadron. Another familiar face was Roy Corry, who had served with Carl on Midway.

VMF-223 was a part of Marine Air Group 23. The group consisted of two fighter squadrons and two dive-bomber squadrons, with many young, inexperienced pilots flying antiquated planes that lacked combat capability, such as the Brewster Buffalo and the SBD-2.

In July the squadron commanders were told that their units were to participate in a special mission and training began to intensify. The crews didn't know it, but they had been selected to go to Guadalcanal and support the Allied offensive there.

Robert Sherrod, in his book *History of Marine Corps Aviation in World War II*, detailed the problems facing Air Group 23 as it prepared for combat:

> The forward echelon—one fighter squadron (VMF-223, Captain John L. Smith), and one dive-bomber squadron (VMSB-232, Major Richard Mangrum)—would have to be flown to the Gua-

dalcanal airstrip from a carrier. And the pilots had not yet been taught to land and take off from a flight deck. . . .

> VMF-223 and VMSB-232 not only were squadrons without carrier experience, but nearly all the pilots were fresh from flight school where they had piled up about 275 hours apiece, mostly in SNJ trainers. (The veteran Japanese Navy pilots they had to face averaged 800 hours flying time even before Pearl Harbor.) Five of Mangrum's 15 pilots had had some practice bombing the target ship *Utah;* his ten newest dive-bomber pilots had done no dive bombing when the group's orders were being issued at Pearl Harbor. . . . Smith's fighter pilots, excepting the two Captains (Rivers Monell and Marion Carl) and a veteran enlisted pilot (Tech. Sergeant John D. Lindley), were second lieutenants ranging in age from 19 to 21, who had been in the Marine Corps a few months.

> For their intensive last months' training, described by Mangrum as "flying the pants off them," both squadrons had to [make] do with their old planes. Just before sailing on board the escort carrier *Long Island* on 2 August for Guadalcanal, Smith's squadron received brand new 4F4-4's with two stage superchargers. . . . Mangrum's squadron turned in its old SBD-2's, which had been reconditioned after seeing their best days in the Coral Sea battle, and was furnished with SBD-3's which had self-sealing tanks and armour plate.

Marine pilots John Smith, Bob Galer and Marion Carl, left to right, shortly after being awarded the Navy Cross. When asked who was the best pilot he observed on Guadalcanal, Marine ace Joe Foss replied, "There were three of them actually: Marion Carl, John Smith and Bob Galer; all three of them were hotshots. They were there before us—they were there when it was really rough going." National Archives

On the afternoon of August 20, 1942, the *Long Island* launched thirty-one planes nearly 200 miles out from Guadalcanal. The Wildcats were launched first, followed by Mangrum's Dauntlesses. Once in the air the planes headed toward Guadalcanal, 1 hour and 20 minutes away.

In the 1943 issue of the *Marine Corps Gazette*, United Press correspondent Robert Miller recorded the reaction of the Marines on Guadalcanal as the planes from the *Long Island* arrived:

> Finally the day arrived when the magic word was passed around—"Our planes arrive today." And sure enough in they came, just before sunset, the SBDs first and the stubby-winged fighters trailing them for protection.
>
> Pandemonium broke loose that afternoon. Every Marine within a mile of the beach sprinted through the coconut trees to get a clear view of the incoming planes, and the shore was lined with half-crazy troops who waved, yelled and screamed at the sight of them.
>
> . . . A great interest in the planes was also noticed in the prison camp. The camp's number one boy, a Japanese laborer who understood and spoke English, cocked an eye skyward when the planes roared overhead the first time, shook his head sadly and remarked philosophically, "Tojo make trouble—now he catch hell."

Once on Guadalcanal the Marine fliers wasted little time getting into action. The first large-scale clash between the Marine Corps fighters and the Japanese took place on August 24, 1942. At 1400 hours fifteen Japanese bombers escorted by twelve Zeros were observed heading toward Henderson Field. Forewarned, fourteen Wildcats were waiting for the Japanese over the water north of the airfield.

Carl, leading the Wildcat formation, directed his planes away from the incoming Japanese bombers to gain more altitude so that he could attack the bombers from above. Once above the bombers the Marines would be in good position to dive through the Japanese formation. Flying the number 4 position in one of the flights was 2d Lt. Mel Freeman, a VMF-212 pilot who had been on Guadalcanal for only three days. Looking down, Freeman saw dark-painted twin-engine bombers that resembled the American B-26. Looking back up, he was startled to see the Wildcat flown by Carl peel off into a beautiful overhead pass. Carl, flashing through the Japanese formation, blasted one of the bombers and started it burning on his downward dive.

The battle became a swirling free-for-all as the Wildcats dove on the Japanese bombers. Richard Tregaskis was at Henderson Field when the jubilant Marine pilots, still pumped up from their life-and-death encounter with the Japanese, landed. He recorded the scene in his prize-winning book *Guadalcanal Diary:*

> I went to the airport immediately after the "all clear" and waited for our fighters to come down. Most of them seemed almost hilariously elated as they taxied in one by one and jumped down from their cockpits. For most of them, it was a first victory over the enemy. . . .
>
> A smiling, handsome lieutenant told me how he and other fighter pilots had knocked down two enemy bombers apiece. The pilot was Lieut. Ken Frazier. . . . "I took the left side of the formation and Carl (Lieut. Marion E. Carl of Hubbard, Ore.) took the right. I let one have all my guns and he exploded. Then I moved my sights up a little and let go at the second guy. A sheet of flame came out of one of his motors."
>
> Lieut. Frazier had, naturally, been excited by the experience. He could not surely say how many enemy bombers there had been or whether they were one or two motored craft.
>
> Col. [Charles L.] Fike, the graying executive officer of the Marine fliers, was taking notes on their stories, arranging a tally of victory. The memo on his notebook pad showed a total of ten bombers and eleven Zeros shot down in the fight.

Carl was VMF-223's big scorer for the day, shooting down two bombers and a Zero. On the

John Smith (who commanded Marine VMF-223), Richard Mangrum (who commanded Marine Bombing 232) and Marion Carl, left to right. "The true measure of John Smith's value," wrote Thomas Miller in his book The Cactus Air Force, *"is found not in heroism—of which he had much, but in tactical skill. He was a true professional and that was what it took to make fighter pilots out of a dozen boys in fifty days. His friend and rival, Marion Carl, totally different in temper[a]ment, but no less skilled as a pilot and leader helped him to make 223 the pre-eminent squadron of the early days on Guadal[canal]."* National Archives

debit side the squadron lost three pilots to Japanese aircraft during the action.

The two bombers shot down by Carl on August 24 were the first of eight he would eventually shoot down during his tenure on Guadalcanal. During a January 1990 interview, he discussed his method of attacking Japanese bombers:

I never attacked a Betty except from an overhead pass. I always made an overhead. I may have adjusted it once or twice for a high-side attack. The overhead was so effective and so risk free I saw no point in making attacks that were less effective.

The Zeros always followed the Bettys, usually a couple thousand feet above or trailing. By making an overhead you could come down, and by the time the Zeros woke up as to what was going on it was too late to do anything about it.

Normally, if the Zeros didn't come in to jump us and force us to dive out, we would climb back up and make another overhead, but that took time because you had to get ahead of the bombers and 2,000 feet above them in order to make a proper overhead. Then you turned toward the bombers right straight head-on and 2,000 feet above, and when you got almost directly over them you rolled over on your back and came straight down.

You had to realize as you were coming down that the bomber had a forward velocity. I would always put the pipper (the Grumman gun sight had rings with a little black dot in the center; the dot was the pipper) ahead of the nose by 20 to 30 feet, and then I would just let that pipper drift back and when I went by the bomber I was 50 or 100 feet behind the tail.

There was no way you could hit that bomber if you didn't allow that pipper to get too far ahead of the bomber. I never had any problem with it, but unfortunately other pilots did.

Some pilots didn't like the overhead. They were always afraid they were going to run into the bomber, and I'd explain to them over and over again, you can't hit that bomber if you do what I just told you to do—that's put the pipper ahead of the nose and let it drift back as you come down. As you fire you could correct your aim with your tracers—if your tracers aren't hitting the bomber you're not leading it enough, and it doesn't hurt to overlead it on the initial part of the pass.

The nice thing about the overhead pass was that we were using incendiaries, and when you're coming down from straight above, some of those bullets go right through the gas tanks. You've got six guns firing . . . and all you have to do is set a gas tank afire and that's the end of that airplane. They wouldn't always blow up, but they'd catch fire and you knew they couldn't get back to base when they were on fire. I never followed them down. Once I had a fire started I didn't monkey with that bomber anymore.

On the morning of August 26 the Japanese launched another attack on Henderson Field. At 1135 hours sixteen twin-engine bombers with a strong escort of Zero fighters were reported heading toward Guadalcanal. At 1203 the Japanese bombers were over Henderson Field. Richard Tregaskis was standing at the edge of the airfield as the Japanese bombers came over and he described the action in his book *Guadalcanal Diary:*

Today we heard the bombs screeching down as loud and close as they were yesterday. Then we piled into a small foxhole. This time I remembered to support myself slightly on my elbows to avoid concussion, in case one came too close. Some of our people have been so badly shaken by close ones that they have suffered shock and prolonged bleeding from the nose. . . .

This morning Miller and I jumped up rather quickly after the sticks (of bombs) had cracked down, and before the dust columns of the explosion had settled saw reddish flames leaping into spreading brown smoke at the far edge of the field. . . .

Somewhere up in the sky the crescendo, protesting wails of zooming and diving motors could be heard and the clatter of machine guns. We knew many of the Japs would never get back.

Thirteen Wildcats had taken off from Henderson Field to attack the Japanese bombers and fighters. Led by John Smith, the Marines shot down thirteen enemy planes, with Marion Carl claiming two Zeros destroyed.

The ubiquitous Tregaskis was waiting at Henderson Field as the Marine pilots brought their F4F Wildcats in. Walking on the edge of the runway, he encountered Carl.

Marion Carl came in, grinning happily, to tell us that he had shot down his fifth and sixth planes—both Zeros. The lads call him the Zeroman, literally a very unflattering title but in this connotation quite agreeable to Carl.

The other pilots seem to have great respect for Carl. They don't mention it to him, but one of them told me today: "What a pilot! He's a natural. Always relaxed."

On August 30 the Japanese sent a large number of fighters to attack Henderson Field. They were evidently trying to force a showdown between the Wildcats and the Zeros because no bombers were used in their formation. They were undoubtedly disappointed at the outcome, as the Marines shot down fourteen Zeros, including four by Carl and three by Smith.

With these victories Carl brought his score to eleven Japanese planes shot down. Although extremely successful in fighting the Japanese over Guadalcanal, Carl never considered shooting down a Zero to be an easy task while flying the Wildcat.

You had to have the advantage on the Zero in order to shoot it down. If it's straight one-on-one and you are both starting even, so to speak, and you're at low altitude, you're in bad shape, because the Zero was faster and could outturn us.

In a dogfight the whole mass of airplanes are losing altitude. You start at fairly high altitude, because usually we would start at 20,000 feet. There was usually some cloud cover, and you dive, shoot one down, and look around and see where there was another one; if you found one in a favorable position, you jumped him.

On this day I got three at higher altitudes and was heading back home when I saw a Zero on the tail of a Wildcat, right down on the water. The Wildcat was going straight and level and there wasn't a damn thing he could [do] but sit there and take it. I could see little puffs of smoke coming out of the Zero from the 20 mm cannon he was firing.

I just happened to have enough altitude. I started at 5,000 feet and dropped right behind the Zero and shot him down. The Zero pilot never saw me, he was so goddamn busy shooting up that Wildcat.

The air battles over Guadalcanal from August 24 through August 26 went a long way toward destroying the myth of the Japanese Zero as an invincible fighter plane. In *History of Marine Corps Aviation in World War II*, Robert Sherrod described the legend that had grown around the Zero during the early days of the war:

The Japanese Zero at this stage of the war was regarded with some of the awe in which the atomic bomb came to be held later. US fighter pilots were apt to go into combat with a distinct inferiority complex. Tales from the Pacific had filtered back to the US after the Bataan and early New Guinea fighting which attributed to the Zero (and the Japanese pilots) a sort of malevolent perfection that was beyond Occidental comprehension. The Japanese fighter plane had not been mastered at Coral Sea nor Midway. . . . The [Guadalcanal] fighters made a great contribution to the war by exploding the theory that the Zero was invincible; the Marines started the explosion on 24 August.

Although the Zero was a formidable fighter plane, its pilot still had to know its limits and how best to use it in any tactical situation. Mistakes of judgment or poor tactics could lead to serious trouble or death. The Zero pilots on occasion seemed to underestimate or show contempt for the Marine pilots and the combat performance of their planes.

While coming in to land at Henderson Field one day, Carl encountered a Japanese pilot who seriously underestimated his opponent. Carl described the action that followed:

I had my wheels down when a Zero shows up on my tail. I don't know where in the hell he came from, but the first thing I know I've got a bunch of tracers past me. Here I am with my landing gear down. On the Wildcat, getting the gear up was twenty-eight

An F4F Wildcat on Henderson Field, Guadalcanal. "The Wildcat was a very rugged airplane," recalled Marion Carl, "but it didn't have the performance of the Japanese Zero. The Japanese bombers would come over Guadalcanal at [20,000] to 22,000 feet and the Zeros slightly above. We would normally climb up to meet them. We very seldom had an altitude advantage. As a result we were always getting shot up. Our main mission was to shoot down those bombers. We could make one pass, maybe two, and then we had to defend ourselves and it was every man for himself." National Archives

turns of a hand crank. So I shoved the throttle to the firewall and started cranking up the wheels. I then dove for the antiaircraft battery, which was right at the edge of the field.

Well, they scared him off and he took off toward the ocean, which was a mile or so away. Meantime I've got my wheels up and I took out after him. Well, I had no chance of catching him—he could outrun me. But he decided to make a fight of it. He turned around and came back.

So now we're meeting head-on and we meet head-on just about over the beach. He then suddenly decides to hell with his head-on stuff and decides to pull up. If he'd pulled up a little sooner he would have gotten away with it, but he did it a little too late. I stood that old Wildcat on its tail at about a 90 degree deflection shot that blew him up right over the beach. I had about a thousand or more people that saw that one. One of the Marines brought me the oxygen bottle of that Japanese airplane and I think I still have it.

As day after dreary day went by on Guadalcanal the Japanese of the Eleventh Air Fleet never varied their schedules. Between 1000 and 1400 hours Henderson Field could count on having an air raid. The methodical Japanese rarely let the defenders of Henderson down. Fighter Command met the attacks by keeping a small group of fighters airborne. When Condition Red was sounded, the field was cleared of planes and more Wildcats were scrambled to join the battle.

On September 9 Carl led an intercept of Japanese Betty bombers attacking a ship convoy. The Japanese were approaching at 20,000 feet and actually overflew the island because of heavy cloud cover. Because of the overflight the Marines had time to gain an altitude advantage. Carl described the action that followed:

I got two bombers, one on each pass, and was pulling up for a third one when the next thing I know I'm being hit from behind. A Zero had apparently come up from below. Next thing I know I have smoke and fire in the cockpit. I didn't hesitate. I pulled open the canopy, rolled the airplane over on its back and out I went. I bailed out at about 23,000 feet. I thought, *I'm not going to stay in this cockpit and fry,* so out I went. One way I did not want to go was to get burned to death.

Carl landed in the ocean and was in the water for 4 hours before a native boy paddled out to rescue him. He then spent four days with the natives while a Fijian medic named Eroni helped him to recover from his ordeal.

One of the natives had a small motorboat and Carl helped him to get it running. On September 14 Carl and Eroni, using the motorboat, made it to safety. It had been a dangerous journey, as many Japanese troops were in the area.

One of Carl's last missions over Guadalcanal took place on October 3. The pilots had just finished noonday chow and were sitting around reading a bunch of outdated magazines when they were given the report that Japanese planes were approaching from 145 miles out at 12,000 feet.

As the pilots rushed onto the field the ground crew had the 4F4-4s warmed up and ready for action. Carl was first to take off, followed by William Watkins and Frazier. Lt. Col. Joe Bauer, flying with VMF-223 on this day, led the second section. "We poured the throttle to those Grumman Wildcats," wrote Carl in the book *United States Marine Corps in World War II,* edited by S. E. Smith, "to get upstairs in a hurry and succeeded in reaching 34,500 feet before the raid reached the vicinity of Henderson Field."

At this point the pilots received information that the Japanese had turned back. "So I'm looking around," recalled Carl; "it looked like it was going to be a dull day and we could go back and land."

Looking down to his left, Carl spotted eleven Zeros flying at 11,000 feet toward Henderson Field. Turning to the attack, he led the Wildcats down in a loose spiral, keeping between the Zeros and the sun.

Marion Carl has been called the ultimate fighter pilot. "When you first see an opponent," stated Carl, "you have to react instantly and properly. If you haven't been trained to do this, if you haven't figured out what to do, somebody's on your tail and you're in trouble." National Archives

Once in position to attack Carl dove on a Zero flying in the rear of the formation. Closing to about 100 yards, he fired a short burst and watched the Zero explode and plunge toward the sea, ablaze.

Carl had latched onto the tail of a second Zero when he made the same mistake he had made at Midway: he pulled the trigger too soon in the steep dive and all his guns jammed. Discretion being the better part of valor, he withdrew from the fight to recharge his guns.

While Carl was withdrawing, Lieutenant Colonel Bauer made a high-side rear attack on a Zero. As Bauer began firing, the Zero burst into flames. Picking out another Zero, Bauer pulled up inside and began firing. "It was a bull's eye. This Zero also plummeted to the sea in flames."

After ducking into a cloud Bauer emerged from the other side and found a Jap fighter below him. "This Nip never knew what hit him. He also went blazing into the sea."

Lt. C. G. Winter, who had dove to the attack with Carl, got on the tail of a Zero and followed him through a series of violent maneuvers. Finally able to close to within 25 to 30 yards, Winter opened up with all his guns. "This time he connected. The Zero blew up and pieces of airplane literally filled the air for a few seconds." Seeing no Zeros around, Lieutenant Winter dove down and joined up with Carl.

[Ken] Frazier, who was Carl's wingman, dove on a Zero. The Zero saw him coming and began to climb. With his height and speed advantage Frazier pulled to within 50 yards and fired. "This Jap plane blew up, one wing falling. Frazier had to maneuver quickly to avoid hitting it, but one small piece hit his windshield, cracking it," wrote Carl.

Climbing upward, Frazier saw a Zero trying to latch onto the tail of a Wildcat. "The Jap saw Frazier coming and pulled up into a loop. Frazier was right behind him, shooting all the way over. Coming out of the loop and close on the Zero's tail, Frazier's guns went into action and this plane blew up into a thousand pieces," according to Carl.

After the reports were analyzed, the intelligence officers were sure that the pilots of VMF-223 had downed nine Japanese planes, while only losing one Wildcat. Bauer led the way, claiming four Japanese planes shot down. The victory by Carl was his sixteenth.

On October 10 VMF-223 flew its last mission over Guadalcanal, escorting SBDs and TBFs to strike Japanese shipping. Squadron commander John Smith downed his nineteenth Japanese plane on this mission.

During its tenure on Guadalcanal, VMF-223 had sustained some forty-three percent casualties among its own pilots. The squadron was credited with 93.5 planes, of which 50.5 were twin-engine bombers and forty-one were Zero fighters. Smith and Carl shot down more twin-engine bombers over Guadalcanal than did any other Marine pilots throughout the war: ten and eight, respectively. Along with Smith and Carl, six other 223 pilots were ranked as aces.

The officers and enlisted personnel of VMF-223 were relieved and sent back to the United States to train new pilots and crews. Richard Mangrum, John Smith and Marion Carl reached the West Coast on October 21 and were given a hero's welcome by the media and public through war bond rallies, magazine stories and other public relations opportunities.

After a few weeks of publicity tours Carl found himself in New York City attending a party at the Waldorf-Astoria hosted by the Grumman Aircraft Corporation. While there Carl was introduced to an attractive young lady who was a professional model. It was love at first sight, and after five dates Carl found himself a married man.

Shortly after his marriage Carl was ordered to the Marine air station at El Toro, California. While there, as was his custom, he flew every airplane in sight. Flying the Lockheed P-38 Lightning was an experience he remembered vividly:

Maj. Marion Carl in front of an F4U Corsair. "The Corsair," recalled Carl in Barrett Tillman's Corsair: The F4U in World War II and Korea, *"was a great mount, head and shoulders above its contempor[ar]ies. An airplane like the Corsair only comes along occasionally."* National Archives

I had a friend down at San Diego who I went to Oregon State with who had a P-38 squadron. I went down and flew with them a couple of times. He wanted me to teach them overhead runs in a P-38. After damn near killing myself I decided they couldn't do it. "John," I said, "you and I can do it, but if you're trying to teach this to your green second lieutenants you'll have a few dead ones real quick." That airplane was the cleanest airplane I'd flown up to that time and was the first airplane I flew that got into compressibility. When you get into compressibility you're in for a rough time. On my first pass that damn thing was bucking like something I'd never experienced before. I kept at it until I was able to get it down, but you had to do everything just right.

Carl and his squadron were then ordered to Midway Island for two months training with the F4U Corsair. "I had a lot of fresh kids who could barely fly the airplane," recalled Carl. "Some of them pulled some stupid ones in the airplane and got themselves killed."

VMF-223, with Carl in command, was ordered to Vella Lavella Island in the central Solomons in December 1943 for a second tour of duty. While leading escort missions to Rabaul on December 23 and 27 Carl managed to shoot down two more Japanese planes, bringing his victory total to eighteen Japanese planes destroyed.

Another proficient destroyer of Japanese airplanes was also stationed on Vella Lavella at this time. Greg Boyington, the commander of VMF-214, shot down his twenty-fifth Japanese plane on December 27. With that victory the pressure was on Boyington. His claim of having shot down six Japanese planes while with the Flying Tigers in China had been accepted and he was now only one victory short of Joe Foss' Marine record of twenty-six victories. Time was running out for Boyington, however. His squadron was scheduled to finish its third combat tour in mid January 1944, and if Boyington was to break Foss' record he would need to fly as many missions as he could in the short time remaining.

On January 3, 1944, Boyington landed his Corsair at Vella Lavella after an unsuccessful combat mission. In his best-selling book *Baa Baa Black Sheep*, he recalled the events that followed:

Never had I felt so tired and dejected.... Another futile attempt was behind me. The bullet holes in my plane were a far cry from the record I was striving to bring back. I was dead tired, I had counted upon the day ending, but a pilot had crawled up on my wing after I cut my engine, and he had something important to say.

Marion Carl was scheduled to take several flights that afternoon to Bougainville, where they were to remain overnight, taking off the following morning for a sweep. He said, "Greg, I want to give you a chance to break the record. You take my flight because you're so close I think you are entitled to it.

I've got seventeen, but I still have lots of time left and you haven't."

... He had just been promoted to Major, and it was true that many chances were coming up for him. Great person that Marion Carl is, he was trying to give a tired old pilot a last crack at the title, even though it was at his own expense.

Carl's version of his encounter with Boyington at Vella Lavella was slightly different:

Boyington and I were at Vella Lavella together. The day he got shot down we traded flights. He came to me and said, "I've got twenty-five airplanes to my credit, I'd like to at least tie, if not break, Joe Foss' record." So I traded him flights.

Whichever way it happened, Boyington, in Carl's place, led the sweep to Rabaul the next day. The Marines encountered fierce resistance from an estimated force of sixty Japanese fighters. Boyington managed to shoot down a Zeke during an overhead pass but was soon lost sight of in the swirling dogfight that followed. Landing at Torokina after the battle, the Marine pilots compared notes. They had managed to shoot down six Japanese planes, but Boyington and his wingman, Capt. George Ashmun, were missing. Ashmun was lost, but Boyington was picked up by a Japanese sub.

Carl remained in command of 223 for only thirty days after the Boyington incident. Then he was unexpectedly transferred to the staff of Marine Air Group 12. "It was the end of my shooting," recalled Carl, "and I objected to the transfer very strenuously, but it didn't do any good."

With the end of World War II Carl returned to the United States as the sixth-ranking ace in the Marine Corps. For his valor in the skies over the Pacific he was twice awarded the Navy Cross.

After the war Carl applied his remarkable flying talent to flight testing. In 1945 he began his career in flight testing and in 1947 he became the chief test pilot for all carrier-type aircraft. "I was in the carrier section for 5½ years," he recalled, "and I put in over 3,000 hours in flight testing. I flew more than anybody in the section, even though I was head of the section."

As a test pilot, Carl had the opportunity to set the world speed record on August 25, 1947, when he flew the Navy's D-558 Skystreak 650.6 mph.

The D-558 Skystreak was similar to the X-1 rocket plane in shape, the main difference being that the Skystreak was powered by a jet instead of a rocket engine. The X-1 could only be launched in the air from a mother ship. The D-558 was designed to take off conventionally from a runway and was slower than the X-1 but could stay aloft longer. Between the two designs, it was thought that the aerodynamics in the unknown and trouble area at or just below the speed of sound could be studied.

Three jet-powered D-558 Skystreaks were built. In August 1947, shortly before Chuck Yeager flew the X-1 through the sound barrier, Navy commander Turner Caldwell, flying the D-558, set a speed record of 640.7 mph.

Carl had originally thought he would be the only pilot involved in the Navy's Skystreak project. His previous experience made him a natural choice to fly the D-558. His training in jets had been extensive even for 1947. After his original check-out in a P-59 at the Naval Air Test Center, Patuxent, Maryland, Carl had flown the P-80, including landing and taking off from a carrier. He had also flown the North American XFJ-1, McDonnell's XFD-1 and the German Me 262 jet fighter. He was therefore surprised when he arrived at Muroc, California (now Edwards AFB) to find Caldwell involved in the project.

So when I show up at Edwards, there's Caldwell, who is senior to me. Caldwell had never flown a jet and I had more jet time than anybody in the Navy or Marine Corps. Caldwell managed to check out in a P-80 and had three or four flights in it before the speed trials came up.

Once at Edwards both Carl and Caldwell had to wait for the Skystreak to be operational. After a short delay they were informed the plane would be available the next day. Once the plane was ready they had to decide who was going to make the first attempt at the world speed record.

So here was a dilemma: who is going to fly the airplane first? So I said to Caldwell, "I'll make a proposition to you and you can take your choice. You can take the airplane up tomorrow and fly it, or whoever doesn't fly it tomorrow gets to wait as long as he wants to for a higher temperature." Now this is August and 77 degrees [the predicted high for the next day] is a damn cold day for the desert. The temperature should have been close to 100 degrees. Optimum temperature for the speed trial was 104 degrees.

Turner Caldwell says, "I'll take it up tomorrow."

So he takes it and goes 640 mph and that's a new world speed record.

Carl had watched Caldwell's flight carefully and had noticed that although Caldwell got 100 percent rpm on the takeoff, he did not get 100 percent rpm during his flight.

Carl then went to the Westinghouse representative and asked him to change the governor on the Skystreak to get 100 percent rpm over the course. The representative told Carl that he could not change the governor. Carl was not about to take no for an answer; he knew he would need full engine power to break the record.

Maj. Marion Carl, third from right, near the nose of the P-80. Carl was the first Marine pilot to land a jet on an aircraft carrier. He did this on November 1, 1946. On occasion Carl landed a P-80 and later took off from the carrier. He also flew the German Me 262 jet plane after the war, as well as North American's XFJ-1 and McDonnell's XFD-1. National Archives

I said all I needed was a screwdriver on the damn governor. "Well," he says, "I don't want you monkeying with my engine."

"Look," I said, "I guarantee you I'll control it so it won't exceed 100 percent because the throttle overrides the governor."

Knowing the Skystreak would get 100 percent rpm over the course, Carl prepared to make his flight for the record on August 25. Takeoff time was scheduled for 1130 hours using the same plane that Commander Caldwell had flown while setting the record.

The cockpit of the Skystreak was no place for the faint-hearted or claustrophobic, recalled Carl:

The jet engine, air intake ducts and test equipment occupy most of the fuselage, leaving very little space for a cockpit. With only a pad on the floor, my head touched the top of the canopy when it was closed, making it impossible for me to wear a crash helmet. On the official runs I did not wear goggles on my helmet, for goggles rubbed the windshield when I pushed them up on my forehead. Also I could only turn my head only about 30 degrees before it would wedge inside the canopy.

Carl's flight lasted only 18 minutes from takeoff to landing; included a total of four runs over the course, two each way; and covered a distance of about 180 miles. His average speed for the four runs was 650.6 mph. Final speed was determined under the international rules of the Federation Aeronautique Internationale. These rules required Carl to stay below 246 feet going across the measured 1.86 mile course.

When asked how it felt to travel at the unheard-of speed of 650 mph only 50 to 100 feet above the ground, Carl replied in a December 1947 *Flying* magazine article "I Hold the World's Speed Record":

One thing I can say for certain, you really feel like you're getting someplace. You're keyed up—for regardless of how much confidence you have in the airplane you suspect they wouldn't be able to find all the pieces if something went wrong at that speed, or if you made an error in judgment, or overcontrolled with 100 feet or less between you and the ground.

In the early fifties Colonel Carl was assigned to test a full pressure suit, designed for flights above 50,000 feet. The "space suit" was designed for the Navy by the David Clark Company of Worcester, Massachusetts. The Clark Company had an extensive background in the manufacture of girdles and brassieres. Having conquered that market and with a detailed knowledge of the structural loads the human anatomy could place on a garment, the company president, David Clark, became interested in building a pressure suit, which was a new challenge to his inventive mind.

After more than a year in design the new suit was scheduled to be tested in the fall of 1952. At this point Colonel Carl fractured his back in a jet accident and the tests had to be delayed.

In August 1953 Carl was ready to fly again. The world that year was celebrating the fiftieth anniversary of flight, and the Navy, eager for publicity, wanted Carl to test the pressure suit while trying to set two new flying records. Scott Crossfield, in his book *Always Another Dawn*, recorded Carl's arrival at Edwards AFB:

One day in the summer of 1953 Marine Colonel Marion Carl arrived at NACA. Carl is one of the most fabulous aviators in history. . . . Carl had never flown a rocket airplane. But Walt Williams called all of us into the office to announce that the Navy was borrowing the Skyrocket for a few days. Colonel Carl would try to beat Bridgeman's altitude record of 79,000 feet and set a speed record of Mach 2.

The Douglas Skyrocket was a research airplane with a rocket engine capable, it was hoped, of speeds up to Mach 2 and altitudes of 90,000 to 100,000 feet.

Carl was helped immensely by Crossfield, a veteran NACA test pilot. Crossfield threw himself into the project enthusiastically, as he wrote in his book *Always Another Dawn*.

One reason was that Carl, a big lanky guy, was immensely likeable and a superb aviator, in my book. I had to admire his guts. There weren't many pilots in the world who would deliberately jump in the Skyrocket and go for broke. We stayed up late at night. I told him every detail of the Skyrocket, all her quirks and strong points, what to beware of, just how to balance on that knife edge in the thin air. . . . In many ways this was superfluous: he had done considerable cramming before he came.

The Skyrocket would be launched from a B-29 at around 30,000 feet. The first flight was almost a catastrophe and Carl never was launched. He related his close brush with disaster:

You wait in the B-29 until you get up to altitude, then you climb into the cockpit of the D-558 and you hook up, and when you think everything is all set you start the countdown from ten. They also at this time disconnect you from all the main systems in the B-29, including oxygen.

On this particular flight by the time they got to eight I realized I didn't have any oxygen. In the Skyrocket the oxygen system was out—and here I am, sitting at 33,000 feet. I tried to break into the countdown and couldn't. He wasn't releasing the button on the intercom so I could break in. Fortunately Crossfield was watching me. I started waving my hand across the front of my face and finally they got the word and stopped the count at two.

On the third flight the D-558-II was carried by a B-29 to 32,000 feet. Just after leaving the ground Carl had put on the pressure suit. At 10,000 feet he was strapped into the cockpit of the Skyrocket; it was a tight and uncomfortable fit for the big Marine.

I'm 6 feet 2 inches and wearing a full pressure suit. This was the first time a full pressure suit had been used for this in the United States, and that pressure suit was bulky. Hell, it was the first attempt at this sort of thing and the suit was big and clumsy and hard to do anything in. In fact, when it was inflated, you could only move your fingers, your arm a little bit and your wrist just slightly, and the same thing with your feet. When you put the pressure in the suit it just stiffened everything up so that you weren't able to do very much. But you could do enough to control the airplane, because you don't have to attack those controls with a lot of vigor at high speed.

After waiting in the Skyrocket for more than 30 minutes Carl was launched. Once on his own he put the Skyrocket into a ballistic trajectory and began what he felt was the most difficult part of the flight.

The hardest part was staying on that damn schedule going up. Once you're going up—every time you hit a certain altitude you're supposed to be at a certain indicated air speed and you have to be right on, not off 5 miles an hour or so. That's the ticklish part—not the most dangerous part, but the most difficult.

Although his limited supply of rocket fuel was spent when the Skyrocket reached 75,000 feet, the plane's momentum propelled it more than 1½ miles farther to establish the altitude record. Carl in-

stinctively knew he had broken Bridgeman's record, although he would have to land before confirming the fact.

I knew before I even landed that I had gone higher than Bridgeman, because I knew that I had flown a perfect profile and that I'd gone over the top with a lot more speed than Bridgeman had—which meant I'd gone higher; how much higher I didn't really know.

Carl didn't achieve full control of the plane coming down until he was at 20,000 feet. By that time he was more than 100 miles from Edwards and looking for a place to land. Even though he was without power, Carl had no trouble landing.

Coming down was easy, just like flying another airplane dead stick. I had 13 miles of runway on a dry lake bed and they had a mark on it and I always managed to put down within 1,000 feet of that mark.

Carl had flown to 83,235 feet, breaking Bridgeman's record by a healthy margin. When asked almost fifty years later if flying the Skyrocket was a special challenge for him, he gave this reply:

I didn't think much about flying the Skyrocket. You have to remember I was used to climbing into a lot of different airplanes. I wasn't like those guys at NACA who were on a project, who might fly two or three different airplanes. Hell, I've flown 250 different types and models of airplanes, everything from sailplanes up to rocket-powered jobs. It's just one of those things that I've never had any trouble adjust-

Marion Carl, on left, in front of the Navy's D-558 Skystreak. On August 25, 1947, Carl set a world record in the Skystreak, flying 650.6 mph. "It was not a difficult plane to fly," wrote Carl, "and it does not require a superman. All in all, it is a beautiful airplane, well built, and one that flies like an airplane should at those speeds." National Archives

ing. One day I might be flying a supersonic airplane and the next day I'd be flying a puddle jumper.

I never doubted my ability to handle any airplane; that never concerned me.

Crossfield, who had watched Carl break the world altitude record in the Skyrocket, summed up Carl's performance during the flight with these words of praise:

Ever since, I have held Carl in highest regard. In five brief Skyrocket flights he had shattered the world altitude record. His record is usually omitted from most aviation-record summaries. I think that is because he was a Marine. But Carl, in no sense a small man, had never raised the point himself.

In 1955 Communist China was threatening an invasion of Quemoy and Matsu. These islands were more than 100 miles from Nationalist Formosa and within 5 to 10 miles of mainland China. Admiral Carrey, the chief of naval operations, contributed to cold war tensions by telling reporters that he and his staff expected a Chinese attack on the islands within a month. Dwight Eisenhower warned the Red Chinese that any attack on Formosa or Quemoy and Matsu would have to run over the Seventh Fleet.

It was against this background of international tension that Carl flew several photo-recon flights over Red China. He missed the first photo-recon flight over the Chinese mainland but recounted the second flight, which he led:

We're on our way in, and I have a wingman and both of us are flying photo airplanes with no guns. Without any warning from anybody I happen to pick up two MIGs, either 15s or 17s, coming up from below. . . . I just happened to pick them up. They were behind [us] a couple of miles at seven o'clock. Without hesitation I turned into them and dove right toward them. When I met them I passed right over them, head-on, and my wingman was right with me. Then I rolled that Banshee over on its back and went right straight down with the speed brakes out, and that old Banshee was really bucking because it wasn't used to that kind of treatment.

I got down to just above the ground and I pulled up and scooted for home just over the treetops. Well of course the Red Chinese radar, which had been guiding the MIGs, lost me when I went down to the ground and because it was kind of hazy that day the MIGs lost me too. I did it all so quick I don't think they ever figured out what happened to those two airplanes.

After landing back on Formosa, Carl called headquarters and said that if the photo-recon flights over China were to be successful they would have to be done differently. Carl wanted four Banshee fighters for escort and wanted to be able to fly the recon flights at any altitude.

The high command agreed to Carl's suggested changes and the photo-recon flights went ahead as scheduled. Carl, who was the only fighter pilot in the squadron, flew a fighter on subsequent missions and escorted the photo plane.

To further enhance the success of the photo-recon flights Carl convinced the high command to let Americans operate the Nationalist radar stations in the Pescadores. On the next flight Bill Hardy, a former fighter pilot with thirteen aircraft to his credit, manned the radar that was monitoring Carl.

As Carl approached the Chinese mainland he radioed Hardy simple instructions:

I said, "Bill, all I want from you is the vector and the distance from me to any Communist airplanes you pick up. Don't waste your time telling me what to do. I'll know what to do. All I want to know is where in the hell they are."

Using Carl's strategy and with the assistance of the Nationalist Chinese radar, the photo-recon flights were successful.

"We never had another interception after that," recalled Carl.

Sometimes they sent up two or three flights of MIGs to get us but they never found us. Their own radar was trying to tell them how to find us but we always managed to screw them up.

We made seventy-seven sorties over Funkien Province in China. I probably flew a little bit more than any of the others, because I usually flew a fighter. I was always kind of hoping, to tell you the truth, that I'd run into a MIG.

One of Carl's last major assignments was in Vietnam. He served there as a landing force commander for two amphibious landing operations—the only two landings ever made there, as far as he knew. Neither landing was opposed and on one the Marines were met by flower girls.

While in Vietnam Carl served as an assistant wing commander, with the rank of brigadier general. Not much fighting was going on at that time, so Carl, a qualified helicopter pilot, went looking for trouble.

I got in the habit of going out over in the country in a Huey gunship. I'd take a Huey, what they called a dirty slick, because a Huey gunship fully armed has rocket pods on it, and I'd say, "Take the damn pods off, all they do [is] slow me up, and I can't hit anything with them anyway."

I did, however, have four forward-firing .30 caliber machine guns plus two waist guns. I'd always take somebody along as a copilot and most of the time it was my aide, who was a first lieutenant.

I flew the gunship and taught my aide how to fly also; in case I took a round, he could put the damn thing down or fly back to base.

I flew 110 flights in the Huey gunship and about eight or nine flights in F-4 fighters. All the fighter flights were just dropping bombs; at that time we weren't allowed out of South Vietnam.

With the Huey gunship I'd do a little strafing, but I always had to be careful not to get into trouble because I wasn't supposed to be flying. Eventually the word got back to the commandant that he had a brigadier out there flying tactical missions in a Huey and he sent an order out grounding me.

Carl retired from the US Marine Corps on June 1, 1973. He had achieved the rank of major general and logged more than 14,000 hours flying time in more than 250 different types and models of aircraft.

Living in Oregon, the legendary pilot recently reflected on his storied career:

Looking back, I've felt I was very fortunate in having certain opportunities most pilots never have—also being in a position to take advantage of those opportunities. I was never backwards about pushing myself whenever I saw an opportunity available.

What really got me started was that I was the first ace in the Marine Corps. When I came back from Guadalcanal there were not many aces around at the time and I got a lot of publicity.

As far as combat and test pilots go, there's not many of them that have a better record than I have.

I thoroughly enjoyed flight testing. A lot of the people who worked with me and for me got killed. I have had four pilots who flew my project airplanes get killed. In other words, the airplane was basically my project, but while I was gone out to Edwards or someplace and it was flown temporarily by someone else they got killed.

The philosopher Spinoza wrote, "All things excellent are as difficult as they are rare." Marion Carl was one of those rare people who instantly overcame difficulty to achieve, time and time again, excellence.

Taking publicity photos of the Skystreak. Marion Carl is in the center, looking down at the cockpit. The Skystreak was built solely for research and carried over 500 pounds of test equipment. "The exterior coating of the Skystreak," wrote Carl, "is an enamel, *with a glass like finish. Skilled workmen worked tirelessly, rubbing it to a jewel like smoothness, for at 600 mph, skin friction is an appreciable item."* National Archives

Chapter 4

Jerry Collinsworth, American Spitfire Ace

Jerry Collinsworth won his wings in March 1942. After talking his way out of an assignment to bombers he was assigned to the 31st Fighter Group. One of the first American fighter groups sent to England, the 31st was equipped with the famous British Spitfire Mark V. Piloting the British plane, Collinsworth soon found himself flying combat in support of the Dieppe raid in August 1942. After the invasion of North Africa the 31st was assigned to combat duty at Feriana, Tunisia. During his tenure in North Africa, Collinsworth managed to shoot down six German FW 190s and damage two others. After being wounded in a freak accident in Sicily he returned to the United States. For the remainder of the war Collinsworth was involved in training pilots to fly the P-47 Thunderbolt. He retired as an Air Force colonel on October 31, 1970, and settled in Phoenix. Unless attributed to another source all quotes are from a September 1988 interview with Jerry Collinsworth.

On June 12, 1942, members of the 31st Fighter Group, US Army Air Force, set sail for the United Kingdom to enter the Second World War. Upon arrival in England the group proceeded to Atcham Air Base near Shrewsbury, Shropshire, England.

Arriving at Atcham with the other members of the 31st Fighter Group was a young second lieutenant from Texas, Jerry Collinsworth. Expecting to be equipped with P-39s, Collinsworth and his fellow pilots were shocked when during a night briefing they were informed that they would receive a British fighter, the Supermarine Spitfire.

Although not disappointed about losing his chance to fly P-39s, Collinsworth was unfamiliar with the Spitfire Mark V. He remembered vividly his first close-up inspection of the famous British fighter:

I stood and looked at the Spitfire parked on the runway at Atcham. I looked at it hard and it kind of looked like an ugly duckling in a way.

I was very surprised when I grabbed the wing tip and found I could shake the airplane.

I was more surprised when I noticed that the propeller was wooden. I thought all airplanes had to have steel propellers.

Although not initially enthused with the airplane, Collinsworth would fly it through some of the fiercest air combat of World War II. He would complete his tour with the 31st after flying 125 combat missions. He would be awarded two Distinguished Flying Crosses and the Air Medal with seventeen oak leaf clusters.

Jerry Collinsworth grew up in Berger, Texas, an oil boom town located in the Panhandle. Graduating from high school in 1937, he entered Texas A&M University in the fall and lasted for a semester. Withdrawing from the university because of poor grades, he took a job working as a laborer in the Texas oil fields. After six months of hard work he was sufficiently motivated to reenter college, this time at Texas Tech University.

In May 1941 Collinsworth joined the US Army Air Corps, and in August he was sent to Hemet, California, to begin primary training. Collinsworth eventually received orders to report to Alexandria, Louisiana, for training in B-25s. After a short period there he was assigned to the 31st Pursuit Group, which was forming up in New Orleans.

The group began training with P-40s; however, this was only temporary, as it was soon reequipped with P-39s.

Despite its many advanced features, the P-39 was not a high-performance fighter plane. Collinsworth was blunt in his assessment of it: "I didn't like the P-39. It just didn't seem to perform as we expected fighters to. The center of gravity was right

Jerry Collinsworth in 1945. By the end of his combat tour Collinsworth would shoot down six German *planes, with one probable and one damaged.* Jerry Collinsworth

behind the pilot where the engine was. I put in 125 hours in the P-39 in a little over two months."

Flying fighter aircraft while training was a dangerous occupation, and Collinsworth remembered several close calls while flying the P-39:

One time I was flying and we were shooting at ground targets on the beach at Lake Pontchartrain. I zeroed in and fixated on the target, as so often happens to young pilots, and all of a sudden the ground was very close and I pulled back as hard as I could. I splashed mud on my windshield that had been kicked up by my bullets. . . . It was that close.

Another time I was dogfighting a fellow right over a swamp west of Lake Pontchartrain. I hit his prop wash and it flipped me over on my back at 50 feet and I could look up and see the trees. I was inverted and I remember thinking, *So this is how you get killed,* but I pushed the rudder real quick and I snapped upright and got out of that one.

In May 1942 the ground echelon departed New Orleans for Fort Dix, New Jersey, to begin overseas processing. At this time the 31st Pursuit Group was renamed the 31st Fighter Group and became part of the Eighth Air Force. In June the ground echelon sailed on HMS *Queen Elizabeth* for Europe.

Meanwhile, the air echelon had been practicing long-range flights from Grenier Field, Manchester, New Hampshire, in anticipation of flying across the Atlantic in its P-39s. When these plans were canceled, the air echelon left New York by ship and arrived at Atcham Air Base on June 25.

Now stationed at Atcham, Collinsworth and his fellow 31st Group fighter pilots began training in the Spitfire Mark V. This superb single-engine fighter had a liquid-cooled engine and carried two 20 mm cannons and four .303 inch machine guns in the leading edge of its wings. It was extremely maneuverable but it was neither as fast nor as efficient at high altitudes as the German Me 109 or FW 190.

Learning to fly the Spitfire was not an easy task for Collinsworth and his fellow pilots.

Our biggest trouble with the Spit was learning to coordinate the rudder with the brake system—it didn't have brakes in the rudder pedals like our airplanes.

We damaged about twenty airplanes because of this in the first three or four weeks—nothing serious, but once you got the hang of it there was no problem.

After several weeks of concentrated training the various fighter squadrons of the 31st FG became operational. Collinsworth and the other members of the 307th Squadron were sent to Biggin Hill for their initial combat missions.

The experienced British led the eager Americans on several missions out over the English Channel, attempting to introduce the fledglings to combat gradually. Collinsworth vividly remembered these early missions:

The British sent a wing commander called Thomas down to lead us out over the Channel three or four times just to get the feel of it.

They told us some of the things they had learned the hard way in combat: "Keep your head on a swivel, and never get by yourself, never get less than a two-man element."

Spitfire Mark IXs and P-51 Mustangs of the 31st Fighter Group line the runway at Castle Volurno, Italy, in 1944. The 31st FG, which served under both the Twelfth and Fifteenth air forces in World War II, *scored 571 air-to-air victories and produced 33 aces.* John Fawcett

I remember an old British pilot said, "Chaps, where there's one there are quite often two or more."

This saved my life one time, I am convinced.

The defensive patrols of the 31st came to an abrupt end on August 19 when the group was called on to support an Allied landing by ground troops on the coast of France at Dieppe.

The RAF and the 31st FG engaged in heavy fighting over Dieppe. When it was all over, the 31st had flown 123 sorties, losing eight Spitfires to enemy action and having seven more damaged. Overall, the Allies lost 103 aircraft for the day and claimed forty-eight enemy fighters shot down.

Collinsworth flew three sorties over Dieppe on August 19, landing on one occasion with only 8 gallons of gas left in his Spitfire. For the inexperienced Collinsworth the day was an education in combat flying.

I saw lots of German planes that day, but I never fired my guns; I just flew around wide-eyed and the next morning my neck was stiff and sore from twisting and turning while watching for German airplanes.

We flew cover for the ships to try and keep the dive-bombers off of them. The first mission we went in at 10,000 feet, so the FW 190s just went to 12,000 feet, came diving through, dropped their bombs and went back to France.

Pink Lady, *an American P-40, taxis through the North African sand while ground crew member Paul Dunn sits on the wing. Jerry Collinsworth recalled one occasion when the French landed at his base: "In came the Lafayette Escadrille, the French unit with new P-40s. I remember seeing one Frenchman step out of the cockpit with a long white silk scarf, big black shiny boots and a bottle of champagne."* Paul Dunn

The next mission they moved us up and the Germans just moved a little higher—that's the way it went for three missions. This was all a big new world to me—6½ months before, I was a civilian in college.

Coming back from the last mission over Dieppe, Collinsworth found himself flying line abreast to the squadron commander. Looking up, Collinsworth saw a FW 190 coming down rapidly from behind. "It looked like it was 200 yards back; I was so excited that when I hit the mike button all I could stammer was ah . . . ah . . . ah."

Despite having the advantage, the FW 190 rolled over on its back and did a split-S, diving away without firing a shot. The squadron commander, recalled Collinsworth, "never knew what happened until we got back and I told him."

The period following the Dieppe raid was a quiet one for the 31st FG. For several weeks the group flew relatively uneventful missions along the coast and strafing hops across the English Channel. Little enemy air activity was encountered during this time, with the exception that Maj. Harrison Thyng, who would become an ace in World War II and Korea, added to his score by engaging a Ju 88 bomber and claiming it as probably destroyed.

In late September the 31st FG enjoyed a change.

We were taken off ops [operational status]. We had no idea as to why, but we didn't object to it too much, because they told us to go out and practice low-level navigation. To us young fighter pilots that was an open invitation to inspect any and all castles at window level. And man, I bet I inspected at least fifty of these castles in England, from about 50 feet up, vertically and horizontally, flying rapidly by.

Throughout September and October plans for the invasion of North Africa—Operation Torch—were being finalized. In late October Colonel Hawkins, the group commander, informed all officers of the 31st that the group was about to leave England for an unknown destination, that this would be a top-secret move and that all group members were pledged to secrecy.

The invasion of Northwest Africa would feature three Allied landings: one at Casablanca, one at Oran and one at Algiers. The 31st was tentatively scheduled to provide air cover for Gen. George Patton's divisions going into Casablanca.

The 31st had left its original Spitfires in England. Upon landing at Gibraltar the men of the 31st picked up their new "desertized" Spitfires. These planes were painted tan with a blob of dark brown interspersed here and there. They also featured larger air scoops with dust filters.

As the invasion of North Africa progressed, the news came in that the main French resistance was being encountered at Oran. Plans were quickly changed and the 31st was ordered to land at Oran's Tafaraoui airfield.

After the pilots had landed, they learned that the airfield had just been captured a few hours before by American paratroopers who had been dropped from C-47s flown from England. Prisoners taken by the airborne troops were still on the field under guard, waiting to be moved to prisoner of war camps.

Even though the 31st FG reached North Africa on November 9, Collinsworth wasn't able to join the group until the end of November. He arrived at La Senia Airdrome with a group of nurses from the 12th General Hospital. This was rough duty, but Collinsworth figured someone had to do it. Although the rest of the pilots were glad to see him, the nurses, for some reason, seemed to receive more attention.

In mid February 1943 Erwin Rommel launched his famous offensive aimed at Kasserine Pass. The American ground troops were not only outnumbered but also green and inexperienced. Rommel struck the American troops at their weakest points and began to push them back.

The pilots of the 31st did all they could to help halt the German offensive. Dogfights took place often as the Allies battled the Germans to establish air supremacy.

On February 15 Collinsworth was flying near Faid Pass with the 307th Squadron. While they were patroling the area a call came over the radio of German planes at four o'clock high. "I looked up," recalled Collinsworth, "and sure enough there they were, four German FW 190s."

Waiting until the Germans were fairly close, Collinsworth and his squadron mates suddenly broke away from them. Collinsworth gave this description of the air battle that followed:

I turned and we were heading right toward each other head-on. The German was in a shallow dive and I was in a shallow climb. Then I could feel the bullets hitting my airplane and I remember thinking, *You son of a bitch; if you can dish it out, I can too!*

I pressed the firing button—you could fire the two cannon or fire the four machine guns or fire them all—I pushed down on the button and fired them all; it made a big racket, but nothing seemed to happen to the German plane.

I was almost ready to release the firing button, thinking I had missed him, when I noticed the fire

The famous Spitfire Mark IX. "With the Spitfire IX we had a great airplane," remembered Jerry Collinsworth. "We could still outrun the German, but *now could also outturn him and outclimb him. Boy, does that change your outlook on life."* John Fawcett

start to flicker on his wings; then he poured out black smoke and pieces of flame shot out the right cowling, and it was over in a split second—he started windmilling and belly-landed into the desert.

I got excited and started to holler, "Hey, I got him, I got him!" and then somebody with a very quiet voice said over the radio, "Shut up!" so I did.

During the height of Rommel's offensive, Collinsworth and his wingman flew over Kasserine Pass. Scooting under some low clouds, Collinsworth saw tracers coming up from the ground. "I looked over and I could see these pink desert-colored German tanks shooting at us; they didn't hit anything, but I was sure glad I was up high and not on the ground in front of them."

As his offensive began to wane and in the face of growing Allied persistence, Rommel began to with-

John Fawcett, standing by a Spitfire Mark V-C, from 2nd Squadron, 52nd FG. The 2nd Squadron was called the Beagle squadron, which was a takeoff on the Eagle Squadron. Note the beagle on the nose of the Spitfire behind Fawcett. The 52nd FG was the second American group to receive Spitfires upon its arrival in England. Like the 31st FG it was also transferred to Africa as part of the Twelfth Air Force.
John Fawcett

draw. Even though the Germans were now in retreat, the 31st FG was still actively engaging the enemy almost every day.

On March 8 Collinsworth once again met German fighters in a wild encounter that he aptly described as "a real barn burner."

On this day Collinsworth was flying with three other American Spitfire pilots near Kasserine Pass. Weather conditions were poor, as it was raining lightly and visibility was only about 1,000 feet. Merlyn Mitchell was leading the flight and Collinsworth was flying in the number 3 position.

As the flight leader made a sharp left bank Collinsworth swung too wide, and as the flight came out of the turn Woody Thomas, the wingman, cut inside and took the element lead, with Collinsworth positioned behind.

At this point Collinsworth noticed they were receiving fire from the ground.

I could see the tracers coming up at us. As Woody began to throttle back and slow down, I advanced the throttle, and I hadn't pulled past him more than 100 feet when I heard guns going off behind me. I looked back and Woody was on fire—I watched him roll over on his back, go in and blow up. The FW 190 that got him had apparently been coming in off me and when I pulled in front of Woody he shot him up instead. It was 5 seconds that was the difference; it saved my life but cost Woody his.

After observing Thomas crash Collinsworth hit the mike button and hollered, "German in the clouds!" "I didn't know how many there were," recalled Collinsworth. "All I knew [was] that this one was right above me and I knew Woody was dead."

Pulling up into the low-hanging clouds, Collinsworth managed to evade the German attacker. After a few seconds he gently pushed the inside rudder and nosed the Spitfire back out of the clouds.

Coming out of the clouds, Collinsworth found himself behind the FW 190, which was diving to join a dogfight taking place below on the deck. The German pilot soon noticed Collinsworth above and behind him.

I saw the black smoke come out as the German took off and dropped down to 50 feet. He had everything to the firewall; I could see the black smoke pouring out.

We had an emergency boost on our engine. You could use it for 5 minutes in emergencies. I took off on this emergency boost and we were both going flat out. I began to slowly close on him and he suddenly racked the Focke-Wulf into a tight left turn. I remember thinking, *Friend, you are not about to outturn this Spitfire.*

Now above and inside the German, Collinsworth pressed the firing button and started shooting. "One cannon was jammed, so I was sawing because one cannon in one wing was firing and one wasn't." With the Spitfire's nose moving back and forth Collinsworth tried to correct by hitting the rudder pedals. "This all happened, just like bang, bang."

Shortly after Collinsworth started firing, the Focke-Wulf snapped over on its back. Thinking that the German pilot was going to do a split-S and come up behind, Collinsworth rocked the Spitfire the other way to keep the German in view. "Just as I rocked up and looked down, I forgot we were at 50 feet doing about 375 mph. He was too low so he hit the ground and blew up."

Collinsworth found himself right above the deck; "If there had been any grass I would have been mowing it." He throttled back and began to breathe normally once again. Suddenly he noticed another plane 500 feet above and in front of him.

As he warily approached the plane Collinsworth could see it was a German Me 109. Climbing slowly, "[I] put everything forward and began to move up underneath the German. I was just getting ready to fire when I remembered what a Britisher in England had said: 'Chaps, where there's one, there's quite often two.'"

Doing a quick 180 degree turn, Collinsworth was startled to see a Focke-Wulf pass right over him. "Had I continued the attack I would have pulled up right in front of his guns."

Turning west, Collinsworth pointed the Spitfire for home. His breath came in short gasps as he tried to calm down after his brush with death. Landing at his base, he was sorry to learn that flight leader Mitchell had also been shot down during the surprise attack.

Mitchell had been hit by the great German ace Kurt Buehlingen, who shot down 112 Allied aircraft during World War II. He spent three years as a POW in Germany before returning home.

For much of its stay in Tunisia the 31st FG was stationed at Thelepte Airdrome. Conditions at Thelepte were primitive, unlike the relative luxury the staff was accustomed to in England. The airdrome had at one time been occupied by the Germans, who had constructed a number of underground huts on the perimeter of the field. These huts were of crude construction but they offered satisfactory protection against German air attacks and the violent Tunisian sandstorms. They housed

John Fawcett in the cockpit of a Spitfire Mark VIII at Palermo, Sicily, Italy, in August 1943. "The Spitfire was the most natural flying airplane that was ever made," claimed Fawcett. "It was the perfect design for a fighter interceptor. It had better maneuverability than any plane, except perhaps the Japanese Zero." John Fawcett

two to four officers, and the enlisted men occupied pup tents, widely dispersed some distance from the field.

Food for the group often consisted of cold C-rations. Water was scarce; it had to be transported 45 miles from Tebessa by truck. Each person was allowed only 1 gallon per day for drinking, cooking and washing. Few men bothered to shave.

Occasionally, the Tunisian sandstorms, called siroccos, became so violent that it was impossible to walk against the wind. When a sirocco appeared, the aircraft had to be securely tied down and the aircraft guns had to be placed in wraps and the barrels stuffed with cloth to prevent the infiltration of sand. "The old timers," according to the 31st Fighter Group history, "were not kidding when, later, they would tell the new arrivals from the states, 'You should have been at Thelepte, it was r-e-a-l-l-y r-o-u-g-h, there!'"

In early April Collinsworth and several other pilots were escorting a group of A-20s on a bombing mission. On the way out after the bombing run the flight leader spotted a group of Me 109s climbing toward the A-20s.

Apparently unaware of the Spitfires, the Germans were 1,000 feet below the A-20s and about to pounce when Collinsworth and his wingman did a barrel roll and dove to the attack.

Boring in behind a Focke-Wulf, Collinsworth opened fire. The German knew he was hit, remembered Collinsworth:

Almost immediately his canopy came back and he started to climb out. I stopped firing, he sat down in the seat and I started firing once again—and this time he really came out. His chute opened fine and he seemed to be all right.

Finding himself alone and close to the ground, Collinsworth scanned the sky for the missing A-20s. Looking up, he observed a lone A-20 at 500 feet trailing smoke out of one engine with three Me 109s boring in to attack.

Pulling his throttle wide open, Collinsworth rushed to help the stricken A-20.

Those three Me 109s made passes at the A-20, when suddenly the A-20 just pulled up vertically and climbed until he stalled out. He came down spinning—I remember seeing one chute get out—before the A-20 crashed. With a helpless feeling I came on home.

In May Collinsworth was on a mission to Tunis. Up ahead he could make out a dogfight taking place. Approaching the battle, he called out a FW 190 at one o'clock. The flight leader called back and said: "O.K. Go get him!"

Pulling up behind the German, Collinsworth sensed it would be an easy kill.

Dave MacMillan and Charles Toud, left to right, stand in front of a Spitfire Mark IX at Pomigliano, Italy. The two pilots belonged to the 309th Squadron of the 31st FG. Many pilots felt the firepower offered by the two 20 mm cannon and four .30 caliber machine guns in the Spitfire was excellent. John Fawcett

I don't believe he had the faintest clue where I came from. As soon as I hit him he bailed out. When I looked around the only thing I saw was him hanging in his chute at about 12,000 feet; all the other planes had disappeared. I was a half-mile away from the German and I turned to go back by him. The German was sure I was going to shoot him, I'll bet. I did go by close enough so I could see the color of his coveralls, and I thumbed my nose at him. Laughing at my foolishness, I headed home.

Collinsworth's sixth and last combat victory came on July 12 on a mission over Sicily.

While flying over the beach Collinsworth noticed a flicker of light off in the distance. Turning to investigate, he picked up a German FW 190 that had just dropped a bomb and was making a 180 degree turn low to the ground.

As he approached the German from above, Collinsworth began diving.

The dust began kicking up behind him, as I was shooting short. I immediately corrected and began to see hits on his airplane. He went into a 45 degree climb and I stayed on his tail shooting. At around 1,000 feet his canopy came off and he bailed out. As I went by him he pulled his ripcord and for some reason his chute fell off him and he tumbled to his death.

While in Sicily the 31st was stationed at an airdrome near Gela. The first three nights there the Germans came over in an old Ford Trimotor and dropped antipersonnel bombs.

One night, to ensure safety against the German night attacks, Collinsworth and a fellow pilot slept in an old abandoned gun pit. Awakening early the next morning, Collinsworth observed an infantryman from the 45th Division walking on the field near him. Approaching one of the German antipersonnel bombs that had failed to explode, the infantryman nonchalantly gave it a kick. The explosion that followed woke up everyone in the immediate vicinity. The infantryman was lying on the ground screaming. The explosion had blown off his leg.

Soon the group was moved to a dirt strip near Agrigento. The Italians had moved out the night before. Shortly after their arrival Collinsworth noticed that a grass fire had started near some of the parked aircraft. Collinsworth and several of his buddies ran over to help put out the fire. Shortly an explosion slammed Collinsworth.

I felt a blow and I remember throwing up my hands and doing a 180 degree onto my face. Johnny ran over and said, "Are you hurt?" I said, "I don't know." He rolled me over and I was pretty well covered with blood. What had happened was that the fire had set off an Italian hand grenade.

Collinsworth was taken to a tent hospital filled with other wounded men. "I had been shot full of morphine," he recalled. "The Doc looked me over and said, 'Well, if you were going to die you would be dead already.'"

Collinsworth underwent surgery that night. He was operated on by a British doctor on a British

Pilot Mike Encinias stands in the cockpit of a Spitfire Mark VIII at Palermo in August 1943. Encinias was shot down on February 19, 1944, and spent the rest of the war as a guest of the German *government at Stalag Luft 1. He retired after being chairman of languages at the University of New Mexico.* John Fawcett

hospital ship. "I was a mess," he remembered. "I hadn't had a bath in three or four weeks."

After a hospital stay of twenty-six days, Collinsworth returned to the 31st to fly a few more noncombat missions before being returned to the States with seventeen other pilots.

Retired and living in Arizona, Collinsworth's pride in serving with the 31st FG is obvious. He is one of only ten Americans who became aces while flying the Spitfire in World War II.

The men of the 31st FG received little publicity during World War II. Many Americans, even today, are still astonished to learn that for a large part of the war several American fighter groups were equipped with foreign aircraft. Flying the borrowed British Spitfire, pilots of the 31st FG ran up a total of 192 enemy aircraft destroyed, thirty-nine probably destroyed and 124 damaged. The Spitfire was, recalled Collinsworth, "a hell of a plane that helped to win a hell of a war."

John Fawcett in the cockpit of his Spitfire Mark IX. Fawcett flew tours with both the 52nd and 31st FGs.

He ended the war with 180 combat missions to his credit. John Fawcett

Chapter 5

The Nine Lives of Perry Dahl

Although he shot down nine Japanese planes during World War II, Perry Dahl was fortunate to survive several incredible mishaps while flying with the 475th Fighter Group. On November 24, 1944, for example, flying in support of B-25s attacking the Japanese fleet, he was rammed accidently by his wingman. Blown out of his P-38, he parachuted into the middle of the Japanese fleet. After making it to shore he was rescued by Filipino guerrillas. He joined the guerrillas on several raids behind Japanese lines. After returning to his unit he led his squadron 1,000 miles across the China Sea and returned after shooting down a Zero near Saigon, Vietnam. Following the war, he served two tours in Vietnam, flying the OV-10 and as commander of the 56th Special Operations Wing. He also served as the vice-commandant of cadets at the US Air Force Academy. He retired in the Florida Keys. Unless attributed to another source all quotes are from a September 1990 interview with Perry Dahl.

On February 29, 1943, Lt. Perry Dahl, a member of the 475th Fighter Group "Satan's Angels," Fifth Air Force, was scheduled to fly a combat mission providing air cover for the Admiralty Island invasion. The 475th FG flew the P-38 Lightning, a plane whose long range made it especially suited for air combat in the Southwest Pacific.

Taking off from Nadzabi, New Guinea, Dahl joined a group of seven Lightnings for the journey to their area of operation. Weather always affected operations in the Southwest Pacific, and 20 miles short of landfall Dahl's group observed heavy rain clouds ahead. The leader of the formation decided the front was too severe to penetrate and turned the group back toward home. As they headed for their base the pilots had no way of knowing that their retreat to New Guinea was now blocked by a huge, severe weather front that had closed in behind them on the outbound leg.

As the weather conditions worsened, Dahl found that visibility was almost zero.

> The weather was atrocious. . . . The leader got us completely lost and we were right down on the deck because the visibility was so bad. We were very inadequate instrument flyers, so we had to stay out of the clouds. The rain came down in torrents and I could hardly see a thing.

In the deluge the P-38s separated, each seeking its own haven. Dahl and four other pilots sought refuge on New Britain and turned to follow the coastline to the airfield on Cape Gloucester.

As the P-38s turned Dahl watched with horror while a Lightning flown by Lt. Harold Howard banked too hard to the right and caught its wing tip in the water. The force of the impact sent the Lightning cartwheeling into the sea, killing Lieutenant Howard.

Approaching the primitive airstrip on Cape Gloucester, Dahl noticed a B-24 sitting at the other end of the field. "I thought," recalled Dahl, "that if he could land so could I."

As Dahl broke off to land a green flare was fired into the air from the vicinity of the control tower. "I threw down the gear and flaps," remembered Dahl, "and came in to land." What Dahl in his eagerness failed to understand was that the green flare was a signal for the B-24 to take off from the other end of the runway.

Dahl landed on one end of the runway at the same time the B-24 pilot was starting to increase his speed for takeoff from the other end. The two planes, traveling in opposite directions, collided violently in the middle of the runway.

> I looked up and saw four propellers coming at me! I was still doing 60 or 70 knots, so I ducked down and my plane went right through his number 1 and number 2 props. One blade hit in front of me on the cockpit and one hit behind me and turned my plane

Perry Dahl in 1942 at preflight school. The method of teaching young people to fly military aircraft remained the same from 1939 through 1945. The sequence was explanation by the instructor, supervised student performance, correction of student errors and then practice. Perry Dahl

Perry Dahl, second from left, as an aviation cadet, class of 1943, at Cal Aero, California. Successful completion of pilot training wasn't easy. From 1939 to V-J Day more than 124,000 students were washed out. This amounted to almost 40 percent of the number that entered the flying course. Perry Dahl

around backwards. Propelled by the violent force of the collision, I went shooting off the end of the runway into a big water-filled gully.

As the P-38 floundered in the water Dahl jumped out onto one wing. The other wing had been torn off by the force of the collision and the plane was sticking almost straight up in the air. Dahl crawled along the remaining wing and jumped off onto the airstrip. Once on land he watched helplessly as his plane slowly settled into the water and was washed out to sea.

Dahl's P-38 was a total loss, the first of four Lightnings he would lose while flying combat. He would end the war as an ace with nine Japanese planes and 280 combat missions to his credit. Some of his exploits during one of these missions can only be described as incredible.

Perry Dahl was born in Canada, but his parents moved to Seattle shortly after his birth. After graduating from a Seattle high school young Dahl attended the University of Washington until he was called to active duty in 1940.

Dahl had joined the National Guard while in high school and served with the 41st Infantry Division. When the opportunity came to apply for aviation cadet training he jumped at the chance. He was accepted and sent to Santa Ana, California, for preflight school. From there he was sent to Bakersfield, California, for basic training and then to school for twin-engine fighter training with P-38s.

After graduating from flying school in 1943 Dahl was sent to Muroc AFB. There he received RTU training with the P-38 in gunnery.

Dahl's next assignment was to the 55th FG in Olympia, Washington, as a replacement pilot. The 55th had a group of veteran pilots who had been sent down from Alaska where they had been flying P-38s.

Orders soon came to the commander of the 55th FG that two replacement pilots were needed to go to the Pacific. The commander arranged a fly-off between several of the young second lieutenants to determine who to send. As a result of the fly-off, Dahl was selected to join the 432nd Squadron of the 475th Fighter Group.

It was late October 1943 when Dahl joined the squadron. He was nineteen years old and perhaps the youngest pilot in the Southwest Pacific theater.

By the middle of October the American forces were set for the invasion of Bougainville. This island was well fortified by more than 20,000 Japanese soldiers. To support the US Marine invasion of Bougainville it would be necessary for the Fifth Air Force to neutralize the Japanese bastion of Rabaul on New Britain.

Rabaul was located on the extreme northeastern part of New Britain. The principal targets for the Fifth Air Force included Simpson Harbor and four major airfields that circled and protected the harbor. On these four fields the Japanese had hard-stands for 166 bombers and 265 fighters.

The Japanese could also send air reinforcements and replacements to Rabaul from a number of nearby air bases. Any air attacks on Rabaul by the Fifth Air Force would meet with determined and formidable resistance from the Japanese air arm.

Another hazard the pilots of the Fifth Air Force would have to face over Rabaul would be intense and accurate antiaircraft fire.

Upon joining the 475th FG Dahl had done some local flying, but he soon found that he was scheduled to fly a combat mission to Rabaul.

Dahl's first combat mission brought him much valuable experience. His survival was due more to his luck than to expertise. His experiences over Rabaul demonstrated why so many pilots new to combat failed to survive.

I had been told to get on my element leader's wing and just stay there. Well, we went up and got jumped and the first thing that happened was that the guy I was flying wingman for got shot down.

The P-38s I had flown in the United States had the trigger on the right-hand side and you pulled the trigger for the .50s and pressed a button for the 20 mm cannon. Well, in the Pacific—they rearranged everything.

I dropped my drop tanks by mistake when I went to call someone on the radio and pushed what I thought was the radio button. I pushed the wrong button and released the drop tanks. All of a sudden both engines quit because after I lost the drop tanks I forgot to reselect the internal fuel. I switched real quick to the other tanks and got the engines started, but I was suddenly all alone. I looked around for help and all I saw was Zeros and airplanes falling out of the sky. I jumped in with a squadron of B-24s because I didn't even know the direction home—I was really disoriented!

Shortly I saw a bunch of P-38s and I went over and joined them for the trip home.

If I fired a shot I'd be surprised. I really flew around the sky in complete confusion.

When I returned home I found that we had lost two guys out of my tent on the mission.

The air battles over Rabaul were fierce engagements that often involved large numbers of planes on each side.

Both the Japanese and the Americans claimed to have the upper hand in the Rabaul air battle. Yet the Japanese suffered the greatest losses and could least stand a battle of attrition. The Fifth Air Force raids failed to completely neutralize Rabaul, "but they did take a heavy toll of [Japanese] carrier planes, badly damage Rabaul's harbor and airfields, and [divert] attention from the developing Bougainville offensive."

It was shortly after the raids on Rabaul that Dahl scored his first victory. He had taken off from Buna and was flying as a wingman when he and the

Perry Dahl joined the 432nd Squadron of the 475th FG as a replacement pilot in 1943. The 475th shot down 551 enemy aircraft in World War II. This was the highest score of any group flying the P-38 in combat. Perry Dahl

flight leader spotted two Japanese planes flying some distance ahead of them.

The flight leader went after one and I went for the other. As I dove down on him I almost overran the guy, he was going so slow. We went in and blew them apart almost simultaneously. It was rather uneventful, really. Once or twice before I had taken deflection shots at Japanese planes. While flying as a wingman you didn't get a chance to shoot too often. I found out real quick the best way to do this thing was to fly right up their rear end and poke that gun right up their butts and kick loose and let the pieces start flying off.

On a mission over Lae, New Guinea, Dahl lost his second P-38. Flying tail-end Charlie in the formation, he lagged behind as the flight climbed toward a group of cumulus clouds. As the flight made a climbing turn he watched his air speed drop to 180 mph, a dangerous predicament to be in while flying a P-38. "I was just hanging in the air like a damn balloon," recalled Dahl, "and we got jumped by a bunch of Zeros."

Dahl realized he was in deep trouble and called out for help over his radio. He rolled the P-38 over on its back and dove for the deck. As his air speed began to climb he looked around and realized he had lost the other members of his formation.

Pulling out of the dive, he saw a lone Zero up ahead. "I thought, *What the hell*," he remembered, *"I'll get one on the way home."*

As Dahl approached the lone Zero he thought it would be an easy victory.

I was very inexperienced and so intent on the lone Zero I forgot to look around. Suddenly I saw gun flashes off to my side and there was a Zero at about 90 degrees shooting at me. When I saw him he was only about 50 yards away on my right. I just threw the right engine of the P-38 up at him to protect me. The right engine and tail boom took all the hits, instead of my being plastered in the cockpit.

Some 20 mm shells hit the vertical stabilizer in my tail and some of the explosive flew up the tail boom and went into the radio. A big stream of white smoke began pouring out of my right engine.

I dove for the deck and outran the Zero and headed for home trailing white smoke all over the sky. The engine soon froze, however, and that ended the smoke.

I got it home on one engine. Once I landed they counted sixty-four bullet holes in the P-38 and sent it to the boneyard.

The 475th FG, which served with distinction in the Pacific, was the only all-P-38 fighter group to fly during the war.

The Lockheed P-38 was one of the few successful twin-engine fighters of World War II. Its twin engines gave it great power. The twin engines also were extremely useful in the Pacific theater because much of the combat took place over water and long distances. If an emergency arose or one engine was knocked out in combat, the plane could make it home on one engine.

The mounting of the 20 mm cannon and four .50 caliber machine guns in the nose gave a fire-power advantage to the P-38 pilot. "With all the guns in the nose," recalled Dahl, "all the bullets went into about a 12 inch circle, with the machine guns throwing about 900 rounds per minute—it had devastating firepower!"

This maelstrom of straight-ahead firepower was particularly effective against the lightly armored Japanese fighters, which also lacked self-sealing gas tanks. Dahl recalled the reluctance of the Japanese pilots to engage the P-38 in a head-on pass:

The Japanese pretty well avoided the head-on pass. They would never take you on in a head-on because of the firepower, and the closing rate in a head-on was terrific. You get a couple of airplanes flying 300 to 400 mph and your closing rate is close to 1,000 mph. Whenever we had the opportunity we would take a head-on against the Japanese.

As Dahl's total of combat missions grew he began to gain skill and confidence in his ability to handle the P-38 in any kind of emergency situation. This was illustrated in a mission over Wewak, New Guinea.

I was flying with John Loisel, who was an ace. It was early in the morning and I was flying his wing and we dove down through a bunch of clouds—he was heading the group—and we got separated; just

P-38 Lightning take off from a Southwest Pacific airfield. "The characteristics of the airplane were really good. If you knew how to use the bird," wrote Perry Dahl. "You couldn't turn with the Japanese because their planes were so maneuverable, but with the P-38 you had a big advantage over the Japanese in other areas." Dennis Cooper

he and I were left and there were a lot of Zeros in the area. I looked up into the rearview mirror and the mirror was just full of red spinner! Somebody was 20 feet behind me. I hit hard right rudder, hard right aileron, and chopped the right engine and the airplane almost pivoted. You could really move—there was no way he could have got a shot. He just skidded out from under me and I fired everything up and dove away. I think if it would have been any other airplane he would have had me for sure. But you had to know how to fly it.

April 3, 1944, found Dahl and other members of the 475th escorting American bombers to Hollandia, New Guinea. Japanese fighters rose to defend their air base and attack the bombers. As the P-38s engaged the Japanese, dogfights broke out all over the sky. Richard I. Bong, flying with the 432nd Squadron, registered his twenty-sixth victory and John Loisel and Perry Dahl each shot down two Japanese planes. In all, the 475th shot down fifteen Japanese planes on this mission.

Although successful on April 3, Dahl shortly lost his third P-38 in combat. Leading a flight of four, he was searching for a Japanese destroyer reported to be in the area.

Looking up, we saw three Zeros come over, looking around. They saw us and tried to run into the clouds.

I caught one of the Zeros and shot him down immediately. While doing this his wingman made a pass at me. I saw him coming and turned into him but I took a couple of hits, one of which sheared the up-lock on the right-hand main landing gear. Coming in for a landing, I couldn't get this gear down all the way, and when I landed, it slowly folded and I lost control and ran up over a revetment and sat down on top of another plane that was being refueled.

On October 20 the Americans began the invasion of the Philippines. The 1st Cavalry Division and the 24th Infantry Division landed on the northern beaches of the island of Leyte. The immediate objectives of the ground troops were the airfields at Tacloban and Dulag. Gen. Douglas MacArthur felt it was imperative that land-based aircraft of the Fifth Air Force be available to cover the ships in the harbor, which were full of troops and supplies waiting to go ashore.

Accordingly, ground echelons of the 49th and 475th groups and the 421st Night Fighter Squadron began arriving on October 24. The historical officer of the 49th FG reported on the status of the two airfields at this time:

Tacloban, furnished with a 6,000 foot steel-matted strip was the most heavily used airfield during the initial part of the Philippine invasion. Dulag, located on the flat flood-plain of the Marabang River, required the efforts of three aviation engineer battalions before it could be made ready

Perry Dahl's P-38 undergoing repair at Buna in November 1943. Dahl arrived on Buna just when the 475th was attacking Rabaul. "The Japanese," wrote Dahl, "would put maybe 100 or 200 airplanes in the air when we would go up there with our three squadrons of P-38s." Perry Dahl

for fighters. However, by November 21, 1944 steel matting had been laid at Dulag and all of the 475th Fighter Group was based there.

A primary duty of the 475th FG during this period was to attack Japanese reinforcements before they could be put ashore on Leyte. Often the Japanese attempted to land troops on Ormoc Bay, almost 25 miles west of the group's Dulag air base.

On November 9 the 26th Division of the Japanese Army attempted to land at Ormoc Bay, screened by a severe weather front. On November 10 the weather had cleared enough for the 475th to be alerted.

Fourteen P-38s scrambled off the steel matting of the Dulag airfield at 0815. Leading the formation was the 475th group commander, Col. Charles Henry MacDonald, a leading ace of the war. Flying in the second flight behind MacDonald was Lt. Perry Dahl, unaware that he was embarking upon an unbelievable and extraordinary mission.

Flying over Ponson Island, the formation sighted two Japanese planes. MacDonald intercepted one and shot it down in flames. Dahl, flying behind MacDonald, described the attack: "I always thought the Japanese pilot jumped out before MacDonald fired a shot. I think he looked up and saw this string of fourteen P-38s coming out of the sky at him and just jumped."

MacDonald had neglected to completely fuel his airplane the night before, so he and his wingman broke for home, to refuel, leaving Dahl to take over as formation leader.

Shortly after Dahl assumed the position of formation leader he looked off in the distance and caught sight of a dozen Ki-61 Tonys flying a tight V-formation beneath a layer of altocumulus clouds.

Dahl led his formation of P-38s up and over the clouds in a maneuver designed to bring the squadron out high and behind the unsuspecting Japanese. As the Tonys emerged from underneath the clouds Dahl and his squadron dove from above. Leading the P-38s, Dahl, diving at a high speed, flew right up the middle of the V and shot down the lead Japanese plane.

During his attack Dahl became separated from his wingman. After dispatching the Japanese formation leader Dahl was locked in a tight turn with another Tony and slowly pulling into firing position. Suddenly he felt a tremendous shock as another plane rammed his, slashing through the twin tail booms at a right angle. Dahl's first thought was that he had been rammed by a Zero, but in actuality it

A youthful-looking Perry Dahl peers out the cockpit of his P-38. Dahl flew many of his missions with Charles MacDonald, commander of the 475th FG. "MacDonald was really deadly with the airplane," *wrote Dahl. "He had flown it a long time and was really a good shot. He was very aggressive and went after the Jap fighters." Perry Dahl*

was his wingman, Lt. Grady Laseter. Laseter, rushing to help, had misjudged the turn. He was killed in the accident.

Dahl, flying a badly damaged P-38, was in serious trouble. He described the events that followed:

> The crash tore off the tail booms. We were over Ormoc Bay; I could look down and see Dulag airfield. I turned the wheel and tried to glide the P-38 over there because we were at 10,000 feet and I could then bail out. Then the right engine fell out and the right wing folded up and fell off and fire shot out! I popped the canopy and fire flashed into the canopy and I got hung up trying to get my chute undone. When I popped the canopy I lost my helmet and the fire burned all my hair off. I stood up in the airplane and was sucked out of the canopy and began to free fall away. Just after I went out, the airplane exploded—I more or less got blown out. One of the flight members said later there wasn't a piece of my P-38 bigger than a square foot after the explosion. The plane really blew—the squadron members hadn't seen me fall out and wrote me off as dead after the explosion.

As Dahl, miraculously alive, floated down he observed a Japanese chute right above him. The Japanese used smaller parachutes and the Japanese pilot was descending faster than Dahl. "I didn't want him to beat me to the water," recalled Dahl, "so I reached up and pulled the shroud, spilling most of the air out of my chute." With the chute partially collapsed, Dahl shot down toward the ocean. Alarmed at his rate of descent, he got the chute to fill again but watched, dismayed, as the Japanese pilot floated into the water. As the enemy pilot entered the water his chute went over him and Dahl

Parafrags drift down toward parked Japanese airplanes. The parafrags [parachute bombs] were used effectively at Rabaul. The B-25s would fly in at low range and open fire on the antiaircraft positions from long range. Once over the target they would drop their parafrags over the revetments. Smithsonian Institution

75

noticed he was dead. "He was probably dead when he fell out of his plane," observed Dahl.

As Dahl neared the water he had to fall through a hail of tracer fire from the Japanese ships below, which were trying to defend themselves from air attack by American B-25s.

Somehow he managed to land in the ocean without being hit by the swarm of bullets passing around him. Once in the water he unbuckled his chute and inflated his Mae West and one-person dinghy.

As Dahl, badly burned and shaken from his ordeal, slowly climbed into his small raft he found himself in the middle of a group of Japanese ships.

They were heading south and didn't pay any attention to me and in 20 or 30 minutes they were out of sight. I was badly burned, and the only things I had were a sea anchor and medical kit. I sprinkled sulfa all over myself. I also gave myself a shot of morphine and put the sea anchor out. There is no way you can stay afloat on the ocean in a one-man craft without a sea anchor—the raft will flop over.

I also cut several panels out of the parachute for a tent or cover and let the rest float away.

Dahl's squadron, assuming he had been killed, had returned to base. He was now alone in the middle of Ormoc Bay.

Late in the afternoon Dahl noticed a single airplane off in the distance. Thinking that perhaps help had arrived, he was disappointed when he

Perry Dahl at Dulag, Leyte, in 1944. During many of his first missions, Dahl flew as a wingman. "I flew tail-end Charlie most of the time," he recalled, "and my duties were just to stay with my element leader —in this position you don't get many targets." Perry Dahl

realized the plane was a Japanese Zero. The pilot of the Zero noticed Dahl and made a couple of circles over the raft and dove to begin a strafing run. Dahl flipped the raft over and hid underneath as machine gun bullets sprayed the water around him. He wasn't hit but a bullet went through the raft, leaving a small hole. After the Zero flew away Dahl righted the raft and found he could still keep air in it by laying across the hole with his feet in the water.

As night closed around him Dahl knew he was in a perilous position. Seemingly deserted by his squadron, and with painful flash burns over his face and lips, he had little hope of rescue.

Alone, on the vast expanse of the ocean, with the black of night surrounding him, he would catch snatches of sleep. At one point in a deep sleep he suddenly sat upright. He was sure something had bumped the side of the raft. Suddenly alert, he squinted into the dark night trying to figure out what his raft had bumped against. He saw a large form in the water and a wave of terror swept over him. Sharks! Through the murky, lightless night he could see the sharks circling. They would bump the raft as they passed, forcing Dahl to jerk his feet up out of the water.

The night slowly passed with Dahl watching for sharks and drifting in and out of consciousness. At first light he noticed ships off in the distance.

First thing I saw were all of these antennas on the horizon. They were Japanese ships and they were heading right toward me. I was badly burned on the right side of my face and my right arm was burned all black. I laid on my left side with the burned side showing and played dead in my boat. Several of the Japanese ships went by so close the raft was almost turned over in their wake.

A Japanese destroyer escort approached the raft and Dahl could hear the crew cut the engine as they drew close. Out of one partially opened eye he saw the Japanese put out a pole to draw the raft over to the ship. He recalled the events that followed:

I felt at this point it would be good to be captured because at least I would get a drink of water. I was parched! Just as I was pulled over, the destroyer escort cut loose with a 5 inch gun right over my head. They were firing at American B-25s, which were coming to attack again. When they fired the 5 inch gun it so startled me that I stood up in the raft and found myself face to face with a Japanese sailor, whose eyes were as big as saucers. I fell back into the water and the destroyer escort under attack took off. As the ship pulled away a sailor on board fired at me with a machine gun and one slug just nicked me in the back of the head. That was the last I saw of the Japanese Navy.

The attacking B-25s were from the 38th Bomb Group. The thirty Mitchells that made up the strike force came in at a low level, causing chaos as the

Japanese destroyers zigzagged around the transports, trying to protect themselves and at the same time keep the B-25s away from the cargo ships. The bold ambush foiled the Japanese attempt to land troops and supplies at Ormoc.

The attack cost the Americans seven B-25s. Dahl watched, horrified, as Japanese antiaircraft fire hit a B-25 and sent it diving toward the ocean with fire streaming out of its bomb bay. The B-25 bellied in and tore up and sank quickly. "No one got out alive," recalled Dahl, "and all that was left was a pool of oil on the water."

For the remainder of the day Dahl drifted toward the west side of Leyte Island. He was dehydrated from the searing sun, and the salt water would splash over the side of the raft and fall on his burns, cracking them open. Perhaps the worst torment was that he had been without water for almost two days.

Late in the afternoon the raft caught a big wave and finally hit the beach. Dahl climbed out, glad to be once again on dry land. He quickly hid the raft and tore off all his insignia of rank. Walking up a jungle trail, he sought cover as a firefight broke out between Japanese soldiers and Philippine guerrillas hiding in the bush.

With night coming on rapidly Dahl knew that he was weak from his ordeal and must find help or die. He soon noticed that a person was standing out on the trail about 15 feet away. Dahl kept waiting for him to move on but he just stood there silently watching and listening. Finally Dahl could stand the tension of waiting no longer.

I pulled out my .45 caliber pistol and shot at the back of his head. I had forgotten, however, that I was loaded with bird shot and not a regular slug. The bird shot was encased in cardboard—and the force of this hitting the back of his head knocked him to his knees. He turned around and saw me and with his big machete chopped down the foliage I was hiding behind. As he came toward me I saw he was a Filipino and I said, "Americano, Americano." He answered in perfect English. "Why in the hell didn't you tell me you were an American?"

Dahl had fortunately fallen into the hands of Filipino guerrillas. Had he been captured by the Japanese it is almost certain that he would have been tortured and killed.

After the American forces were driven out of the Philippines, guerrilla resistance to the Japanese occupation had slowly taken shape. The largest group of Filipinos was known as the Huks and was led by Luis Tarluc, a fire-eating Communist.

Other guerrilla leaders in the Philippines included some Americans who had escaped from Bataan or from POW enclosures at Santo Tomas University and Cabomatuan. One American-led force grew to over 6,000 people in northern Luzon.

The Japanese, often stung by the guerrilla attacks, labored to stamp out or disrupt the resistance network that had been built throughout the Philippines. Their efforts intensified as American liberation forces edged closer to the islands. In the remote regions heavily armed patrols regularly beat the bushes, and in the cities the Kempei Tai, the ruthless Japanese secret police, searched, bribed, arrested and tortured in an effort to stamp out armed resistance.

To support the resistance movement the United States, by means of submarine, delivered weapons, ammunition and explosives to the guerrillas.

By the middle of 1944 every major island, as well as many of the smaller islands, had organized resistance forces in action. On the eve of the Allied invasion more than 182,000 well-organized and armed guerrillas stood ready to help liberate their homeland.

Dahl lived with the guerrillas in the jungle for more than thirty days. They afforded him excellent care and slowly nursed him back to health. To heal his injuries, "they boiled coconut oil mixed with

A Japanese torpedo bomber plunges toward the sea. "You had to be aggressive, as a fighter pilot," wrote Perry Dahl. "It was interesting to note that 15% of the pilots got 85% of the kills. You had to be aggressive—you always had lots of opportunities to get out of there." US Navy

sulfa and after it cooled poured it all over [his] burns many times a day." Receiving good food and rest and a pet monkey, Dahl began to regain his strength.

After two weeks Dahl felt strong enough to go out on several raiding parties with the guerrillas. "They assigned me two bodyguards," he recalled, "and they dressed me all up like a guerrilla. I had the two bandoliers around my chest and a big white horse. We were raiding Japanese positions and we didn't want them to know I was an American."

Many of the guerrillas with Dahl had been trained by the Americans and were survivors of the Bataan Death March who had escaped. The guerrilla war against the Japanese was a bitter one with no quarter asked and none given. Dahl remembered the treatment given to captured Japanese prisoners:

When we would catch a Japanese there was little mercy shown. After the interrogation they would take the Japanese prisoners back close to Ormoc—which was pretty close to a Japanese base camp. Then with a machete they would cut the tendons on

the back of his knees, so the Japanese would have to crawl back to camp.

These guerrillas were tough! They would make a living getting shark liver. They'd get in their little boat and go out in the water with a monkey. They would slit the gut of the monkey open and throw him over the side. When the sharks would come to get the monkey, they would jump onto the back of the shark and with their knife split the belly of the shark open. They would retrieve the shark's liver for cod liver oil and sell it.

Dahl's luck ran out when a raiding party he was with was ambushed by a Japanese patrol. His two bodyguards were killed and he was forced to hide in the jungle for a week. With little to eat he was forced to exist on abandoned Japanese rice, bananas and a few lizards he was able to trap.

Finally the long ordeal ended when he accidentally ran into a party of American scouts and they were able to radio a PBY to land and return him to freedom.

Dahl returned to the 475th FG on December 10. He weighed 68 pounds, down considerably from the 140 he weighed when he began his fateful mission over Ormoc Bay on November 10.

In February 1945 the 475th moved to Mindoro to begin support of ground operations on Luzon. In March it moved again, this time to Clark Field near Manila. For the rest of the war the group would fly mainly ground support and long escort missions over large expanses of water. These would include strikes against targets in China, French Indochina and Formosa. Some of these missions would be 1,000 to 1,200 miles in length and would keep the pilots cramped in their cockpits for up to 11 or 12 hours.

Often these missions involved little action, just long hours of flying, according to Dahl.

It was a long time to sit and you wanted to be sure the relief tube was working before you took off. Most of the time there wasn't any action; you just sat there droning through the sky with nothing to do. I can remember Cal Anderson. I used to look over at him and he would take all kinds of things to eat along and I remember he would lay out what looked like a little tablecloth on his lap and he would pour a little cup to drink. The big joke was that as soon as he had everything laid out you would call out over the radio, "Bandits at three o'clock," and would all the food fly.

On March 28 Dahl led a group of P-38s on a 12 hour escort mission to Indochina. A B-25 Pathfinder aircraft led the Lightnings to the Indochina coast, where they joined up with other B-25s that were to attack a group of Japanese ships.

After a 45 minute search the Japanese ships were sighted. Taking his group of P-38s down to 7,000 feet, Dahl sighted twenty Japanese planes flying cover for the ships. In the air battle that

Douglas Van Ness Parsons, the commanding officer of the 41st Squadron, 35th FG. Parsons was a graduate of Princeton and led the squadron on many of the 1,000 mile raids flown by the Fifth Air Force against the Balikpapan oil targets. Glen Brewin

followed, Dahl was able to bring down a Japanese fighter with a 60 degree deflection shot.

Returning from the mission, Dahl called over the radio to check the fuel status of his squadron. His wingman radioed back that his fuel was low and he probably wasn't going to make it back. He told Dahl he was scared to death because he would have to ditch in the ocean and couldn't swim. Dahl, talking calmly over the radio to ease the fear of his wingman, carefully explained how to parachute out of the plane and the proper procedure to inflate the Mae West.

The jittery wingman bailed out. As he entered the water his chute went over him and it was obvious to Dahl that he had not followed any of the rescue procedures Dahl had outlined over the radio. Dahl made two circles over the downed pilot and radioed for a PBY to attempt a rescue. As he returned home he passed the PBY on the way out and gave it a heading. Unfortunately, upon its arrival the patrol craft could find no trace of the pilot.

In 1945, after flying 280 combat missions with the 475th FG, Dahl returned to the United States.

Once a civilian he went back to the University of Washington to complete his undergraduate degree in journalism. After graduation he worked for a Seattle newspaper until he was recalled to active duty in the Korean War.

A Japanese destroyer under attack by a low-flying B-25. "Attacking an armed surface ship is the most dangerous thing in the world," wrote a World War II pilot, "because you can't dodge their fire." US Navy

During the Korean War, he served in France as a flight maintenance officer. Upon returning from France he was assigned to Norton AFB in San Bernardino, California. While serving at Norton he was offered a regular commission in the US Air Force and decided to make it a career.

After the completion of his tour at Norton, Dahl commanded a radar squadron in North Africa. He found himself at one point in command of 150 French Foreign Legionnaires. The camp was located on the Algerian border during the conflict between Algeria and France. Running an isolated, armed camp in the middle of the desert was a tough job, and Dahl was glad to be sent to Washington, D.C., for staff duty.

Dahl volunteered to go to Vietnam and flew 102 missions, many when he was over fifty years old. He flew the Rockwell International OV-10 Bronco, a light armed reconnaissance aircraft. The OV-10 was a twin-engine high-wing monoplane with twin tail fins connected at the top by a long tail plane. Armament consisted of four 7.62 mm Gatling guns

and two Sidewinder missiles. The OV-10 could also carry four 500 pound bombs or napalm.

Dahl was the commander of a direct air support unit in the III and IV corps areas. At one point he went into Cambodia and taught the Cambodians how to "pop smoke on the ground" so that they could receive close air support.

After service in Vietnam Dahl was assigned as the deputy commandant to the Cadet Wing at the US Air Force Academy in Colorado Springs.

Dahl ended his remarkable military career in 1978, returning from the Air Force with the rank of colonel. During his Air Force tenure, he was able to fly nineteen different types of military aircraft.

Dahl recently looked back on his long military career and made the following observations:

> There's only so much you can do in a P-38 in combat. You see those guys in movies doing all those loops and chasing each other—you don't see that in combat.
>
> I was young during the war. We'd fly at 30,000 feet without pressurization suits for hours on end and

Perry Dahl, third from left, greeting Gen. Lucius Clay, second from right, at Ben Hoa, Vietnam, in *1970. Dahl volunteered to go to Vietnam and was still flying combat missions at age 50. Perry Dahl*

pull 8 or 9 g's without g-suits. I was an ace before I was twenty-one, and now you can't even get near an airplane until you go through college and training and you're twenty-four or twenty-five.

It was a great experience, having the whole country behind you in World War II. When I came back from Vietnam—I took the cadets from the Air Force Academy to a parade in Washington, D.C., and those beatniks spit all over us.

Since 1978 Dahl has been living in active retirement on Plantation Key, next to Key Largo, Florida. He is the master of ceremonies at each 475th FG reunion and has forgiven the Japanese enough to purchase a new Honda.

The Rockwell International OV-10 Bronco. This unique airplane was used in a variety of roles in Vietnam. It had a maximum speed of 281 mph.

Other features included a superb all-round view for the pilot and observer seated in tandem ejection seats. Perry Dahl

Perry Dahl is hosed down after his last combat mission, in Thailand in 1973. Dahl flew 102 missions in the OV-10. Perry Dahl

Perry Dahl celebrates his last combat mission. He flew a total of 328 combat missions in World War II and Vietnam. Perry Dahl

Perry Dahl, second from left, at the ceremony honoring his retirement from the Air Force in 1978. Dahl's military decorations include the Silver Star, the Distinguished Flying Cross, the Meritorious Service Medal, the Air Medal with 16 oak leaf clusters, the Purple Heart and the Cross of Gallantry with Palm. Perry Dahl

Chapter 6

The Legendary Career of Joe Foss

Growing up on a South Dakota farm, Joe Foss became an avid outdoorsman and hunter, skills that served him well in World War II. After graduation from college he entered the Marine aviation program. October 1942 found him on Guadalcanal flying the F4F Wildcat. In only sixty-three days of combat he managed to shoot down twenty-six Japanese planes, becoming the first American pilot to tie the score of the great World War I ace Eddie Rickenbacker. Foss led a charmed life in the skies over Guadalcanal, several times having to crashland and once ditching at sea but never being touched by Japanese bullets. The postwar years only added more luster to the Joe Foss legend. He was elected governor of South Dakota, became a brigadier general in the Air Force Reserves and became president of the American Football League. He has also served as president of the National Rifle Association. Unless attributed to another source, all quotes are from an April 1989 interview with Joe Foss.

The F4F Wildcat climbed slowly into the hot and humid air over the island of Guadalcanal. As the plane fought for altitude pilot Joe Foss was busy manually cranking up the retractable landing gear and mentally preparing himself for combat. Foss and the other members of his flight were aware that a group of Japanese bombers was approaching Guadalcanal from the east at about 24,000 feet.

Foss, a twenty-seven-year-old Marine captain, had arrived in Guadalcanal on October 9, 1942, with Marine squadron VMF-121 from the escort carrier *Copahee*. Now, only four days later, he was beginning his fourth combat mission. It would prove to be a mission he would never forget—one with excitement and terror enough to last a lifetime. Death would almost claim him; he would owe his survival to what he would call his incredible

luck and the toughness and durability of the Grumman F4F Wildcat.

Foss was eager for combat and the opportunity to shoot down a Japanese plane. He had earlier remarked to a fellow pilot that he was going to get one that day. Leading the second flight while Maj. Duke Davis led the first, he "felt excited and good, like a kid waiting for a big dish of ice cream," according to a 1942 *Life* magazine article by John Field.

Climbing to the left of the bombers, Foss and the other members of the flight noticed a group of Zeros off to the right. Foss led his flight along the edge of a cloud bank, hoping the Zeros wouldn't notice the Marine fighters.

Intent on catching the Japanese by surprise and relatively new to air combat, Foss soon made a mistake that almost cost him his life.

> In my excitement I guess I forgot to turn the radio on or maybe it wasn't working. Anyway, one of my boys flew alongside, waved urgently, looked up and pointed. Thinking he was pointing at the Zeros we'd already seen, I smiled and waved back.

Suddenly Foss was aware his wingmen were gone. Jumped from above by Zeros, the other members of the flight had dove out of formation, leaving Foss blissfully alone. Another Zero, which had been hiding on top of a cloud, came down on Foss' tail and sent a stream of tracers a few inches from his head.

The Japanese plane flew past Foss owing to the great speed of its dive. The pilot then made a fatal mistake by pulling up directly in front of the Wildcat. Foss pulled up after the Zero, lined it up squarely in his sights and gave the Japanese plane a short burst. "With a great flash," wrote Walter Simmons in *Joe Foss, Flying Marine*, "he blew into a thousand pieces."

While maneuvering to shoot down the Japanese plane Foss had lost air speed and this made him an easy target for three Japanese planes that came boring in viciously, their guns blazing. Foss, wrote Simmons in *Joe Foss, Flying Marine*, pushed the Wildcat over into a dive and "saw oil fly from [his] oil cooler, and a hunk of wing ripped out by a cannon shell." As the Wildcat raced for the ground the motor burned out and the pistons stuck.

The Zeros chased Foss right to the edge of the field, and he didn't dare slow up for his landing approach. As he came over the edge of the field he was doing 150 knots, 150 feet above the ground. Less than 90 knots was considered safe for such an approach.

An ambulance was rushed out to the field, wrote Simmons in *Joe Foss, Flying Marine*, "to pick up the pieces—if any." Foss would need all his skill as a pilot to bring in the heavily damaged Wildcat.

> I swung wide to land and I was coming like a greased pig and the three of them were still chasing me. They came right on over the field and I dropped gear: on the old Wildcat you usually wound the landing gear down; I didn't wind it down, I just tripped the rachet—and I got my arm out of the way so it didn't chop it up in pieces—and let her drop.
>
> At the speed I was going, I could use a lot of brakes on that grass field and just almost be skidding—but I ran out of space and I had to kick it. By some miracle I managed to stop before running into the river or the stump patches at the edge of the field.

Relieved to be back alive, Foss felt he owed his good fortune to more than luck. "I always say that God is a great pilot; he got it in there, because I was sure figuring I was in a sorry situation." Although untouched by Japanese bullets, he counted over 200 holes in his Wildcat.

Later at supper Foss thought over the day's action. True, he had downed his first Zero, "but," he said, "[I] had made a boob out of myself getting him." Even though the pilots of his squadron had shot down three bombers and four Zeros during the day, Foss felt that they had, more importantly, all learned some good lessons.

Looking back from the perspective of forty-seven years, Foss could see that his first narrow escape was a turning point in his life.

> I think the first time I shot down a plane and then got shot down caused me to do some thinking. You see, I was twenty-seven years old and the average age of the kids I flew with was twenty. Then, after my crash landing when all these kids were beatin' me on the back and saying, "Nice going!" that's when I realized, *I can't back out of this deal.* See, I was ready; when I got the first airplane and they got me, the score was tied and I thought, *Boy, I'll settle for a trip back to the farm—why did I ever leave?* But then I realized I couldn't let those kids down.

As Foss and his fellow pilots went to bed after the hectic events of the day it was probably fortunate that they had little or no idea of the ordeal that awaited them.

On the darkened bridge of the Japanese battleship *Kongo* Vice Adm. Takeo Kunita began to discuss with his staff gunnery officer, Commander Yamagi, the details of the operation planned for that night. Kunita and Yamagi knew that 900 plus 14 inch bombardment shells were ready in the battleships *Kongo* and *Haruna* to hurl against the Marines around Henderson Field.

The Japanese plan for the battleships, screened by the light cruiser *Isuzu* and four or five destroyers, was to approach Guadalcanal between Santa Isabel and Florida islands. Once in good position they would open fire and attempt to destroy the Marine planes and installations on and near Henderson Field.

Shortly before midnight, October 13, 1942, the drone of a low-powered observation plane was heard over Henderson Field, and at a few minutes after 0100, October 14, sixteen 14 inch guns broke the nighttime silence with a monstrous thunder that echoed from the mountains of Guadalcanal. A bright flare fell from the Japanese observation plane, affording the pilot and Japanese observers in the hills a clear view of the airfield. The first 14 inch shells exploded in orange-red sheets of flame to mark the target.

To Foss, sleeping soundly, the terrific explosions came as a complete surprise, wrote Walter Simmons in *Joe Foss, Flying Marine*.

> The thing started so suddenly we almost broke our necks getting into foxholes—and what fox-

In 63 days Joe Foss shot down 26 Japanese planes in the skies over Guadalcanal. National Archives

The F4F Wildcat in flight. "I wouldn't be here today," *of people who badmouthed the F4F but I would say*
remarked Joe Foss, "except for the Wildcat's dura- *for the time, compared to what it was going against,*
bility. I got hit a lot of times with it. There were a lot *it did all right."* Smithsonian Institution

holes! There had been no good, tough shelling lately, and because of hot weather nobody had been inclined to do much digging. Duke Davis and I shared a hole 6 feet long and about 18 inches deep.

The ground was shaking and pitching from the violent concussions. We were shaking too—we just about beat each other to death that night.

As the Japanese ships threw salvo after salvo at the island, the Marines crouched low in their foxholes and wondered at the fury for the attack. The ground shook as the shell patterns walked back and forth over the airfield and surrounding area, shattering planes and storehouses, setting off fuel dumps, knocking down trees, killing people or tearing their bodies apart with jagged shell fragments.

For Foss, huddled in his tiny foxhole, wrote Simmons in *Joe Foss, Flying Marine* the Japanese attack became an event he would never forget.

Japanese planes overhead were dropping occasional white parachute flares and bombs. Fires set by the shelling lighted our area like day. A hundred yards away captured Jap gasoline in drums blazed with periodic explosions that shook our back teeth.

At the height of the bombardment the express train roar of the bursting salvos was so loud that it overloaded the capacity of the human ear. Those two hours [of the shelling] were simply indescribable. Nothing like them can be imagined.

Finally at 0230 the Japanese battleship commander ordered a cease-fire and retreated according to plan. The *Kongo, Haruna* and escorts slipped around Savo Island and headed northward for the fleet rendezvous.

In the morning the Marines crawled out of their foxholes and looked in disbelief at the scene surrounding them. All about were yawning chasms and wrecked equipment. Only forty-two planes—thirty-five fighters and seven dive-bombers—remained operational out of ninety. The aviation gas supply, critically low before, was nearly all gone. Forty-one men were dead, others wounded.

During his first hectic days on Guadalcanal, Foss had managed to survive four combat missions and a major Japanese naval bombardment. He had shot down a Japanese Zero and had been badly shot up in turn, just managing to bring his severely damaged plane home. After the terror-filled days he could be excused for wondering if he would survive the war and ever see home again.

Home to Joe Foss was South Dakota. He was born on April 17, 1915. His father, Frank Foss, had a farm on a knoll, set on rolling land east of Sioux Falls. Frank was a stocky, genial, big-hearted man who had a local reputation as a boxer and wrestler, and he taught those arts to both his boys: Joe and Clifford, two years younger.

Foss' father was killed the year Foss was a senior in high school. In a June 1943 *Life* magazine article, Foss remembered the tough Depression years that followed his dad's death:

Luck and guts were all that saved us on the farm during the drought. Dad died in the fall of 1933. He was coming home from the fields at night and stumbled over an electric wire torn down by a storm. We had a good farm—300 acres with 150 pigs, some cows, chickens and plenty of corn and oats. The house is up on a little hill with a nice view in all directions.

But it was rough going after Dad died. It was the very next year the big dust storms started—in

1934, and they kept on in 1935. The crops and stock all died. Even the box elders died.

But we pulled through somehow. I remember Mother after it was all over, sitting in the living room close to the old potbellied stove, looking up at the family pictures on the walls. There were more lines in her face but her arms were still muscular. And she was cheerful. She said "There'll be rain next year." There was.

In high school Foss' hobby was the band, in which he played the baritone saxophone. The band was a good one and represented South Dakota at the Century of Progress Exposition in Chicago in 1933.

In the fall of 1934 Foss enrolled at Augustana College in Sioux Falls. College wasn't much fun for him.

I was running the farm then and had to jump into the car after classes and tear home to work. At the end of the year a college education seemed totally unnecessary and I quit.

The next year Foss tried to make a go of it as a farmer. It was a disastrous dry season, the farm failed and he found himself working for 51 cents per hour at the Morrell Packing Plant in Sioux Falls.

His job at the packing plant opened Foss' eyes to how hard an uneducated man had to work to make a living in the Depression years. He decided to return to college.

Continuing his education at the University of South Dakota, Foss worked in a butcher shop and as a filling station attendant to pay expenses. In his senior year he helped organize the first Civil Aeronautics Administration flight training program at the university and was in the first group to win their wings. His family knew nothing about this until the day he flew over the farm; dove low over the field where his brother, Cliff, and a cousin were working; and gave them a big wave.

In June 1940 Foss received his degree from the university. He had hoped he would be able to get into the Marine Aviation Program—a tough thing to do at the time. Deciding to give it his best shot, he hitchhiked to Minneapolis, about 300 miles away, to apply for enlistment. With him on this trip was Ralph Gunvordahl from Burke, South Dakota. Gunvordahl would later win fame as a member of the Flying Tigers. Out of twenty-eight men who applied for the Marine Aviation Program that weekend, Foss and Gunvordahl were the only two accepted. "Later," he recalled, "we hitchhiked back home through a snowstorm, our eyes still dilated from drops that had been put in them."

In August Foss hitchhiked to the naval air station at Pensacola, making the trip in three days on $6.87. After seven months of training he was commissioned a Marine second lieutenant on March 15, 1941, and received his wings on March 29.

In May 1942 Foss spent six weeks with a reconnaissance squadron at San Diego. During this time he did little flying. "I wanted to fight," recalled Foss, "and reconnaissance planes have no guns on them." Complaining about not being placed in a fighter squadron, Foss was told he was too old to fly. Finally his persistence won out and he was sent to an aircraft carrier training group.

On August 1 Foss was named the executive officer of VMF-121, stationed at Camp Kearney, California. Events moved fast after that. On August 9 he was married at La Jolla, California, to June Shakstad, his high school sweetheart. On August 17 he was promoted to captain and by the thirtieth he was on his way to the Southwest Pacific theater of war.

While the US naval forces were engaged in the Battle of the Coral Sea the Japanese landed on Guadalcanal, one of the southernmost Solomon Islands, and began to build an airstrip. The presence of Japanese bombers on Guadalcanal threatened the supply lanes from America to Australia. A major amphibious assault already agreed on in Washington was rushed into action. On August 7, exactly eight months after Pearl Harbor, the 1st Marine Division went ashore on Guadalcanal. The landing itself was easy and the airstrip, renamed Henderson Field, was taken.

Almost the only outside help available to the Marines came from the air. By August 20 Henderson Field was completed and Marine major John L. Smith flew in with nineteen Grumman Wildcats followed by twelve dive-bombers. In the next few days some Army P-40s also landed, and still later came torpedo planes and Navy fighters. Often

Joe Foss and fellow Marine pilots of VMF-121: Lt. Roger Haberman, Lt. Cecil Doyle, Capt. Joe Foss, Lt. William P. Marontate and Lt. Roy Ruddell, left to right. National Archives

planes from all three services would fly together on one mission.

The Japanese were determined to recapture Guadalcanal. From mid August to mid November they attempted four progressively more powerful and dangerous combined offenses to wrest the island from the Americans. All four failed disastrously. Although Marine, and later Army, foot soldiers and Navy ships took a prominent part in these four battles, the decisive role was played by the Marine, Navy and Army pilots and their aircraft flying from Henderson Field on Guadalcanal.

During the long voyage to the Southwest Pacific, Foss and his squadron mates were briefed on the conditions they would find on Guadalcanal. "More than anything else," recalled Foss in Simmons' *Joe Foss, Flying Marine*, "we were interested in reports on the Japanese Zero fighters, about which we had heard almost everything and didn't know what to believe. Those were the days of the big Zero scare."

No doubt the Mitsubishi Zero was an outstanding combat plane. It was not a mere copy of Western aircraft, as wartime propaganda claimed. It was the result of the efforts of a brilliant design team and of specifications so demanding that the firm of Mitsubishi had no competition for the contract.

The Japanese Navy had wanted a carrier-based fighter that would equal in speed and exceed in maneuverability and range any foreign opponent likely to be flying before 1942. The Zero was completed in 1937. It was streamlined, low-winged and only 5,500 pounds. Its engine could only deliver 875 hp, but with its light weight and large wing area it could still outclimb and outmaneuver most British and American fighters then in use. When equipped with a belly gas tank, it could remain airborne for nearly 12 hours and had almost twice the combat radius of the F4F Wildcat.

The Japanese paid a high price for the Zero's range and maneuverability, however. The pilot was provided no protective armor plating, and the gas tanks were not self-sealing, giving the Zero a high tendency to explode when hit. Although the extra belly tanks gave the Zero an advantage in range over a Wildcat, they reduced the plane's speed and ability to maneuver. All the Japanese fighters flying from Rabaul to attack Guadalcanal had to carry belly tanks, which reduced their advantage over the F4Fs. With only two slow-firing cannon of low muzzle velocity and two rifle-caliber machine guns, the Zero lacked the firepower of the American fighters it would encounter over Guadalcanal.

The Japanese naval pilots Foss and his squadron mates fought against were among the best and most rigorously trained in the world. Thomas Miller, Jr., in his book *The Cactus Air Force*, briefly described the training they had to undertake:

Training for Japanese naval aviation included doing somersault dives from a high diving board to the ground, supporting oneself by one arm from the top of an iron pole for ten minutes, swimming under water for a minimum of one and a half minutes and wrestling in matches where defeat meant automatic expulsion. Japan's ace enlisted pilot Saburo Sakai competed for entrance to the training program with 1500 others—only he and 69 other men graduated. Typically, two-thirds of each class washed out. In a land where the concept of the Samurai, the faithful hereditary warrior, still gripped the imagination, and the Navy was considered the premier service, these skilled and proud aviators were all considered heroes. Their numbers were kept small, so that it became incumbent upon these elite flyers to survive, in spite of the vulnerability of their planes, if air superiority was to remain in Japan's control.

American Army and Marine pilots were also well trained and proud but lacked the combat experience the Japanese had gained since their invasion of China. The first-line Navy fighter in 1942, the Grumman F4F-4 Wildcat, was not a superior aircraft even by 1942 standards. It was almost 50 mph slower at combat altitude than the Zero and had only eighty percent of the Japanese plane's climb rate. Because it was 2,500 pounds heavier, the Wildcat had a much shorter range and was far less maneuverable than the Zero. The Wildcat's peculiar narrow tracked landing gear made it "look rather like a knock-kneed bumblebee on the ground" wrote Barrett Tillman in his book *Wildcat*.

The Grumman had many excellent features, however. Its armament of six .50 caliber machine guns was far superior to the Zero's firepower. If it was heavy because of its exceedingly rugged construction, which included armor plate and self-sealing tanks (Navy and Marine pilots referred to the manufacturer as the Grumman Iron Works), it was still far more likely to survive battle damage and make it home.

Even though Foss and his fellow pilots knew they would be facing a formidable foe, they were confident. Foss recalled their attitude in *Joe Foss, Flying Marine* by Walter Simmons:

We knew our planes had many virtues. We also had confidence in our long tactical training, which was better than [that of] the Japanese. Our hands —to put it in language a bit overstuffed—were trained to make guns destroy anything our eyes could see.

Foss flew to Gaudalcanal from an escort carrier. "We got there just after a bombing raid," he recalled in a 1942 *Life* magazine article written by John Field. "The island looked like one of those tropical islands in a Dorothy Lamour picture—only she was missing."

Lamour can be pardoned for not being on Guadalcanal in 1942. The war-torn island was not a place that anyone in his or her right mind would have wished to visit for a vacation or brief rest.

Americans knew little about the Solomon Islands in the years before World War II. The Solomons had never figured in the prewar plans of the US Navy. The Marine Corps possessed information on almost every group of Pacific islands except the Solomons. The few Australians contacted by the Navy described Guadalcanal as a bloody, stinking hole, which was exactly what it was.

Located between the latitudes of 5 and 11 degrees south, the Solomons are wet, hot and steamy. The seasons vary little except that more rain falls from November to March, when the northwest trade winds blow, than during the rest of the year. The islands are jagged, lofty and volcanic; on Guadalcanal the mountains rise 8,000 feet above the sea.

Ronald Spector, in his book *Eagle against the Sun*, described the conditions under which the Marines fought and lived:

> Thick tropical rain forest covered most of the island, a fantastic tangle of vines, creepers, ferns, roots and giant hardwoods; this reduced overland movement to a mile or two a day—and visibility to a few yards. The jungle was the domain of giant ants, three-inch wasps, spiders, leeches, and above all the malarial mosquito.... The constant dampness and humidity produced fungus and skin infections in abundance, while the smallest lapse in sanitation was likely to produce a virulent form of dysentery that rendered men too weak to move.

Foss landed on Guadalcanal at a time when the Allied victory was in doubt. Shortly after he arrived, the naval picture became so bleak that Adm. Chester Nimitz admitted, "We are unable to control the sea in the Guadalcanal area." Nimitz saw a great danger in this, adding: "Thus our supply of the positions will only be done at great expense to us. The situation is not hopeless, but it is certainly critical."

After scoring his first victory and surviving the terror of the Japanese night bombardment, Foss was again in action against the Japanese during the midmorning of October 14, 1942.

Foss scrambled to intercept a Japanese bombing attack and then found himself alone owing to a faulty engine. Unable to land because twenty-five Japanese bombers were busily plastering the field, he sought safety by hiding in the clouds over the mountains.

Looking up, Foss noticed a Wildcat diving right in front of him with a Zero hot on its tail. He described the action that followed in Simmons' *Joe Foss, Flying Marine*:

> The Grumman dove into a cloud and the Zero swung directly in front of me unknowingly. All I had to do was kick the plane around a little, and he was full in my sights. My touch on the trigger was delicate.... The Jap's wing blew off, and he whirled into a cloud and disappeared. Afterwards I saw the plane burning on the side of a mountain. It was Zero number 2 for me; I never got one any easier.

Later the same day Foss led a raid on a small Japanese convoy of six troop transports, accompanied by warships that were attempting to land troops north of Santa Isabel Island. He flew through heavy antiaircraft fire to strafe the decks, which were packed with standing soldiers. "It was a slaughter," recalled Foss, in *Joe Foss, Flying Marine*. "I wish some of the boys we lost at Pearl Harbor could have been there to see it."

The vicious air attack on the Japanese ships accentuated the bitterness of the war in the Pacific. Fighting a fanatical enemy that asked for no quarter and gave none, the Marines developed a deep hatred for the Japanese. Foss' attitude was no exception to this rule.

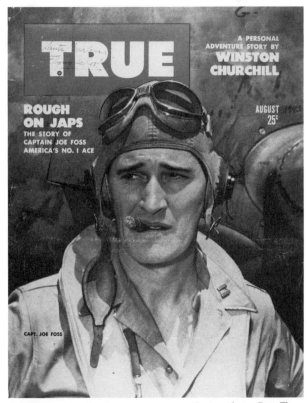

Looking much the veteran combat pilot, Joe Foss graces the cover of the August 1943 True Magazine. *"At Henderson, Foss always flew one of the chubby F4Fs, occasionally with the bravado number 13. His only lucky bit of clothing was an old hunting cap faded almost white. He liked to grow dark and scraggly goatees. He set his teeth on a cigar when he flew."* Smithsonian Institution

I really wasn't fond of the Japanese in any way, shape or form. The tales that came from the ground troops about the way the Japanese butchered people when they captured them. . . . Of course they knocked off one missionary and two of the sisters on Guadalcanal—and they did some pretty awful things to them.

So I didn't feel bad about fighting that outfit. They had no code of ethics at all when it came to war.

I told my boys, "We aren't going to shoot those cookies when they bail out—they're in enough trouble as it is." Some people wanted to argue with me about that. They said, "Kill 'em and they won't be back!" I said, "You're in enough trouble when you bail out in this country wherever you go—if it's over the ocean you got the sharks to contend with, if you land back in the jungle you aren't in too good of shape—so forget it and concentrate on shooting at somebody else."

One morning Foss slept late but was awakened by a dogfight taking place high overhead. Emerging from his tent, he was just in time to watch several burning Japanese planes falling from the sky. "One stricken bomber," he recalled in *Joe Foss, Flying Marine*, "dropped its load into the sea near Tulagi, raising tall columns of water. At the same time the crippled plane floated down out of the sky like a burning bit of paper."

"One Zero pilot got on the tail of a Wildcat over Henderson Field and for a time it looked like curtains for the Grumman," recalled Foss. The two planes roared through the sky, diving, turning, climbing, but the Grumman pilot couldn't shake the Japanese plane off his tail. Finally the American pilot pulled out quickly from a long swoop and the Zero overran, disappearing from view behind a hill.

In a moment the Zero was back, remembered Foss in *Joe Foss, Flying Marine*, "climbing like an elevator as ground fire boxed him in." The Japanese plane managed a brief escape, only to be brought down in flames by machine gunners near the beach.

As this incident illustrates, Henderson Field was a busy and exposed place. Here the Marines lived, fought and often died. The airstrip was about 3,800 feet long after enlargement by the Marines. The field ran northeast-southeast in the center of a grassy plain about a mile square. The plain was bounded on the south by low ridges rising out of the jungle, on the north by Savo Sound and on the other two sides by coconut groves. The Marines of the 1st Division were dug in around the airfield on three sides. To the south, where the jungle started, was no well-defined line, only a group of outposts. From the middle of Henderson Field it was only a short distance to the front lines in any direction except south. Foss and his fellow pilots, who had air battles of their own to fight almost daily, were also close observers of every ground action.

"The pilots and aircrewmen," wrote Thomas Miller, Jr., in *The Cactus Air Force*, "lived in tents in

Japanese sailors cling to the side of their sinking escort vessel. Flying Leathernecks, *a 1944 book, contained the following account of one Joe Foss mission against Japanese shipping: "Foss and his men had been continuously strafing Jap transports.*

It was a slaughter so dreadful that the Marine fliers sometimes could not keep from vomiting overside when they saw the sheer ungarnished death that their bullets and bombs brought." US Navy

the strip of coconut grove between the field and the beach—'Mosquito Grove' they called it."

The pilots slept two to six to a tent. "Some of us," recalled Foss in Simmons' *Joe Foss, Flying Marine*, "always were out before dawn, ready for surprise attacks." Standing ready, the pilots watched the ground crews start the planes and check magnetos, props, engines and tabs. Ordnance crews checked the guns and kept the ammunition pans full.

After breakfast was the endless vigil of the ready tent. Walter Simmons in his book *Joe Foss, Flying Marine* details the waiting

> where some of the boys lay comfortably on cots [recalled Foss] and others just sat on the backs of their necks. A phonograph blared out some old tune. Sometimes there were fairly recent (only a few months old) magazines or newspapers, to read. We played checkers, cribbage, or ace-deucy. . . . Sometimes we just sat and shot the breeze, or discussed tactics by the hour. Often we'd sleep in the daytime, since the Japs kept us awake so much of the night.
> Occasionally there was a scramble, or maybe we were alerted by a bogey. . . . For lunch at noon there was invariably soup or stew, with crackers. Supper was at four. . . . Afterward two eight man flights remained on duty until dark. The other men were free, which usually meant a shower. . . . The shower was something to look forward to all day.

Clothing on Guadalcanal was kept simple, the men usually wearing flight suits or khakis. To shield their eyes from the bright tropical sun they wore baseball caps—dark blue for pilots, red for mechanics; Foss wore an old canvas hunting cap. Clothes were rarely taken off because Japanese aircraft conducted a raid almost every night. The sound of an approaching Japanese plane was the signal for the crews to run from their tents to the nearby foxholes and slit trenches. For an hour or two the enemy plane—which the Marines called Maytag Charlie or Washing Machine Charlie or Louie the Louse—would fly back and forth overhead, dropping a small bomb now and them.

Those night nuisance raids were a cunning device, recalled Foss, in *Joe Foss, Flying Marine*:

> to rob us of sleep, and make a liar out of the gent who spoke of the Japanese sandman bringing sweet dreams. On the night of October 16th, for example, a crazy Jap swept so low over the field that his rear gunner was able to strafe with a machine gun, doing little damage but being a great bother so far as sleep was concerned.

Near the end of the first full week on Guadalcanal Foss knew he wouldn't have to worry about missing his share of combat in World War II. "The air was filled with danger," he recalled in *Joe Foss, Flying Marine*. "Night and day bombing attacks, shelling from the jungle and the sea, the spatter of snipers' bullets—all these were our steady diet."

The morning of October 16 had seen 1,500 shells from the heavy cruisers *Myoko* and *Maya* plaster Henderson Field. This was the third straight day of Japanese naval bombardment and the losses of planes and material were heavy. The three-day total included twenty-three SBDs destroyed or requiring major overhaul with six F4Fs, eight TBFs and four P-39s damaged.

The almost continuous Japanese air offensive against Guadalcanal continued on October 18 when fifteen Bettys and nine Zeros were reported coming in.

As the Japanese planes approached, a mishap delayed the takeoffs of Foss' last two men and the first five planes circled over the field waiting for them. On one turn Foss noticed five planes below, not two. Simmons in *Joe Foss, Flying Marine*, details the action that followed:

> On closer view I could see three of them were Zeros [recalled Foss]. They were flying a few feet behind the Marines with the apparent idea of knocking off those two planes and then any others they could surprise.
> We slid gently down behind them and started shooting. I picked the Zero farthest to the left. My first tracers set him afire, and he tipped over into a spin and went in.

Other Zeros dove to the attack from above and a wild dogfight ensued. Foss singled out a Zero and attempted to get behind him to no avail. Realizing he was pitted against a tough opponent, Foss attempted a side shot and scored hits on the Zero's motor. The Japanese plane began smoking, but Foss was unable to follow it down because he was immediately jumped by another Japanese fighter.

Foss approached the Zero head-on, holding his fire as the distance between the two planes rapidly narrowed. Suddenly the Zero pulled up to avoid a collision. "As he did so," recalled Foss in *Joe Foss, Flying Marine*, "I had barely shot at him when he burst into flames. He did a tight wingover, burning fiercely, and I pulled off and saw him far below, going down in flames."

As the Zeros scattered, Foss looked off into the distance and observed the approach of the expected Japanese Betty bombers.

The Mitsubishi Type One, or Betty, was a good medium bomber. It was nearly as fast cruising at altitude as the Grumman F4F flying at maximum speed. It was also capable of enormous range, "but that was a mixed blessing," wrote Thomas Miller in his book *The Cactus Air Force,*

> for its great fuel supply was made possible by two six hundred-gallon gas tanks, located in the roots of the wings between the engine nacelle and the fuselage. Since to armour them would reduce their capacity by almost half, the tanks were totally unprotected. A hit in either one would blow up the plane killing the seven man crew.

To get into better position to attack the Japanese bombers, Foss climbed to meet them on a 180 degree course to make a run on the right rear bomber. Soon, high above the bomber formation, he was in the tactical position he preferred to begin his attack.

> I liked to get out in front and above and turn back toward them and do an absolute straight overhead —where you can come right straight down on them. In fact, you were on your back and coming down. I tried to almost run into them—I didn't want to hit them, but I wanted to come that close.
>
> A gunner shooting at you doesn't have any chance to aim at you then. A vertical pass on anything is one that is almost impossible to defend against.

As Foss made his vertical dive the bomber suddenly exploded below him. He later learned that Ens. Red Thrash, a Navy pilot, had shot down the bomber before Foss reached firing range.

Pulling up through the smoking debris, Foss made an attack on the next bomber in the echelon. His short burst into the plane started smoke but caused no fire or explosion.

The next attack by Foss was successful, related Walter Simmons in his book *Joe Foss, Flying Marine*.

> I dove and came up under the left wing of the V-formation [recalled Foss] taking a belly shot at the last plane in line. It was a direct hit, which caused an explosion and fire on the left motor.
>
> I was right under him, my nose pointing straight up and the plane in a complete stall. It was impossible to miss.
>
> He went down at a 45 degree angle. Bombers all go down the same way when you get them. There's a big burst of fire, which dies down, goes *whoooosh* again, dies down and repeats. Pretty soon a wing drops off and the bomber goes into a final spin.

Incredibly, three of the bomber crew members survived the crash without a scratch.

Foss took a reprieve from air combat the next day and hiked the short distance to the front lines to look around. He did this on several occasions, usually trading candy or cigarettes to the ground troops for captured Japanese flags, sabers, pistols or rifles.

The brief rest from air combat was soon over for Foss. On October 20 his flight took off to intercept eighteen oncoming Zeros. A Zero singled Foss out and dove straight at him in a head-on attack. The enemy opened fire, his machine gun and cannon shells streaming beneath the Wildcat. As the dis-

Joe Foss—kneeling at right, first row—and fellow Marine pilots on Guadalcanal. During the 1½ years of fighting in World War II, the Marines had six of the leading aces: Joe Foss and Greg Boyington with 26 Japanese planes each, Capt. Robert Hanven with 25, Lt. Kenneth Walsh with 20, Capt. John Smith with 19 and Marion Carl with 16. National Archives

tance closed between the two planes the Zero pilot decided to turn out. Foss bore around hard and latched onto the Zero's tail.

Foss put a long burst into the Japanese plane's wing base and watched the Zero blow up in a shattering roar.

Instantly Foss was engaged with another Zero. Neither pilot was able to gain the advantage until Foss did a quick wingover and made a deflection shot at extremely close range. Foss' bullets slammed into the side of the cockpit, apparently killing the pilot, for the Zero began to twist downward until it splashed into the channel, raising a towering plume of water.

With this double victory Foss had shot down seven Japanese planes in eleven days. Much of his success was due to his superior combat tactics and his ability to shoot.

> I understood lead from the time I was just a kid and having a gun in my hand much of the time and shooting at running targets—rabbits and anything else I was after. So I had the advantage of understanding how to lead a target. I sometimes think that the guy[s] I was fighting against didn't understand it too well because they ended up shooting behind you all the time or under you. They never seemed to be able to direct their fire right on you.

Foss often conserved precious ammunition by cutting out two machine guns and using only four in combat. He also learned the value of conserving ammunition by working in close before opening fire. Running out of ammunition at critical times cost him at least four victories.

Despite his rapid string of victories, Foss didn't lose his respect for the Zero fighter plane. He felt that in its own way it was the best fighting plane in the world at that time, a feeling he still held in the early nineties.

> The Zero could fly much higher than the Wildcat; [it] could cruise faster too. The first time I saw a Zero he made a run on me and then pulled straight up doing slow rolls. It looked to me like he was absolutely vertical; that sort of startled me, to see somebody do that.
>
> See, you had 5,900 pounds in the Zero and the Wildcat weighed 8,900 pounds. You take that weight difference and you know that they could outmaneuver you easily.

One could not deny that the Japanese flew first-rate combat planes. One also could not doubt the bravery and tenacity of the Japanese pilots. What many Marine pilots did come to wonder at over time was the inflexibility of the Japanese tactics and the sometimes utter foolishness of their flying.

"Our boys developed an amused contempt for Jap flyers," recalled Foss in *Joe Foss, Flying Marine*. Often while on the ground the Marine pilots would look up and laugh as the Japanese planes put on their aerobatic circus. "Look at the crazy dopes!"

the Marines would shout as the Japanese went through their itinerary of slow rolls, wingovers and intricate loops.

Because of the Japanese pilots' poor tactical training, the Marines felt they passed up a lot of good chances to down American planes in combat. To Foss the Japanese tactics were somewhat of a mystery.

> I'd have to say they could sure handle their airplanes. I just don't know how smart they were! They sure pulled some dumb ones, like trying to show off when they outnumbered you. They had to let you know they could really maneuver their airplane and they would get a little too close and get snapped. But they handled their airplanes well, and as has been borne out since, some of them had good records. However, they achieved a good share of their victories before they got to our area.

Despite the start of the rainy season, the weather was good enough on October 23 for the Japanese to attack Guadalcanal with the largest force of bombers in several weeks: sixteen Bettys escorted by a force of twenty-eight Zeros. The Japanese arrived at 1130 hours. Col. Joe Bauer, who

Twenty of the Japanese planes Joe Foss shot down were elusive, hard-fighting Zeros. Foss was always careful to give much of the credit for his impressive score of victories to his wingman, Thomas Furlow. Furlow on several occasions shot down Zeros that had Foss in their sights. National Archives

had taken over as the new fighter commander, scrambled every plane he could: twenty-four F4Fs and four P-39s. Bauer was determined to protect Henderson Field and meet the Japanese on their own terms. "When you see Zeros, dogfight 'em," he told his pilots.

Foss, leading his flight to the attack, spotted five Zeros. The Japanese turned toward the Americans, who swung around to meet the attack.

As the F4Fs began to close in, Foss took a good look around and picked up a pack of eighteen to twenty Zeros in a full dive. Quickly leading his flight into a turn Foss dove to pick up speed.

The Zeros pitched into a flight of F4Fs led by Duke Davis and a wild dogfight ensued with both sides turning, diving, climbing and firing at each other.

Foss spotted a Grumman shooting at a Zero. Following the Wildcat was a Zero firing its machine gun and cannon.

Foss hurried to the rescue of the Grumman by swinging in behind the Zero. Closing the distance, he waited until he was only a few feet away and then fired his machine guns. Simmons, in *Joe Foss, Flying Marine*, describes the scene.

Poof! He blew up and disintegrated. No words can [ever] picture the explosion of a Zero, or exaggerate the thrill it gives you [wrote Foss]. The motor goes off in a crazy lopsided whirl. The pilot pops out of his cockpit like a pea that has been pressed from the pod. The air is filled with dust and little pieces, as if someone had emptied a huge vacuum cleaner bag in the sky. The wing section, burning where it had joined the fuselage, takes a long time to fall. It goes down like a leaf—sailing, then almost stopping as it attacks the air, sailing again, and attacking the air again.

Foss looked around and found the sky "filled with wild dogfights." Latching onto the tail of a Zero, he followed it through a dive and an ill-advised loop. Cutting inside the Japanese plane, he had the Wildcat on its back when he let loose with all six machine guns. A converging hail of machine gun fire riddled the Zero and it blew up "in a great beautiful burst."

Diving to gain speed, Foss noticed a Zero that appeared out of nowhere. The Japanese pilot was foolishly climbing at an angle while breaking into a slow roll. Closing in on the unsuspecting enemy, Foss once again fired a burst into the Zero. "There was a lovely, blinding flash," wrote Foss, "and the pilot popped out nearly hitting my Grumman." Narrowly avoiding the falling pilot, Foss watched as he plummeted toward the sea.

Soon Foss found himself approaching two Zeros head-on. Flying straight at one, he hoped the Japanese pilot would break and not ram the Wildcat. Soon the Zero broke to the right and Foss got in a short burst that riddled the back of the motor.

Flames were visible from the Zero as it flashed by. A split second later the Zero blew up in a fiery explosion. It was Foss' fourth victory of the day.

Foss now noticed tracers flashing past and a Zero glued to his tail. His troubles mounted when the Wildcat's engine began to smoke. Putting the Wildcat into a dive, he avoided the trailing Zero only to be machine-gunned by another Zero.

Now in deep trouble Foss hurriedly called for help on his radio. Luckily, two Wildcats joined the fight and finished off the Zeros that were trying to cause Foss' demise.

Foss made a long dead-stick glide back to Henderson Field, all the while mentally thanking the Grumman Aircraft Corporation for making such a durable plane that never caught on fire. As he landed and brought the Wildcat to a stop he thought to himself, *This is the fourth Grumman I've brought down in bad shape. Just one more and I'll be a Japanese ace!*, as related to Simmons in *Joe Foss, Flying Marine*.

All the Wildcats returned safely from the battle, although one landed in such a shot-up state that it was immediately rolled over to the boneyard. Seven other Wildcats were shot up in varying degrees. It had been a lucky day for the American pilots.

Thomas Miller, Jr., in his book on the air war over Guadalcanal, *The Cactus Air Force*, summed up the situation that existed at this time:

Joe Bauer's assessment of the situation had been proven right. It would have been suicide for an F4F to dogfight a Zeke a month before, but the attrition of September and October's hard fighting had cost the Japanese their best fighter pilots, and their replacements lacked experience and skill.

Then came October 25, a grisly Sunday forever memorialized in Marine annals as Dugout Sunday. It was a day, reported the April 3, 1943, *Saturday Evening Post*,

when the fate of all the Americans on Guadalcanal hung by as slender a thread as war gives an army and lets it live. It was a time of dank, dark days for the whole venture and those in high places were sick with the fear that all which had been sacrificed so f[a]r might have been a burnt offering to disaster.

Back home in America it was being said that our boys in the Solomons were caught like rats in a trap.

A postmidnight attack against Marine ground positions was only the beginning of what was supposed to be a coordinated land, sea and air attack to recapture Guadalcanal. The Japanese air attacks were heavy, wrote Robert Sherrod in his *Classic Marine Corps Aviation in World War II*.

Headquarters lost count of the air raids, and the war diary (assembled some time later) simply notes that: Enemy fighter planes were over Cactus at irregular intervals throughout the daylight hours. Our Grummans were almost continuously in the air, landing, refueling, reloading and taking off again time after time.

At 0800 Sunday the Zeros began to come over. The fighter strip was so muddy that it was a full hour before Foss and four others managed to take off. Almost immediately they were in a dogfight with six Japanese planes.

Foss raced to attack a Zero that was closely following a Wildcat. Seeing Foss dive after him, the Japanese pilot racked his plane into a tight turn and came racing head-on. As Foss fired, the Zero pulled almost straight up into the air in a steep climb. Foss, above the Zero, followed the climb and closed to almost pointblank range.

Now behind the Zero, Foss was just getting ready to fire. He describes the scene in Simmons' *Joe Foss, Flying Marine.*

> . . . I saw him crawl out on the right wing. He was hunched over, so close I could see the details of his blackish-green gabardine flying suit and his helmet. . . . I wanted to blow the plane out from under him, but he just managed to jump clear as I shot. My fire went right into the tail, traveled the length of the plane and blew it up. The pilot hurtled by with a swish and I lost sight of him.

After several futile attacks on other Japanese planes Foss noticed a Zero circling above. As he climbed to the attack the Zero took the challenge and dove toward him. Soon, wrote Simmons in *Joe Foss, Flying Marine,* the Zero was right in front of Foss.

> Huge red dots are on each side of his wings and fuselage, his plane a dirty gray below, rust-colored on top. On my first short burst, smoke started pouring out of him. He made a frantic turn out over the sea and started to lose altitude. . . . I let him go and watched as he kept smoking . . . till he plunged into the sea.

Learning that five of the six attacking Zeros had been shot down, Foss came in for a landing, satisfied that he now had thirteen Japanese planes to his credit.

At midafternoon Foss and his flight took off once again to engage a large group of approaching Zeros. In the dogfight that followed, Foss closed to short range on a Zero and blew it up with a short burst.

Joining another group of swirling planes, Foss found a Zero coming straight at him, firing wildly. As the Zero started to pass, Foss made a right turn, swung onto his tail and fired the six .50s. The Japanese plane blew up.

While coming in to land Foss spotted two other Zeros, and after a game of cat and mouse in the clouds he was able to slip onto the tail of one. "I eased up to within a few feet," recalled Foss in *Joe Foss, Flying Marine,* "and blew him into a million jagged worthless pieces with one burst."

After downing his fifth plane Foss ran out of ammunition and headed back to Henderson Field only 6 miles away.

Upon landing, Foss was approached by another pilot, who, laughing, said, "You don't fight fair," according to Walter Simmons in *Joe Foss, Flying Marine.* "You get up so close to the Zeros that it would be impossible to miss. Why, you actually leave powder burns on them."

Foss' score now stood at sixteen Japanese planes shot down. He was only ten planes away from tying Capt. Eddie Rickenbacker's World War I record of twenty-six. Although he would eventually tie Rickenbacker's record and for a time be the leading American ace of World War II, Foss was never interested in trying to break Rickenbacker's record.

> I think some people today have the idea that it was a contest to see who could shoot down the most airplanes. It was no contest; the idea was to get rid of every sucker you could, so they wouldn't be back another day to get you—whether it was a Betty bomber, dive-bomber or Zero.
>
> You didn't care who got credit or how—we just wanted to get them, and we cheered whoever got them, whether it was by ground fire or somebody in the air.
>
> I never knew in all of this how many airplanes Eddie Rickenbacker had. I knew he was a great ace, but I sure wasn't worrying about Eddie at that time. The only thought all of us had was to get rid of those

Japanese vessel under attack. The Marine pilots would attempt to bomb the Japanese ships but more often would fly in low and strafe, using incendiary and armor-piercing bullets. "The bullets from the planes tore through not only one but four or five Japanese soldiers at a single blast," wrote Capt. John Dechant. US Navy

bums; they were dangerous to have around, they wanted to kill you.

As I would say, "War just isn't safe, it's dangerous!"

October 25, 1942, saw the end of a two-week-long Japanese air offensive. The cost of victory for the Americans was high. At the end of Dugout Sunday only twelve fighters were fit to fly. The pilots were drained and exhausted. For the Japanese the two-week period had been a disaster. Their losses totaled twenty-five twin-engine bombers and close to eighty fighters. The Japanese Eleventh Air Fleet was finished. Its power was so reduced that it was never again able to undertake a major bombing mission against Henderson Field.

As October neared its end the American foothold in Guadalcanal was still tenuous. Between October 22 and 27 the Japanese launched a series of ferocious ground attacks in an attempt to break through the Marine lines surrounding Henderson Field. In these attacks the Japanese lost 2,000 men and failed to penetrate the Marine defenses. Even though the lines held, the Americans still only occupied a stretch of land 3 miles deep and 6 miles long on an island 25 miles wide and 85 miles long.

That the American position in the Solomons was desperate was underscored by the October 27 headline of the *Chicago Tribune,* which read, "Japs Launch Huge Drive on Guadalcanal Yanks." On October 28 the *Tribune,* in a rare front-page editorial, called for the Roosevelt administration to put General MacArthur in command.

The pessimism over the outcome of the Guadalcanal campaign evidenced by the editors of the *Chicago Tribune* and many home front citizens would have surprised Foss and his fellow pilots. In Guadalcanal, on the cutting edge of battle, the Japanese were showing signs of weakening, relates Simmons in *Joe Foss, Flying Marine.*

> How the enemy replaced his plane losses was a mystery [recalled Foss]. Yet he sent his Zeros over almost endlessly. After a time the strain showed, not in planes but in pilots. They were obviously less experienced, less well-grounded in tactics. . . . the second team.

The bitterness of the struggle had not filled Foss with despair or the doubt of defeatism but had forced him to come to terms with the heart-pounding uncertainty of life on Guadalcanal. The man who had once been considered too old to be a fighter pilot was now a seasoned veteran, confident of his ability and flying skills. John Field, in a 1943 *Life* magazine article, gave the home front readers a look at life on Guadalcanal for Joe Foss and his fellow Marines:

> After the long hours of flying, the boys would gather in Joe's tent for a drink. Nearby Marine artillery fired at Japs in the hills, and the bursting crunch blended with the buzz of mosquitos around their ears. They played cards, shot craps, read over worn letters from home. But mostly they talked—long, profane, sentimental conversations about home and war and hunting. Joe especially talked.
>
> With Gregory Loesch he talked about hunting in Colorado; with Bill Freeman about hunting in Big Bend country. With Oscar Bate he talked about the day when Bate would come to visit him on the ranch he was going to buy after the war. With Squadron Leader Duke Davis he talked about changes and improvements in the Grumman fighter.
>
> With all of them he would have a drink. "Joe could drink with any of us," they say. "But like the rest of us he had sense not to drink too much. None of us wanted to get killed the next day. But drinking relaxed our nerves and helped us sleep. It was hot, there were bugs everywhere, and the Japs bombed us every day. Money didn't mean anything, but whiskey was important in our lives. It sold for $100 a quart.

The bull sessions and the whiskey helped to relax the tension of air combat. But staying alive in the air over Guadalcanal required getting wise to the value of little things, recalled Foss in *Joe Foss, Flying Marine,*

> such as keeping our planes clean inside and out. Dirt on the outside cuts knots off a ship's speed. It also conceals bullet holes and mechanical faults. . . . Inside, dirt is dangerous because in maneuvering a pilot might get an eyeful right in the middle of a dogfight. The windshield, particularly, should be spotless.

In late October a period of bad weather limited air activity, and Foss used this quiet interlude to hunt for Japanese snipers with some of his fellow pilots. Because of the small size of the Marine perimeter Guadalcanal had no secure rear area. Often Japanese snipers would penetrate the Marine defensive lines and raise hell in the rear area camps.

On one occasion Foss heard a fellow pilot cut loose with his Tommy gun. "I yelled," recalled Foss in Simmons' *Joe Foss, Flying Marine,* "and asked if he had hit anything." The Marine yelled back that he had seen movement in the bushes but couldn't tell for sure what it was. "That was enough for me— I left," remembered Foss.

On November 4 Foss flew as part of a protective patrol over the harbor while transports unloaded supplies. Unloading operations went peaceably until noon, when Japanese planes appeared in the distance. The intruders were shortly driven off and the needed supplies continued to come ashore.

At 0915 hours on November 5 a report was received that twenty-seven Japanese high-altitude bombers and fighters were approaching Guadalcanal. The transports again interrupted unloading while the Marine fighters climbed to the defense.

Foss first sighted the enemy when he suddenly noticed the shattered fuselage of a bomber go by, straight for the ground. Ground fire from the big

American guns below had knocked down five bombers and a Zero from the attacking force. The Japanese bombers failed to reach the harbor, dropping their bombs in the jungle while beating a hasty retreat.

After Foss had landed, a Marine officer told him he had been watching the falling bomber fragments with his field glasses. While doing this he had spotted the back half of a bomber fuselage coming down with a man trapped inside. "The fuselage was like a tube with both ends blown out," recalled Foss in *Joe Foss, Flying Marine,* "and Captain Finney could see this thing spinning over and over all the way down, with this man vainly trying to escape. He went right in and never did get out."

For the most part early November was relatively quiet, with little air action. An occasional night raid by Maytag Charlie was usually the only Japanese air activity, and his desultory bombing harmed no one. The arrival of much-needed gasoline and other supplies was welcomed.

The waiting ended on November 7. It began quietly when an American dive-bomber scout plane reported eleven Japanese warships north of Florida Island steaming toward Guadalcanal. The Japanese intention was to land troops at night to reinforce the Guadalcanal garrison. Foss' flight, along with two others, was sent up as protection for US dive-bombers whose mission it was to bomb the Japanese ships.

Gaining altitude, Foss turned the attack force north to search for the Japanese convoy. As they flew toward the target the Americans encountered rain squalls and heavy clouds. Suddenly streams of tracers shot in front of Foss, aimed at the flight ahead. Below at 4,000 feet were six Japanese float planes. called out, "Don't look now, boys, but there they are."

Foss and his flight dove to the attack, he recalled in *Joe Foss, Flying Marine.* "They never saw us," he recalled. "I nailed a plane on the right side of their flight—hit him in the motor." This float plane was Foss' seventeenth victory.

It was over in a matter of seconds. The six Zeros had been quickly blown to pieces. Aside from dropping fragments—and parachutes—the Americans were alone in the sky.

Looking around, Foss counted five empty chutes dangling in the sky. He described the scene

Posing for a publicity photo on the wing of an F4F: Roger Haberman, Bill Freeman, Thomas Furlow, *Joe Foss, Gregory Loesch, Presley, Bill Marontate and Oscar Bate, left to right.* National Archives

in *Joe Foss, Flying Marine*. Glancing up, he observed a sixth chute

> with an enemy pilot dangling in the harness. At that moment the Jap unbuckled himself and jumped out. He passed me on his back, falling headfirst at a little angle. Seconds later he hit the sea and threw up a big geyser of water.
>
> The other five flyers had apparently done the same, although none of us actually saw them. The reasons for such suicidal tactics were a mystery. I never saw either side shoot at a parachuting man in the Guadalcanal area.

Moving back up in formation, Foss found himself in the tail-end Charlie slot. Proceeding with the attack, the Wildcats pulled ahead of the dive-bombers in order to begin strafing the decks of the Japanese destroyers, which were now visible below.

Before beginning his dive Foss looked around and saw another Japanese plane—a scout biplane—off in the distance. Instead of sticking with his flight he decided to go after the biplane. To Foss the biplane looked like a sitting duck. It would be, he thought, an easy victory. The biplane proved to be a tough opponent, however, as he related in *Joe Foss, Flying Marine*.

> When I made a pass at him . . . I realized I'd overrun him. He was throttled way down, hardly moving. I passed him to the right and when I did his tail gunner opened up. His bullets cracked into my plane. I looped to the right, got some altitude, dove down and came up under him. My .50s sawed off his right wings—and he dropped. As I came up again I saw another biplane above me. He apparently had not seen me, so I dove to pick up more speed, then came up and got him too.

His eighteenth and nineteenth victories behind him, Foss knew it was time to turn for home. His gas was running low and the Grumman was riddled with holes. As he looked around the empty sky he knew he would have to head home alone, and storms were forming up ahead of him.

Confident of the direction home, Foss hadn't bothered to check his compass. When he did he realized he was 30 degrees off course. Ahead loomed a big rain squall, and Foss suddenly realized he was in trouble and far off route.

In a moment the motor quit, caught hold again and then conked out cold. "I tell you my hair stood up so straight it raised the helmet right off my head," recalled Foss in *Joe Foss, Flying Marine*.

Starting the engine again, Foss found that visibility was bad and all he could see were squalls, especially over the islands. "These storms were dark," he recalled, "and looked too nasty for me with a bum engine. By then, too, I wasn't even sure which island was which."

A big cloud loomed ahead and Foss turned to the left. Finally the motor quit again and Foss found himself with a dead engine at 13,000 feet. Spotting an island off to his left, he began a slow glide, realizing his only chance was to get as close to the island as he could before he crashed into the sea.

Gliding in, Foss pushed the canopy all the way back. He banked to the right and decided to hit the water about a mile from the shore. He had been trained to skid along the swell of the ocean for a smooth ditching, but things didn't go as planned, as he related in *Joe Foss, Flying Marine*.

> When I hit, the storm had broken and it was raining hard. The plane went down like a rock. I had forgotten to undo the leg buckles of my parachute and my right leg was jammed under the seat. With the whole ocean pouring into the cockpit, somehow I undid the buckles and wrenched my leg out. But for what seemed like a long time I was underwater.
>
> Finally the inflated Mae West jacket shot me to the surface and I began swimming toward a point of land maybe 5 miles off. To keep the sharks away I broke a bottle of chloride I had in my pocket. But I didn't seem to be getting closer to land. And I had swallowed a lot of seawater.

Night began to close in and Foss still seemed no closer to land than when he started. In the dark he could see glowing phosphorescent patches in the water. "I thought they were made by sharks' fins," he remembered in *Joe Foss, Flying Marine*. "They nearly scared me to death."

After nearly 3 hours in the water he observed a few canoes approaching. Not knowing if they were full of natives, Japanese or Americans, he kept quiet. Finally somebody called out in English, wrote Simmons in *Joe Foss, Flying Marine*. "Look over here." Realizing that they weren't Japanese, Foss called out, "Over here!"

On the way to shore Foss and his rescuers passed the peninsula toward which he had been swimming. Tommy Robinson, an Australian saw-mill operator who had pulled Foss into the canoe, told Foss he was lucky not to have reached the peninsula. To get to the mainland Foss would have had to ford a stagnant stream, which was filled with man-eating crocodiles. "No doubt I would have walked right into the mouth of one [of] those cheerful customers," recalled Foss in *Joe Foss, Flying Marine*.

That night he slept in a Catholic mission and had a dinner of fresh steak, yams and goat's milk. Shortly he boarded a PBY Catalina for the return trip to Guadalcanal. Landing, he went directly to the fighter tent and had a grand reunion with "his boys." Before long he was back in combat, none the worse for wear.

On November 9 Foss was awarded the Distinguished Flying Cross by Adm. William Halsey. "Three of us got the DFC that day," remembered Foss, including "Big Bill Freeman, a member of my flight, and Lt. Wallace Wethe, a member of our squadron."

Foss attended the ceremony in his flight suit, so he could go right back to the field and take off as soon as possible. The citation, according to Walter Simmons in *Joe Foss, Flying Marine*, read:

For extraordinary achievement while participating in aerial flights with Marine Fighting Squadron 121 in the Solomon Islands Area. During the period October 13 to October 20, 1942, inclusive, Captain Foss shot down six enemy Zero fighters and one enemy bomber in aerial combat. His constant aggressiveness, skill and leadership during these engagements were worthy of the highest tradition of the Naval Service.

During the night of November 11, an American task force positioned itself close to the Japanese positions on Guadalcanal. At dawn the task force began a heavy bombardment, which went on for hours.

Intelligence alerted the flyers on Henderson Field that Japanese torpedo planes had been ordered to attack the US flotilla. "We knew the planes were coming," recalled Foss, "but did not know exactly from where."

That afternoon Foss' flight was at 29,000 feet over Florida Island. In a 1943 *Life* magazine article Foss described the action that followed:

We hadn't sighted the Jap torpedo planes, but we were looking for them. Ahead of us was a big cloud bank miles up into the sky with its underside at about 22,000 feet. I figured the Japs were in that cloud, so we kept our eyes on it. But they must have been able to sneak out when we weren't watching, because when we saw 22 of them they were almost six miles below us at 500 feet, heading straight for our destroyers.

So we pushed on over and headed down. Straight down. Like the damn[ed]est roller coaster you ever saw. For 29,000 feet. Our windshields frosted over and we had to scrape them off to see. They had Zeros for high cover, and we went by those Zeros ZWWWWWT! We broke out of our dive to the rear of the Torpedo bombers and raced up on them still going like bats out of hell. We level[ed] off at 50 feet and went in shooting. I hit one bomber's right motor and set it afire. Without waiting to see it drop, I skidded to the left and caught another bomber. I got him in the left motor. We went through our own ship's AA fire like greased weasels, picking off the Japs one by one as we raced up on them. Only one of the 22 Japs got away. I could have blown him to hell because he was directly underneath me, but by that time I was out of ammunition and almost out of gas.

What licked the Japs was that terrific dive from 29,000 feet.

As Foss raced home he counted twelve Japanese bombers floating on the water, several of them with crew members standing on the wings.

Foss' three victories during this battle brought his total of Japanese planes destroyed to twenty-two.

On the morning of November 12 Foss took off at dawn on a scouting mission. His objective was to track a Japanese battleship accompanied by a cruiser and five destroyers that had been located near Savo Island.

The location of the battleship pinpointed, Foss was ordered in the afternoon to lead a near-suicidal decoy mission against the Japanese ships. He was instructed to engage the ships' guns so that a second wave of American torpedo bombers could come in clean and destroy the battleship.

Foss' eight-plane flight went out carrying 100 pound bombs and came in over the enemy fleet at 12,000 feet, then peeled off to the attack. Foss made the dive at a ninety degree angle, a method of attack he favored.

Like I told the kids, make sure you're going absolutely vertical—in fact, go a little more than vertical and they can't get you with their guns. Somebody from another ship might get you but from the one you're attacking they don't seem to be able to shoot straight up. I know that in my first pass I got so interested in that battleship that it looked like a milking machine. It had a big bunch of guns and they were pumping away.

I could see they were shooting underneath me and I got so interested that I almost hit the superstructure. I had to kick it to the side and still almost hit the water getting out of there.

Passing a few feet from the superstructure of the battleship, Foss made a sharp turn to the right.

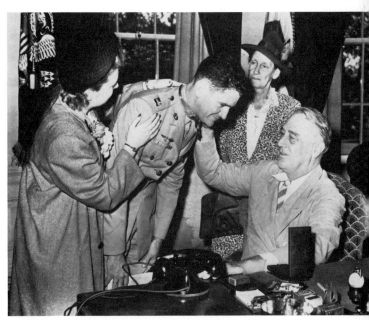

President Franklin Roosevelt, aided by Mrs. Foss, places the Medal of Honor around the neck of Capt. Joe Foss. The captain's mother, Mary Foss, looks on. The award ceremony took place at the White House on May 11, 1943. National Archives

Upon his return to the States, Joe Foss was reunited with his family and given a hero's welcome. "The welcome I got in Sioux Falls is something I'll remember all my life," wrote Foss. "I guess a fellow is concerned most of all about what the home folks think about him. In this city of 41,000 a crowd of 75,000 turned out that day." National Archives

He had intended to turn left but changed his mind. A moment later an antiaircraft shell burst where he would have been had he turned left. Looking back after his close escape, Foss saw the battleship's big guns still shooting into the water, sending up great geysers 50 to 75 feet high to obstruct the aim of the incoming American torpedo planes. The torpedo bombers struck a battleship of the *Kongo* class.

Shortly after noon the next day word was received that fourteen Japanese transports and cargo ships were heading toward Guadalcanal escorted by warships. During the first attack against the Japanese force, the warships turned and fled, leaving the transports to bear the brunt of the battle. The first flight of American bombers and torpedo planes set fire to several of the Japanese ships and sank one outright.

Foss and his flight were scheduled to escort the next attacking wave of dive-bombers and torpedo planes. Col. Joe Bauer decided to accompany Foss. It was his third time in the air, as he was usually grounded because of his duties as fighter director.

Coach was the nickname for Bauer. He was loved and respected by the Marine pilots. "Put me on the team, Coach," they pleaded when they wanted to go on a mission. On an earlier mission Bauer had shot down four Japanese dive-bombers in a matter of seconds. It was a stunning accomplishment and would win him the Medal of Honor.

Foss, Bauer and Thomas "Boot" Furlow circled high over the Japanese ships to provide air cover while the dive-bombers and torpedo planes made their attacks. As the American bombers left, the three F4Fs dove down to make a strafing run on some of the surviving transports.

"I came down to 3,000 feet," recalled Foss in *Joe Foss, Flying Marine,* "started shooting and continued down to almost mast height."

The three Wildcats, their .50 caliber machine guns blazing away, hacked a bloody, jagged swath through the packed ranks of the Japanese troops on the transports.

Their strafing run completed, according to Simmons in *Joe Foss, Flying Marine,* the three Marines "went tearing for home, right on the water." Foss noticed tracers coming over his shoulder. He turned and saw two Zeros heading in for an attack. Bauer turned and went head-on at one. Both Bauer and the Zero raced toward each other, firing steadily. Suddenly the Zero burst into flame and exploded.

Foss and Furlow went after the other Zero, but it managed to elude them. After the unsuccessful chase they turned back to get Bauer and go home. When they returned, they found Bauer just swimming out of an oil slick left by his downed F4F.

Foss tried to toss out his rubber raft to Bauer, but it was jammed. He then attempted to call Henderson Field on his radio, but he couldn't get a message through. Circling over Bauer once more, he turned and headed home at full throttle to get a rescue plane.

Returning to Henderson Field, Foss roared into a landing and slipped to the ground looking for Maj. Roe Renner of Bowbells, North Dakota, who flew the J2F rescue plane.

The J2F was an amphibious biplane. The great pontoon and stubby fuselage made it easily recognizable. The plane had no color; years of wear had faded the original blue into a drab, peeled, weathered gray. Nearly forty patches showed on the wings and body where Japanese bullets had made their mark. The Marines not too affectionately called it The Flying Brick.

Foss and Renner took off to attempt a rescue of Bauer. As they headed out to sea it was pitch-black and all they could see were five Japanese ships ablaze under low-hanging clouds. After circling vainly for some time they returned to Henderson Field.

The next morning Renner went out again to search for Bauer. Foss and a fighter escort met

Renner to provide top cover. Soon two Japanese reconnaissance planes appeared and the Grummans turned to the attack.

Foss made a pass at one of the Japanese planes and as he closed the distance the rear gunner began firing. Foss' first burst hit the plane and it began to smoke. With the Japanese plane trailing smoke Foss turned to aid the other members of his flight, but his help wasn't needed, as the second Japanese plane was downed in a fiery explosion.

Looking back, Foss observed the plane he had damaged still flying. As he turned to the attack the Japanese pilot made a sharp bank directly in front of him. At 300 yards Foss fired a long burst that hit the plane smack in the center. With flames shooting out, the Japanese plane pushed over and began to fall. The rear gunner was still shooting as the plane crashed into the sea.

Foss and Renner then searched vainly for Bauer but found nothing except some empty Japanese lifeboats floating lazily along. Bauer was never seen again. Although his disappearance is something of a mystery, Foss had this opinion on his fate:

> I feel the Japanese killed him. They saw us out there and we had been giving them a good working over on that particular mission. When I flew over Bauer he waved to keep going; evidently he didn't want me to give his position away by circling. But the Japanese must have picked him up and killed him.
>
> Colonel Bauer was a tremendous leader—one of those guys that could get the dullest character really enthusiastic about a mission. He was as good as anybody I flew with. When you have a guy like that you can't lose.

The next day Foss found he had a fever of 103 degrees and ached all over. Malaria had penetrated the quinine and Atabrine defenses that the medics gave every person who served in the tropics. "I was so sick I thought I was going to die," recalled Foss.

On November 19 Foss left Guadalcanal on a DC-3. After a brief stop in New Caledonia he was sent on to Sidney, Australia, for rest and a chance to recover from the malaria.

While at Sidney Foss had a chance to meet Clive "Killer" Caldwell, an Australian ace who had shot down twenty German and Italian planes over the North African desert. Caldwell invited Foss to come to an Australian airfield and talk to members of three Spitfire squadrons recently assigned to the air defense of northern Australia.

Foss began his address to the veteran pilots with some blunt advice:

> I understand that several of you guys are aces. Well, congratulations. But what worked against the Germans won't work against the Japs.
>
> I know what you're thinking. You think that if a stiff-necked American can shoot down twenty-three Japs in an 8,000 pound airplane with 1,200 horsepower, then you're really going to clean house in a 6,500 pound airplane with 1,500 horses. Well, it doesn't work that way. If you try to dogfight a Zero he'll eat your lunch.

Telling the Australians not to try to win the war single-handedly, Foss warned, "When you find yourself all alone out there, head for home."

One Australian pilot asked Foss if that were "quite the sporting thing to do." Foss answered, "When I was all alone, I scooted for home. I'm still around. The guys that fought by themselves are dead."

On January 1, 1943, Foss returned to Guadalcanal. He found that many things had changed in the six weeks he had been away. The Americans now had a field with a steel mat runway instead of the old cow pasture. "We had M.P.'s, telephones, good roads, moving pictures—and no excitement," recalled Foss in *Joe Foss, Flying Marine*. "The field had not been bombed since December 14th, and there hadn't been a multiple bombing attack since we left."

Foss didn't realize that the critical period on Guadalcanal had passed. Although the struggle

Joe Foss in 1989. Foss has had a successful postwar career. He was featured on the cover of Time *magazine on January 29, 1990, in his role as president of the National Rifle Association. Joe Foss*

went on until February 9, the days of trial had ended with the November crisis. Combat would continue, but the balance of power had swung in favor of the Americans.

On January 15 Foss' flight escorted dive-bombers to attack a Japanese destroyer and transport. Flying with the Marines were several Army P-39s.

As they neared the Japanese ships the P-39s were jumped by a group of new square-wing Zeros. Three of Foss' flight dove to help the P-39s. Foss remained above, keeping an eye on several circling Zeros.

As the dogfight moved nearer, Foss fired a short burst at a Zero but failed to get a hit. The Zero dove away and Foss let it go. Then in the distance he noticed a Wildcat surrounded by Zeros. He turned to help.

"As I turned," recalled Foss in *Joe Foss, Flying Marine*, "a Zero dove directly in front of me at close range, apparently not seeing me. I gave a short burst that must have been just right, for he exploded at once."

Almost instantly Foss fired at another Zero trying to get behind a Wildcat. As Foss passed the Japanese plane he looked around and was surprised to see it burst into flames and spin down out of control.

Foss then observed Oscar Bate off to his right with a Zero on his tail pulling into firing position. Foss began firing to chase the Zero off. As Foss' bullets crossed in front of the Japanese plane the enemy pilot pulled up and came at Foss head-on, his guns firing.

The two planes raced at each other, cannon and machine guns blazing away, with hundreds of shells somehow failing to find their mark. As the distance between the fighters rapidly closed, Foss could see his tracers going just over the hood of the Japanese plane, as he recalled in *Joe Foss, Flying Marine*.

If they had been a few inches lower they would have brained him. His shots came at me the same way. We were so close I could plainly see the pilot and the green strip in front of the windshield to keep the glare out of his eyes. The cowling was bright red. . . . It was one of the most nerve-racking situations I was ever caught in.

The Japanese pilot, unable to stand the fearsome tension of the collision course any longer, suddenly straightened out, climbed, made a turn around and dove back toward Foss. Once again the two planes came head-on at each other, the Japanese plane diving down and Foss climbing up. Once again unable to bear the strain of the head-on pass, the Japanese pilot turned right, giving Foss a chance to get an inside angle. As Foss fired, the Wildcat's six machine guns roared and the .50 caliber slugs smashed into the side of the Zero's cockpit.

The Zero dove 4,000 feet below, made a big circle to the right and came back once again toward Foss. Just as the Japanese plane passed at about 100 yards, smoke started pouring out. Foss, headed in the opposite direction, was looking back when the Zero, almost a half-mile away, burst into flames and started on down.

Foss dove into a cloud and traveled along its edges for some time to get his composure back. He knew it had been a near thing. Only his steel nerves and the ability to keep his Wildcat on a collision course while roaring straight toward the teeth of the Zero's propellers had saved him. The Japanese pilot had flinched and in turning had exposed his plane to Foss' machine guns.

These were the last three Japanese planes Foss shot down in World War II, but it was a melancholy victory because fellow pilot William P. Marontate was killed during the dogfight. Marontate had shot down thirteen Japanese planes before his luck ran out.

Foss came back to the United States in March, his ship docking at San Diego. From there he was flown to Washington, where his wife met him. "He was feted there and in New York, and given a tremendous parade and ovation in Sioux Falls," wrote John Field of *Life* magazine.

On May 18 Foss was awarded the Medal of Honor by President Franklin Roosevelt at a White House ceremony. The memory of this remained vivid for Foss:

For a farm kid to meet the president of the United States is a thrill! The fact that he stopped and visited and I looked and all these dignitaries were waiting to see him—people that I had read about, cabinet officers and so forth that were sitting out there. He wanted to know all about Guadalcanal, and I'm in a visiting situation with him—that's really a big thrill!

I've met all the presidents since Roosevelt, and I would say that he really seemed to have a way of talking to you that put you at ease—I was able to visit with him easily.

The June 7, 1943, issue of *Life* magazine featured Foss on its cover. He was pictured standing in front of the White House, the Medal of Honor around his neck. The South Dakota farm boy had come a long way.

Foss featured briefly to the Pacific theater of war until malaria once again struck him down.

I picked up a Corsair group and went back overseas. When my outfit was going to the Philippines I was so sick they had to send me home. I once again got that lousy malaria. I came back and went to Klamath Falls, Oregon, and a doctor who had won the Nobel prize for research in tropical medicine gave me a shot of something and I've never been bothered since. I'd had twenty some attacks up to that point and was down to 140 pounds.

Foss has had, by any account, a remarkable postwar career. In 1990 he was the subject of a feature article by Gary Smith in *Sports Illustrated* magazine. Much of the article discussed his career and his presidency of the controversial National Rifle Association.

Guess I've got myself in the middle of another war [said Foss], being president of the National Rifle Association. Well, that's nothing new for Ol' Joe. Knocked 26 Japs out of the sky in World War II, top Marine ace of all time. Got into politics after that, was governor of South Dakota for four years, then ran for the House of Representatives against George McGovern and lost, which shows you what kind of politician Ol' Joe was. Then was commissioner of the American Football League for its first six years, back when the NFL and us were like two cats tied by the tails and tossed over a clothesline—yep, same time I was host of the *American Sportsman* on ABC-TV.... You're talking to a fellow who's been shot down four times, crash-landed nine or more, lived through malaria, arsenic poisoning, hepatitis, arrhythmia and an infection in the lining of my heart that felt like somebody was jabbing an ice pick in my chest—got a pacemaker in there to kick-start that baby now.

As is evident from this quote, Foss considers himself the top-scoring Marine ace of all time. This is a matter of some controversy because the US Marine Corps lists Greg "Pappy" Boyington as its top ace with twenty-eight victories.

However, six of Boyington's twenty-eight victories were earned while flying with the Flying Tigers. Many members of the AVG, including the legendary ace David "Tex" Hill, dispute his record.

I do know that his record with the AVG was 3.5 planes—two planes destroyed in the air and 1.5 on the ground—which he was paid for....

Joe Foss, a great fighter pilot and a decent man, is the rightful owner of the title of the leading Marine Corps ac[e] of World War II, and I hope that the Marine Corps will have guts enough to correct the record.

Foss and Boyington were, according to *Sports Illustrated* writer Gary Smith, involved in an altercation in 1949 over this controversy.

Baa Baa Black Sheep Ace Pappy Boyington . . . attacked Foss in a hotel ballroom full of VIPS [and] drove him against the wall again and again, until Ol' Joe braced his heels against the wall and blasted off, sending them both crashing through chairs, senators, congressmen and mayors. Then Ol' Joe flipped Pappy over backward and drilled his head into the floor, knocked him colder 'n a pickle—and stayed there, pinning the unconscious body, roaring to a friend, "Count the sucker out!"

Ranking Marine ace or not, Foss received an offer from Hollywood in 1955 of $750,000 for the rights to his life story. John Wayne was to play him in a movie titled *Brave Eagle.* Foss took one look at the script and the gooey dialogue the writers had him using to sweep women off their feet and politely turned the moviemakers down.

In 1989 Foss was asked to look back over his life and determine what he thought was the most significant achievement of his eventful career. Was it the twenty-six victories, the Medal of Honor, being governor of South Dakota? His answer came as somewhat of a surprise:

I'm a born-again Christian and so I say the greatest thing that ever happened to me was the day I asked Jesus Christ into my life as lord and savior—all the other things are ant hills compared to knowing where you are going when you die.

During the time I was battling away on Guadalcanal, if someone would say to me at that time, "Joe, if you were to die today do you know where you would go?" I'd fumble around and change the subject.

I know now where I want to go.

Alfred Montagpent, in his *Supreme Philosophy of Man,* wrote:

It is still true that God is the best cure for a troubled mind. "Though wilt keep him in perfect peace whose mind is stayed on thee." This is the gift that God reserves for his special protegees, talent and beauty he gives to many. Wealth is commonplace, fame not rare. But peace of mind—that is his final guerdon of approval, the fondest sign of his love. He bestows it. Most men are never blessed with it, others wait all their lives—yes, far into advance age—for this gift to descend upon them.

Foss—Medal of Honor winner, Marine ace of aces, successful politician—has, it would appear, won his God's approval and received the best gift of all: perfect peace.

Chapter 7

Jim Goodson, the King of the Strafers

James Goodson was rudely introduced to World War II, when the Athenia, *on which he was a passenger, was torpedoed off the coast of the Hebrides. After his rescue he joined the Royal Canadian Air Force and eventually served with the Eagle squadrons and the 4th Fighter Group, US Army Air Force. He became a leading ace of the 4th FG, participating in more than 100 missions. In July 1944 he was shot down during a low-level mission and he was a prisoner until the end of the war. He ended the war with thirty-two victories—fifteen air—to his credit. After the war he served as the vice president of ITT-Europe. He retired in England. Unless attributed to another source, all quotes are from a July 1990 interview with James Goodson.*

It was the summer of 1939 and James Goodson, a native New Yorker, was traveling to broaden his education. By late August his travels had brought him to Paris. Goodson, who was studying modern languages at the University of Toronto, thought this would be a good opportunity to improve his French.

He had picked an inopportune time to be visiting the French capital, however. On September 1 the Germans invaded Poland, unleashing the specter of war upon Europe. Goodson's mother was English and he had an aunt and uncle living in England. He decided it was time to leave Paris and return to England. "[I] was in Paris when the Germans marched into Poland. There was very little excitement over the war and at first they didn't black out the lights about the Arc de Triomphe. I returned to England and found everyone looking for gas masks and preparing for the blackout."

He soon realized that the war was going to reach him wherever he was in Europe. "While staying with my aunt and uncle I was told I had better get out of England because there was going to be a war. Joe Kennedy, our ambassador, was con-

vinced there was going to be a war and England would lose it."

Goodson had a hard time booking passage. "Everyone was trying to leave," he recalled, "but I'd worked my way over on one of the ships in port, and as I knew the men, they got me on."

On the third of September Goodson stood on the rail of the SS *Athenia* as she slowly left port, and a Europe facing the abyss of war. He related the beginning of the journey in his book *Tumult in the Clouds:*

> The loudspeaker announced the lifeboat drill. I dutifully went back to my cabin to pick up my life-jacket and made my way to the deck and lifeboat station. The boat was large, and I calculated that there would perhaps be just enough space for us all, but it would be crowded. The normal capacity of the ship was about 1000, but with returning American and Canadian tourists, English, Scottish and Irish emigrants and Eastern European refugees, there were at least 1,300 passengers.

Shortly after the lifeboat drill Goodson stopped to talk to a fellow passenger, a Scotsman anxious to leave the Old World for the New. Grover Hall wrote of the incident in his 1946 book on the life and times of the 4th Fighter Group, *1,000 Destroyed:*

> Now Scotsmen are supposed to have what is called "fey," a cross between a crystal ball and clairvoyance. It was this "fey" which prompted [the] Scotsman . . . to remark:
> "All my life I have been trying to get to America, but even now, sailing there, I somehow feel I won't make it."
> "Oh, don't worry, old man," soothed Goodson, "of course you will."

By evening the *Athenia,* making good headway, was off the Hebrides. Seeing the ship outlined against a cloudy sky, a German U-boat took aim and sent a torpedo into it. As told in *1,000 De-*

stroyed, Goodson had just mounted a staircase and was moving forward to the third-class dining room when the torpedo struck.

The sauce cook was scalded with his hot sauce. The grill cook was thrown against the grill and had striped grill sears on his back. The first cook was blown to the top deck. As I passed the hatch on which the Scot and I had talked about his premonition, I saw him. He was purple and dead.

Running back to the companionway, Goodson gazed down at a gaping hole filling with a churning mass of water. Floating or struggling in the water, people were trying to make their way to safety. Throwing off his jacket, Goodson jumped in and began pulling terrified people to the foot of the broken companionway, so they could grab something firm and climb out of the water.

As the ship began to list, Goodson, with the help of the crew, began a search of the cabins along the lower passageway. Making his way through the rising water and dark corridors, he "stumbled into what seemed to be a half-submerged bundle of clothing." Turning the object over, Goodson was startled to observe through the dim light the bloodied, lifeless face of a young, dark-haired Scottish boy. His open blue eyes stared sightlessly into the night.

Knowing it was useless to search any longer, Goodson struggled back to the top deck of the ship, leaving "the lower decks to the dead, the darkness and the sea," as he wrote in *Tumult in the Clouds.*

As the *Athenia* began to list to one side Goodson walked up the sloping deck to the higher side. Around him was utter pandemonium. He watched in horror as a lifeboat that was being lowered tipped forward, throwing the screaming passengers to the surface of the sea far below.

Feeling it was time to leave the doomed vessel, Goodson let himself hand over hand down the side of the ship. Before he reached the bottom he lost his grip on the rope and fell. He hit the water feet first, his momentum driving him under. The struggle to the surface and life-giving air wasn't an easy one, according to this passage from *Tumult in the Clouds.*

It seemed to take a long time. I thought I was a good underwater swimmer, but soon I desperately needed to breathe. In the darkness there was no sign of the surface. For the first time I wished I'd been able to get to my life jacket. If I passed out, it would have at least brought me to the surface. Just as I felt I could hold out no longer, I got to the surface. I gasped for breath. The sea was choppy and I got a mouthful of water. It was colder, rougher and more brutal than I had expected.

Despite the numbing cold, Goodson was able to swim to a lifeboat and safety. Climbing in, he witnessed a scene sure to warm the heart of any young man. "I looked around and saw we were surrounded by young girls in various stages of undress. Some had borrowed sweaters and jackets from members of the crew. Others were huddled in blankets," he wrote in *Tumult in the Clouds.*

The young ladies were a group of American college students who had been touring Europe after graduation. Goodson spent the night talking to them and helping them keep warm. If one had to spend the night in a cold lifeboat, this was the way to do it.

Rescue finally came in the form of a Norwegian tanker. Loaded with survivors, it sailed to the nearest neutral port: Galway, on the west coast of Eire. More survivors of the disaster were picked up by British destroyers and other ships.

Many of the Americans who lived through the disaster were returned to England, where they

James Goodson nearly met his demise early in World War II when he was a passenger on the Athenia, *which was torpedoed by a German U-boat. After this introduction to war Goodson joined the Royal Canadian Air Force and then transferred to the No. 133 Eagle Squadron and eventually into the 4th FG, US Army Air Force. He repaid the Germans for his early dunking in the ocean by scoring 15 victories in the air and destroying another 15 German planes on the ground. James Goodson*

were interviewed by Ambassador Joe Kennedy's twenty-two-year-old son, Jack. Few of the Americans, furious over the German attack on the unarmed ship, were satisfied when young Kennedy told them, "We are still neutral and the Neutrality Act still holds."

America may have been neutral, but for Goodson the attack was the catalyst to an undeclared war between him and the Germans, he explains in *Tumult in the Clouds*.

> For the first time I felt an overwhelming fury that was to sweep over me time and time again during the war. No one had the right to cause such suffering to innocent people. . . . No one had the right to cause such suffering, and those who assumed that right had to be stopped and punished. That was the vow; simple and profound; corny and devout.

After an attempt to join the RAF Goodson was advised to go to Canada and join the Royal Canadian Air Force (RCAF). Sailing on *The Duchess of Athol,* he had an uneventful journey to Montreal, arriving in late autumn 1939.

After completing the rigorous and excellent Canadian flying training program, Goodson was sent back to England in 1941. Once there, he found to his amazement that he had been assigned to gliders. His career with gliders was mercifully short-lived, wrote Hall in *1,000 Destroyed.*

Wilson Edwards in the cockpit of his P-47. Edwards flew with James Goodson in No. 133 Eagle Squadron and in the 4th FG. "Goodson came to the Eagle Squadron as a replacement," recalled Edwards in an interview with the author. "He was one of the more eager individuals. He had received good training from the Royal Canadian Air Force; their training was outstanding. He came into the Eagle Squadron with a world of confidence because of the excellent training he had. He was ambitious, but also very thorough." Wilson Edwards

> [Goodson's] instructor did not even pretend to know more than his charges about gliders, and they set out to learn together.
> At first . . . we found the slip-stream was pulling the tail of the tug plane down. We adjusted for this and the slip-stream pulled the tug's tail up. By the time it came my turn to fly the glider, the tug's pilots had got where they'd trip their own release at less than the slightest provocation. A friend of mine crashed in a woman's back yard and she said, "You're just in time for tea."

Transferring out of gliders, Goodson was soon in action as a fighter pilot with the RAF. Much of his flying during this time took place over France on fighter sweeps. Flying the famous Spitfire, the RAF pilots for the first time felt they had a plane that could outperform the German Me 109 and FW 190.

As he became more familiar with the Spitfire Goodson's admiration for the plane grew.

> I think everybody who flew the Spit had a love affair with it—[it was] such a delight to fly, so quick to the response and so tight in the turn.
> It was a delight to fly because it was so sensitive to the touch. You moved the stick just a fraction of an inch and you were doing a slow roll or you were in a bank right away. That was what people liked in the Spitfire, and it was a brilliant defensive airplane.

It was while piloting a Spitfire with No. 416 Canadian Squadron on a fighter sweep that Goodson gained his first victory. Flying as a wingman, he was the last man in the flight and in a dangerous position when a group of Me 109s dove to attack. Breaking hard, Goodson pulled back on the stick and went into a sharp turn, which caused him to black out temporarily. As his vision slowly cleared, he was surprised to see a 109 turning in front of him, the black crosses clearly visible. Pulling his Spitfire into a tight turn, Goodson gained on the German and moved into firing position. Goodson described the action in *Tumult in the Clouds*.

> I peered through my lighted gun sight and saw it moving up the fuselage as I tried to lay off the right deflection. The correct procedure was to give short bursts, but I was too eager for such niceties. I pressed the firing button on the spade grip on the stick and held it, simply hosing the target from stem to stern. I pulled right on through until he disappeared under the long nose of my Spitfire.

Emerging from the combat alone, Goodson turned for home, upset because he had lost his element leader, a serious breach of squadron discipline. Landing at his home base, he was relieved to learn that all the planes in his flight had returned safely. A subsequent review of his gun camera film confirmed his victory and lessened the sting of not covering his leader's wing.

In the autumn of 1942 Goodson was transferred to No. 133 Eagle Squadron. The reassignment to a squadron composed entirely of Americans wasn't easy for Goodson, for he had come to regard the Canadian squadron as home.

No. 133 was the third and last of the three Eagle squadrons put into service by the RAF. The Eagle squadrons formed an unusual group of pilots. As the Germans had marched through France, Britain had found a desperate need for young pilots. To meet this need the commonwealth of Canada, with the approval of the US government, had set up recruiting booths at various American air bases, where flying cadet examinations and flight training took place. Whenever cadets were rejected for physical reasons or for lack of flying ability, the RCAF recruiters welcomed them with open arms.

Ranging in age from fourteen (a boy who had to bluff his way in) to thirty-eight, these pilots were the first Americans to fight the Axis powers. Wearing the uniform of the RAF but with the distinguishing Eagle squadron patch on the left shoulder, the young volunteers became "known throughout England, and the English people opened their hearts and their homes to these Americans," wrote Gene Gurney in *Five Down and Glory*.

Goodson fondly recalled the mood of the British people while he was in the RAF:

> The British were wonderful to us Americans. You have to remember the Fighter Command of the RAF had a great many foreigners in it. There were large numbers of Poles, Canadians, New Zealanders, Free French and Czechs. It was a little different for the Americans because the USA was neutral, but we were treated far better than we expected because a lot of English people resented the fact that the USA was not in the war and was making a lot of money selling England munitions. The English people, however, made us feel very much at home.

Goodson's service with the Eagle squadron was brief because on September 29, 1942, the Eagle squadrons from the RAF were transferred to the USAAF. Nos. 71, 121 and 133 Eagle squadrons were to become the 334th, 335th and 336th squadrons of the US Eighth Army Air Force, forming the 4th Fighter Group.

To recognize their service with the RAF, the top brass of the Eighth Air Force allowed the former Eagle squadron pilots to wear miniature RAF wings over their right breast pocket; the full-sized US wings were to be worn over the left breast pocket.

Even though the transfer to the USAAF had taken place, the 4th FG continued to fly Spitfires. Having no American planes, the RAF had turned the Spitfires over to the 4th and the ground crews simply painted USAAF stars over the red, white and blue roundels of the RAF.

On October 29 Richard "Dixie" Alexander received permission from Don Blakeslee to take Jim Goodson and fly a low-level strafing raid over

Richard "Dixie" Alexander at Debden, England, in 1942. Alexander flew with James Goodson during some of the first missions of the 4th FG over occupied Europe. He later transferred to the 52nd FG and served in the Mediterranean theater of war. He was shot down in May 1944 and ended the war as a guest of the German government. He later settled in Illinois and became a member of the American Fighter Aces Association. Dixie Alexander

France and Belgium. Alexander's logbook noted that the mission lasted for 1 hour and 20 minutes. Alexander, in an interview, noted the following:

> Led Goodson in at Blankenberg, navigation perfect, up Canal Ghent, fired upon two barge-towing boats. Lots of hits, and flying wood, couldn't stay to observe results. Pulled prize boob; went over Flushing, flak—light and heavy—everything but slingshots—never again! Had 15 small-caliber bullets in starboard wing; both got back in good shape, weather foul, had rain; visibility ½ mile, ceiling in spots 100 to 300 feet.

Goodson gave a more detailed and vivid account of the mission in his book *Tumult in the Clouds*. His description of Blakeslee's reaction to the overblown publicity generated by this rather insignificant mission into occupied Europe is classic:

> The historic and picturesque city of Burges was ringed in red on our maps as off limits for bombing, but low-flying fighter planes could pick out individual targets for strafing with deadly accuracy, and it was the locomotives in the marshalling yards which were our targets.
>
> We each picked out an engine with steam up. The flak was more accurate now and we did a lot of sinking and stomping of rudder as we lined up our targets. They were both belching steam, as we flashed over them. We didn't pull up, but hugged the ground, as the flak arched over us, behind us, and all around us.
>
> Suddenly, we were out in the country and there was no more flak. . . . As we roared over the coast road, a lone cyclist was directly in front of me. I had to pull up a lot to be sure the prop didn't hit him. As I flashed over, only a few feet above him, I was surprised to see he was bent over the handlebars

Don Blakeslee, legendary commander of the 4th FG. Blakeslee flew more missions against the Luftwaffe than any other American pilot. He flew more than 1,000 hours of combat and between 400 and 500 missions. Dixie Alexander

> not even looking up. . . . I kicked rudder to dodge the flak . . . and caught sight of the look of amazement on his upturned face, just as the bike swerved and fell, probably hit by a blast of air from my propeller.
>
> In a flash we were over the sea, setting course for home. We had accomplished our mission as planned, but had no illusions about its importance. We considered it more of a training exercise, and our report to the Intelligence office was duly modest. . . .
>
> But we overlooked the fact that this was probably the first purely US fighter mission over France and Belgium and the newly arrived publications corps were hungry for news. It only took about twenty-four hours for it to hit the fan. The *Stars and Stripes* army newspaper led the parade, with the others sounding the same clarion call. It read as if thousands of planes had spread destruction and fear throughout northern Europe, leaving the transportation system in disarray. . . . Dixie and I destroyed all the news items we could find, so I can't be sure of the exact wording, but one of them went something like this: "At dawn today fighter planes of the US Eighth Army Air Force carried out daring low-level attacks on rail, road, and water transport in Northern France and Belgium, leaving behind them a trail of destruction. . . ."
>
> That evening I heard Blakeslee bellowing long before he burst into the mess. We had been steeped in the RAF tradition that any exaggeration . . . was intolerable . . . so I knew what was coming. As he bore down on me he bellowed, "All right! Where's the other half of the Eighth Air Force?"
>
> "He's taking a pee," I said.
>
> When Dixie reappeared, he held up his hand and said: "Let me show you what happened."
>
> He peeled off his tunic, his shirt and his undershirt, and turned around. There was a gasp. In the middle of his back was a lurid red bleeding gash from which protruded the blue handle of a dagger. It was so perfectly done, it was only when we moved closer that we saw it was a beautifully executed tattoo.
>
> "I was stabbed in the back!" he said. Blakeslee turned to me. "What's your excuse?"
>
> "All I claimed was one bicycle damaged. I blew the guy off on the way out!"
>
> Blakeslee was calming down. He saw from the reaction of the others that, if it had done nothing else, the mission had helped build up squadron morale and pride. . . . "Well," he said grudgingly, "I've just seen your combat film, so I'll buy you a drink. From then on the drinks are on you!"

It was about this time that members of the 4th FG began to hear rumors that their beloved Spitfires were to be replaced by a new American fighter, the P-47 Thunderbolt. When the first P-47 arrived at Debden, the 4th's home base, it was met with disparaging and caustic comments from the pilots. Used to the sleek, trim lines of the Spitfire, the pilots of the 4th were dismayed by the P-47's massive size, which made it look more like a dive-bomber than a fighter.

John McCrary and David Scherman, in their wartime book *First of the Many*, documented the distrust the pilots of the 4th FG initially felt for the P-47:

You've heard of the Eagles, the American kids who formed three squadrons in the RAF and then transferred back to the Eighth Air Force. They flew Spitfires in the RAF and kept them for awhile when they shifted from blue to khaki. They loved those Spits, as one of them put it, "with the kind of love that makes babies." It's possible to feel that way about a Spitfire.

Those were the kids who were given the big-bellied Thunderbolts to take into battle. There was damn near mutiny. Orders had to be issued instructing the Eagle pilots to keep their opinions about the plane to themselves. "Don't talk to newspaper men!" It was like that for almost a month.

Almost alone among the pilots, Goodson looked forward to flying the Thunderbolt. A keen student of air warfare and tactics, he realized that a longer-range fighter was needed to protect the bombers and carry the war into Germany.

As the first P-47s arrived in England the top command asked for volunteers from the 4th to check out the new fighters and introduce them to the rest of the group. Only three pilots, Hoppy Hopson, Snuffy Smith and Jim Goodson, volunteered. While checking out in the P-47 they were instructed in the development and use of droppable external fuel tanks, which would shortly stretch the combat radius of the P-47 from 280 miles to 575 miles.

Once Goodson's training was completed, he was given the task of checking out Blakeslee in the P-47. Blakeslee flew the fighter and found it "daunting to haul 7 tons of plane around the sky after the fingertip touch needed for the Spit," wrote Goodson in *Tumult in the Clouds*. Goodson talked to Blakeslee after the flight and tried to sell him on the merits of the plane by pointing out that the Germans would now not be able to escape by diving away, as they had so often in the past.

Blakeslee soon had an opportunity to test the accuracy of Goodson's prediction. On April 15, 1943, he was leading the squadron over Belgium when three FW 190s were sighted. Turning to the attack, Blakeslee watched the Germans adopt their usual tactic of diving away. Putting his Thunderbolt into a dive from 20,000 feet, Blakeslee followed one FW 190 down to 500 feet before finally blowing it out of the sky. It was the first victory for a P-47 in combat.

According to *Tumult in the Clouds*, once back at Debden an enthusiastic Goodson caught up with Blakeslee at the debriefing and shouted, "I told you the jug could outdive them!"

Blakeslee, still the skeptic, replied, "Well, it damn well ought to be able to dive; it sure as hell can't climb!"

Blakeslee may have been unimpressed with the Thunderbolt's climbing capabilities but he would soon come to appreciate the plane's rugged construction and its ability to take punishment and keep flying. Only the ruggedness of the P-47 and superb flying and shooting by Goodson would save him from being shot down.

On August 16, 1943, the 4th FG was scheduled to escort 170 B-17s on a mission to attack the aircraft repair depot at Le Bourget, the main Paris airfield. Also providing support for the bombers were P-47s from the 56th, 78th and 353rd fighter groups.

During the morning briefing, Blakeslee explained to the assembled pilots that the fighters would take off in pairs and climb to an altitude of 24,000 feet to cover the bombers. The lowest squadron would be the 336th, which Blakeslee, whose code name was Horseback Leader, would lead. Goodson was scheduled to lead the second flight of the squadron, which would be positioned just behind and to the left of Blakeslee's lead section.

As the pilots left the briefing Goodson, as related in *Tumult in the Clouds*, remarked to

Lt. Col. Don Blakeslee's P-47 Thunderbolt back in England after having been hit by 68 cannon shells from German fighters. All that saved Blakeslee on this August 1943 mission was the rugged construction of the P-47 and fast action by James Goodson, who shot three German planes off Blakeslee's tail. De Goyler Library, Southern Methodist University

Blakeslee, "With all that mob around the bombers we should be able to do a little free hunting on our own."

"Right!" Blakeslee answered. "That's why I'm flying where I am, and that's why you're flying where you are to give me cover!"

At 0912 hours the planes of the 4th FG were nearing their planned rendezvous with the bombers at 28,000 feet. Suddenly Blakeslee broke radio silence, calling on the radio telephone, "There's a million of them, 190s . . . down there! Horseback Leader to Horseback, continue to join up with the bombers. I'm going down. Goody, give me top cover!"

Always eager to be at the enemy, Blakeslee turned to the attack. Knowing he would need speed, he put his P-47 into a screeching almost vertical dive. As he watched Blakeslee hurtle down, Goodson knew he would have to "move as fast and dive as steeply as [Blakeslee] had." Realizing that if he didn't catch Blakeslee he would be on his own, Goodson wasted no time in plunging after him.

As the Thunderbolts hurtled down, Goodson watched Blakeslee pull out of his dive to come up under the German planes. Blakeslee had picked out two FW 190s and was going after them. Closing the gap, he was almost ready to fire when the Germans spotted him and flipped over on their backs and dove away. Blakeslee, his blood up, pursued the

Five aces of the 4th FG: Lt. Col. Duane Beeson, Capt. Nicholas Megura, Maj. John Godfrey and Maj. James Goodson, clockwise from bottom left, and Maj. Don Gentile, center. via John Campbell

190s. Goodson and his wingman followed, trying to protect Blakeslee's rear, and were soon diving down at over 500 mph. His plane shaking violently from the tremendous speed, Goodson flashed through a squadron of Spitfires and hurtled after Blakeslee.

Gaining on the Germans, Blakeslee moved in close behind one as the other turned away. Goodson, following, noticed 109s and 190s all around and was alarmed when three 190s broke off and cut in behind Blakeslee in an attempt to save the two German pilots Blakeslee was attacking.

Goodson informed Blakeslee over the radio that three Germans were coming in on him at three o'clock high. Fighting the rigid controls of his diving Thunderbolt, Goodson managed to pull up and inside the last 190. Moving in for the kill, he was so close that he was able to observe the yellow nose of the 190 and the black crosses on the fuselage and wings.

Firing a short burst, Goodson watched intently as the armor-piercing and incendiary .50 caliber shells slammed into the German plane. As his bullets staggered the FW 190, he fired three more short bursts, which hit near the starboard wing root. Few German planes could withstand the terrific impact of the Thunderbolt's eight .50 caliber machine guns, and this FW 190 was no exception. "Suddenly there was a flash and a puff of smoke and his wing came fluttering off," wrote Goodson in *Tumult in the Clouds*. "The wing and the wildly spinning plane tumbled past me."

Looking ahead, Goodson observed Blakeslee still maneuvering wildly, trying to shake the 190s. The lead German plane seemed glued to Blakeslee's tail and scored repeated hits on the Thunderbolt. Knowing Blakeslee couldn't last much longer, Goodson yelled over the radio, "Hang on, Horseback, I'm gaining on him!"

Pulling up behind the second FW 190, Goodson moved in close to be sure he wouldn't miss. Aiming for the front of the engine, he pressed the trigger. Goodson relates the resulting action in *Tumult in the Clouds*.

I was too close to miss. The fire was concentrated. Flashes appeared on the engine and continued down the underbelly in four long bursts. . . . The FW went straight into a vertical dive, trailing smoke, and exploded in a field not far below.

Now free to concentrate on the remaining FW 190, Goodson once again radioed, "I'm coming up, Don, hang on!" Closing the gap, Goodson watched helplessly as the 190 fired burst after burst into Blakeslee's Thunderbolt. Knowing he had to fire from long range to save Blakeslee, Goodson triggered a burst from dead astern. Releasing three more short bursts, he saw flashes as the bullets struck the German plane.

Elated, Goodson radioed, "I've got him, Don!"

"The hell you've got him," Blakeslee replied. "He's got me!"

Even though Goodson's bullets were striking home, the courageous German pilot continued the attack. Pulling up close to the enemy plane, Goodson pressed the firing button to finish him off. The eight .50s roared, then fell silent. Goodson was out of ammunition.

Thinking fast, Goodson decided to try to bluff the German into giving up the attack. He pushed the stick forward and moved ahead and to the side of the FW 190. Once in this position he turned straight into the German. Seeing the eight .50s of Goodson's Thunderbolt staring him in the face, the German pilot rolled over on his back and split-essed for the deck.

Knowing Blakeslee was safe, Goodson pulled his P-47 up alongside Blakeslee's plane. He was shocked to observe the punishment the P-47 had taken. He details his surprise in *Tumult in the Clouds*.

> His canopy was wide open, his goggles were on and at times he peered out from behind his wind screen, which was completely covered by black oil. The whole fuselage was streaked with oil. The big white letters *WD-C* on the side of his plane were practically obliterated.

As the planes flew side by side, Goodson asked over the radio if Blakeslee thought he could make it home. "I don't think so," Blakeslee replied. "Oil is spewing all over the plane, and I have to keep the throttle wide open just to keep altitude." Knowing the Thunderbolt's immense hunger for fuel—up to 130 gallons per hour at high cruise power—Goodson recognized that Blakeslee would be fortunate to make it back to England.

Flying behind Blakeslee on the way home, Goodson and his wingman, Bob Wehrman, had to bluff German fighters off on two separate occasions. Finally the three Thunderbolts were able to land at the Manston emergency strip.

After the mission the ground crews and pilots were able to look Blakeslee's battered P-47 over. The damage was incredible and many wondered how the Thunderbolt was able to fly, much less return from the mission. Wilson "Bill" Edwards, a pilot with the 4th FG, observed Blakeslee's plane after it landed and recalled its battered condition in a 1991 interview:

> It looked like it had just gone through an explosion—like an 88 mm shell had gone off with all the fragments and the plane had flew through the center of the burst. There was damage all over the plane.

For his efforts in saving Blakeslee, Goodson, some time later, was awarded the Silver Star—the nation's third-highest decoration for valor. Blakeslee, as related in *Tumult in the Clouds*, was thankful

and a bit more practical, telling Goodson: "I want to buy you a drink. After all, you saved my ass!"

It was a valuable behind that Goodson saved on August 16. Most military historians consider Don Blakeslee and Hub Zemke, of the 56th FG, to have been the two leading fighter group commanders in Europe during World War II.

Another early 1943 mission to Paris illustrated the intensity of air combat between the German and Allied air forces. At this stage of the war Paris was still an important target and was heavily defended by the Germans.

Goodson was leading a section of the squadron for the first time. After takeoff the fighters climbed to 27,000 feet, leveled off and spread into combat formation. As they passed the French coast they could see flak bursts off in the distance. Goodson pointed them out to his wingman, Kendall "Swede" Carlson.

Forming up near Paris, the Thunderbolts began weaving around the bomber formation. The flak was soon bursting all around them. "There was a big, round, sudden flash down in the lead box of

Duane Beeson looks over his damaged P-51 Mustang. "Beeson," wrote Grover Hall in his book 1,000 Destroyed, *"was undoubtedly one of the two or three best test pilots the 4th produced. He set the pace for destroying German planes and his rivalry with Don Gentile did much to get the group started in its record smashing."* De Goyler Library, Southern Methodist University

bombers," remembered Goodson in his book *Tumult in the Clouds*, "and where there had been a bomber there was a big smoke ring."

Soon, off in the distance, the enemy fighters could be seen approaching, about 100 yellow-nosed FW 190s. From dead ahead, five 190s dove down in a head-on attack against the first box of bombers. "They dove in line abreast, all firing," recalled Goodson in *Tumult in the Clouds*. "The leading edge[s] of their wings were winking and flashing." Heavy machine gun fire from the bombers blew the lead 190 apart with a blinding flash. The other 190s continued their attack, closing on the bomber formation at a combined speed of 700 mph. "At the last minute," wrote Goodson, "they rolled on their backs, still firing, and flashed down through the bomber formation." One of the speeding fighters hit one of the bombers head-on. "The blazing mass went tumbling down through the formation."

Diving to intercept the next wave of attacking German planes, Goodson latched onto the tail of a 190 and began firing. The eight .50 caliber machine guns in the Thunderbolt were capable of firing 800 rounds per minute per gun; a short burst of 2 seconds could put over 400 incendiary, tracer and armor-piercing rounds into an enemy plane.

Closing fast, Goodson fired again, and the enemy plane staggered under the impact. As Goodson's bullets struck home the FW 190 fell away, out

The chorus line of Tonight and Every Night *from the Windmill Theater, sitting on the wing of Duane Beeson's* Boise Bee *at Debden. No doubt the 1,500 officers and enlisted men stationed at Debden, most between the ages of 17 and 30, enjoyed the visit of the lovely ladies to the air base.* De Goyler Library, Southern Methodist University

of control. "I saw flame licking along the grey fuselage and over the black cross," wrote Goodson in *Tumult in the Clouds*. "The fire grew until there was just a long flame streaking down."

As the German plane went down in flames the momentum of Goodson's attack carried him through the bomber formation. Sliding under the first bomber, he then passed B-17 after B-17 as he flashed through the group.

Once safely through the bombers Goodson and Carlson began climbing to regain altitude. Leveling off, they observed a straggling B-17 off in the distance under attack by a group of German fighters.

A straggling B-17 was in a dangerous position. Removed from the massed machine gun fire of the bomber formation, it was often an easy target for the German fighters. By the time Goodson and Carlson were close enough to help, the B-17 was in a spinning dive, heading uncontrolled toward the ground. As it fell two crewmen were able to jump, their white chutes blossoming against the sky.

As the bomber plunged toward the earth the enemy fighters followed it down. Goodson could see that the bomber's rear gunner was fighting to the end. "That tail gunner's tracers kept coming until the bomber spun into the woods," wrote Goodson in *Tumult in the Clouds*. "Then there was a flash, and a tall, still column of smoke."

One German fighter circled low over the crash site, his attention riveted on the smoking wreckage. Goodson got in close and fired, observing strikes all over the enemy plane. Too low to recover, the German plane spun off out of control.

His attack completed, Goodson was watching the doomed enemy fighter when he heard Carlson yell, "Break! Break left!"

Goodson, flying low to the ground, now found a German fighter above and behind him, closing in for the kill. He recalled the attack in his book *Tumult in the Clouds:*

I hauled back on the stick, and my head went down, and my eyes dimmed as I started to black out. I heard a "crump." The plane shuddered and started to stall. . . . He was close behind me. I could see the round yellow nose and the grey body with the black crosses, but most of all I could see the flashes that lit up the leading edge of his wing.

I tightened my turn, and fought the plane with stick and rudder as it shuddered and locked on the point of the stall. . . . My head and neck ached as I screwed around to watch the Hun. And he was still out turning me.

Then I felt the "crump" again. He was starting to hit me. . . . I reached down to release my harness to try and [bail] out. Then I heard the Swede: "O.K., I'll have him off you in a jiffy."

I looked back. The Jerry's grey fuselage was covered with flashes. He flicked over and dived down. He went into a field on his back, leaving a trail of fire behind him.

The attack over and thankful for the presence and help of the skillful Carlson, Goodson had time to look his battered Thunderbolt over. His left wing was badly damaged with a jagged hole a foot across, marking where a 20 mm shell had exploded. As Goodson looked behind him he could observe other shell holes in the plane, evidence of how close he had come to being shot down.

Able to fly at only 130 mph, Goodson managed to nurse the injured plane home. Carlson stayed behind him, constantly weaving around his aircraft, on the lookout for German fighters.

Goodson—his gas gauge showing zero—landed at an airfield on the south coast of England, with Carlson touching down right behind him.

Relieved to be home, Goodson knew it had been a near thing and that he owed his life to his wingman.

Wingmen were the unsung heroes of air combat in World War II. They often flew mission after mission without a chance to attack or maneuver for a shot as they covered their element leader's wing. Goodson, in a tribute to Carlson and wingmen everywhere, summed up their importance when he wrote in his book *Tumult in the Clouds*:

No he was no big-time hero, and you probably never heard of him. But there were a lot of guys like him, and when you need someone to loan you a buck, or fly on your wing—or help win a war—they're nice guys to have around—if you know what I mean.

Preinvasion get-together: Lt. Col. Oscar Coen, Major General Kepner, Lt. Col. Jim Clark, Mr. Banks (standing), Gen. Dwight Eisenhower, Col. Don Blakeslee, Gen. Carl Spaatz, Maj. Don Gentile, Brigadier General Auton, Capt. Joe Lang and Colonel Fallows, from the left facing the camera; Brigadier General Curtis, Maj. James Goodson, Lt. Gen. James Doolittle, Capt. Bob Johnson, Comdr. Harry Butcher, Capt. Alfred Markel and Lieutenant Rowles, from the left nearest the camera. Eisenhower visited Debden on April 11, 1944. Blakeslee staged a mock briefing for the Supreme Commander and narrated a combat film. Both Blakeslee and Gentile were awarded Distinguished Service Crosses and Eisenhower took a ride in a 55th FG P-38J droopsnoot. De Goyler Library, Southern Methodist University.

113

In the early days of 1943 the Luftwaffe was a formidable opponent. German pilots had an edge in experience and the advantage of fighting over their own territory. The yellow-nosed fighters Goodson encountered over Paris were the elite of the Luftwaffe and were toughened with the severest discipline of any air force in the world.

Friedheim Taylor and Samuel Taylor described the intense training German pilots received early in the war in their 1945 book *Fighters Up*:

> Until last year [1944] the road to a flying officer's commission in the German air force was beset with tortuous obstacles ingeniously placed before each candidate with Gestapo thoroughness.
>
> Selection of cadets was limited to unmarried youths between the ages of 17 and 24, possessing exceptional moral, mental, and physical qualities. These qualities were tested in a unique preliminary examination which required the candidate to write an essay on love, war and kultur while a noise machine produced a nerve-racking cacophony of hysterical laughter. He was lashed to a revolving wheel and required to do mental arithmetic while counting the revolutions and responding to various signals by means of controls in his hands. Next, the prospective pilot was strapped with electrodes and subjected to shocks while cameras were recording his reaction. . . . At one school, candidates were marched along a cliff some 40 feet above a river. The command was given to dive into the water and those who showed even momentary hesitation were rejected as unsuitable officer material. After the candidate had cleared these preliminary hurdles there followed an intensive flying and military curriculum that gave him approximately 200 hours in the air before going on combat operations. . . . Mortality among students was always high. Out of a class of 60 at one flying school 27 were killed in flying accidents and two had nervous breakdowns.

Goodson and many other pilots of the 4th FG developed a great deal of respect for the German fighter pilots, who often had to attack huge Allied bomber formations protected by hundreds of Allied fighter planes. To Goodson the decline in the quality of German pilots was noticeable. The German pilots he encountered in 1943 were of a much higher caliber than those he flew against later in the war. In a recent interview he discussed the reasons for the decline of the German fighter arm:

> Toward the end of the war we usually had the Germans outnumbered. Also toward the end of the war the Luftwaffe pilots had orders to go after the bombers—because it was the bombers that were doing the destruction.
>
> So very bravely they very often ignored the fighters and just plowed right into the bombers, which made it pretty easy to get on their tail and shoot them down.
>
> I also think that toward the end of the war the Luftwaffe had taken such heavy casualties that the pilots were not as good as we were. There were very few of the early German pilots left. The ones that were left were the ones that racked up these enormous scores of individual enemy aircraft destroyed. But for every one of these there were ten or twenty young German pilots who just hadn't had time to get the experience, and these were the ones we shot down.

In December 1943 the 354th FG arrived in England. This new group was equipped with the P-51 Mustang. Because of his vast experience in combat and as a group leader, Lt. Col. Don Blakeslee was sent to Boxted airfield near Colchester. Blakeslee's task was to lead the group on its initial raids until its own commanders had the experience to take over.

Blakeslee led the group on several missions, but each night he would fly back to Debden. Grover Hall, in his book *1,000 Destroyed*, explained the method behind Blakeslee's madness:

> [He came back] explaining that he couldn't bear the 354th's primitive Nissen Hut station. But probably Blakeslee derived a malicious pleasure in seeing his pilots crowd about his borrowed Mustang, mouths watering, agog and enraptured with his enthusiastic account of the Mustang's combat capabilities.
>
> It's the ship, Blakeslee said.
>
> It's the ship, they repeated after him.

An Allied fighter shooting up a German airfield. James Goodson recalled one occasion when his squadron attacked a German airfield: "[We] caught them totally unprepared. Planes were scattered all around. We made a pass over. Then we came back for another pass. We kept right on coming over until everything was done [that] we could do: planes destroyed and hangars burning." Smithsonian Institution

Blakeslee fell in love with the Mustang; it was reminiscent of the Spitfire. Blakeslee knew he wanted the P-51 for the 4th and put pressure on Gen. William E. Kepner to approve the changeover.

Kepner was opposed to the idea but gave in when Blakeslee promised him that the 4th could switch over and undertake a combat mission within 24 hours. Kepner arranged for Mustangs to be given to the group and in 24 hours the group was off on a mission. "Most pilots have about 200 hours in a front-line fighter before taking it into combat," wrote Goodson in *Tumult in the Clouds*. "We had about thirty minutes."

Goodson considered the Mustang the most remarkable plane of the war. In a recent interview he discussed its merits:

I think the Mustang probably won the war because it had the range as well as the performance, so we could go anywhere that the bombers went.

The P-51 was a most remarkable plane, but it wasn't as much fun to fly as the Spit. The Mustang was not quite as tight in the turn, but it was faster than the Spitfire or the 190 or the 109 and of course it had this remarkable range, but it could also turn pretty well. I've outturned a FW 190 in a Mustang, but more importantly the P-51 had superior performance from 30,000 feet down to the deck and could do this 750 miles from home. When [Hermann] Goering saw Mustangs escorting the bombers to Berlin, he knew the war was over.

"The P-51 Mustang," wrote Grover Hall in *1,000 Destroyed*, "gave the 4th Fighter Group Seven League Boots: the Luftwaffe was presently to find there was no such thing as recoiling beyond American fighter range anymore."

More than 2,000 P-51B Mustangs were ordered for the Eighth Air Force. With the use of external fuel tanks, which could be dropped, the Mustangs were capable of accompanying the B-17s to their targets and meeting enemy fighters on equal terms. The Eighth Air Force's first Mustang escort mission was flown to Kiel, Germany, in December 1943, and later Mustangs would accompany the American bombers on the 1,100 mile round trip to Berlin.

By early 1944 the Eighth Air Force was embarked on an offensive to destroy the German fighter strength to prepare the way for the invasion of Europe. Air armadas of 2,000 bombers and 1,000 fighters went out day after day to Germany. The Germans countered by building their fighter strength to alarming proportions and the stage was set for some of the greatest air battles of all time.

Little subterfuge was used in these titanic air battles fought over Germany in 1944. The American planners didn't want the bombers to spend any more time over German territory than was necessary and usually directed them straight to the target, except for necessary detours around heavy antiaircraft gun concentrations. It would have been difficult, at any rate, to hide the approach of more than 2,000 airplanes, and the Germans had plenty of time to reinforce the target area with heavy concentrations of fighters. To counter this the Americans sent the Mustangs and Thunderbolts out on sweeps hundreds of miles ahead and on the flanks of the attacking bombers. The German fighters, especially the twin-engine types, tried to avoid the American fighters so that they could make concentrated attacks on specific bomber formations. The resulting clash between these two large opposing air forces saw dogfights and wild melees involving scores of aircraft taking place over large distances.

It was reasoned that the one place the Luftwaffe was most likely to defend was Berlin. Bombing the German capital would cripple German morale as well as offer a chance to destroy important strategic targets around the city.

Thus, early in March 1944 the Eighth Air Force began planning to strike the German capital. The first American attempt to attack Berlin took place on March 3, but clouds piled to nearly 30,000 feet caused the mission to be canceled.

Another attack was launched on March 4, and it began to look as if this mission would be canceled also, as clouds piled up at an increasing rate while the heavy bombers assembled. As the bombers flew toward the target, orders to return went out, but one combat wing composed of two 95th Bomb Group

A P-47, machine gun blazing, bears down on a German flak tower. "Personally," recalled James Goodson, "I preferred the Thunderbolt, but few others in the 4th FG did. You see, we'd flown the Spitfire, and the Mustang was a great deal like the Spitfire." Smithsonian Institution

squadrons and one 100th Bomb Group squadron did not receive the signal and continued toward the target.

This small force of thirty-one bombers continued on toward Berlin, escorted by Mustangs of the 4th, 354th and 363rd fighter groups. Leading the Mustang escort was Don Blakeslee, determined to provide cover for the bombers over Berlin.

Near the German capital two sections of the 4th FG became separated and flew blindly into a veritable hornet's nest of German fighters. The nine Mustangs—piloted by some of the great aces of the 4th, including Don Gentile, John Godfrey, Willard Millikan and Vermont Garrison—were forced to fight for their life in the general melee that followed.

The March 4 mission to Berlin proved to be a costly one for the 4th. It managed to shoot down a total of eight German planes but lost four Mustangs over the target and on the way home.

On March 6 the first full-scale raid on Berlin took place, as 730 bombers escorted by 796 fighters were scheduled to attack the Bosch works, the Enkner ball bearing plant and the Daimler-Benz factory.

The March 7, 1944, *New York Times* highlighted the Berlin raid. An article written by James MacDonald carried the following account:

A German train takes a pounding from low-flying Allied fighters. "Strafing was a dangerous business," recalled James Goodson. *"Fortunately our planes, particularly the P-47, could take plenty of punishment. I once brought a Thunderbolt back from Kiel with three cylinders shot out of it."* Smithsonian Institution

A United States Fighter Base in England, March 6
Physically weary but undauntedly cheerful American fighter pilots jumped out of their Mustangs here late this afternoon upon their return from the big aerial attack on Berlin today and almost unanimously they described the day's activities as the "best hunting" they had ever had.

They were so pleased over their "field day" that many of them relegated their hair-raising escapes to second place. They had made the return trip of almost 1200 miles and tangled with score upon score of German fighters over Berlin as they protected the United States bombers that roared in over the target area, yet they could still grin broadly as their roommates came in one after another and reported their kills.

For Goodson March 6 was also a memorable day. Leading his squadron, he helped prevent or break up attacks on the American bombers. For his efforts on this day he was awarded the nation's second-highest decoration for valor, the Distinguished Service Cross.

Despite the heroism of Goodson and other Allied fighter pilots, the Luftwaffe took a heavy toll of bombers during the March 6 mission. When the day's expenditures in aircraft were added up, sixteen B-24s were missing and fifty-three B-17s had gone down, for a total record loss of sixty-nine heavy bombers. Eleven American fighters were lost in the action, whereas postwar evaluations show that eighty German fighters were shot down, almost half the attacking force. The Luftwaffe was slowly losing air superiority, even over its own capital.

On March 29 the 4th FG was flying a target withdrawal support mission to Brunswick, Germany. Rendezvous with the bombers was made near Nienburg and at 1330 hours, near Giphorn, forty-five enemy fighters dove to the attack. Garry Fry and Jeffrey Ethell recorded details of the engagement in their book *Escort to Berlin:* "The Group bounced both formations from 24,000 feet, breaking into numerous engagements all the way to the deck. By 1350 four more Fighters attacked the lead boxes near Celle."

During this mission, Goodson led his squadron on an attack against twenty-plus German fighters. As he followed the Germans down in a steep spiral dive while dodging in and out of a cloud, his whole cockpit frosted up, leaving him on instruments at 1,000 feet.

Working feverishly, Goodson was able to scratch some of the ice off and determine where he was. He describes his situation in *Tumult in the Clouds.*

I found myself near an airdrome of Ju 88s with some in circuit. One was going in for a landing and I gave him a burst with considerable deflection. I got strikes but he continued to land. I came back and hit him again as he was taxiing. This started him smoking, but due to the frost condition of my wind screen it was not until after the fourth pass that I considered him blazing sufficiently to call him destroyed.

I then observed another 88 flying around. I had trouble getting behind him but finally got a few strikes on him from 90 degrees. He was very close to the deck and promptly crashed into a field, but although it was a good prang, I returned and got some more bursts on him, leaving the crash burning.

By mid March German fighters were unwilling to engage in combat unless the situation or odds were favorable. To counter this, Allied fighter pilots had no choice but to go down and get them. As a result, the Eighth Air Force entered into another phase of air war in the many-pronged attempt to destroy the Luftwaffe: strafing.

Roving fighters would return from their low-level strafing missions

with the tips of their propellers folded back from chewing into the ground or into the paved runways of Luftwaffe airdromes. Chunks of high-tension wires were found in air scoops or wrapped around bomb racks, wrote Gene Gurney in *Five Down and Glory.* "One P-51 ace came back with a turnip in his scoop."

In his book *1,000 Destroyed,* Grover Hall informed his readers of some of the dangers faced by the Allied pilots on their strafing missions:

The strafing of airfields across Europe to Berlin and the Baltic is about the most dangerous job that thousands of young American and Allied fighter pilots are doing these days. . . . To shoot up enemy planes on these distant fields, Thunderbolts, Mus-

Lt. Ralph Hofer, left, and James Goodson. "Hofer," wrote Grover Hall in 1,000 Destroyed, *"commenced bagging Huns as unceremoniously as he had enlisted in the RCAF. It was an accepted axiom that a pilot flew 10 to 12 missions before his eyes were good enough to even see a Hun, let alone bag one. But Kid Hofer bagged a 190 on his first mission and astonished all by gaily diving down to strafe a flak boat in the channel."* James Goodson

tangs and Lightnings fly through hundreds of miles of enemy territory and run the gauntlet of hundreds of guns. Some of these guns shoot as high as 40,000 feet, others are set to cross-fire above the growing fields of corn, and even rifles and tommy guns are now aimed at the strafers.

The strafer zooms down and across at speeds ranging up to 450 miles an hour. He flies, perhaps only 10 feet above the ground. He must keep his eyes skinned for obstructions on the airfield, buildings that rim it, and other planes of his squadron knifing through the dust, smoke and fire.

The perilous game of strafing has seen the loss of more aces of the US 8th and 9th Air Forces than any other form of flying.

Terrific speed protects the strafer in the early stages of his attack. As long as he stays low, using the shelter of trees and hills, he is a difficult target. To check his position on the map as he turns homeward, the strafer pilot must often climb high enough to pick out a string of landmarks. The moment he sticks his nose up, like a prizefighter coming out of a crouch, he becomes vulnerable. While he climbs, his speed naturally falls. His evasive action—the bag of tricks that makes him a tough target—becomes restricted and he may feel that he is a clay pigeon for flak batteries.

Goodson, who was designated by one wartime paper as the King of the Strafers, gave his views on the art during an interview:

You see, if you strafed an airfield where you found airplanes on the ground, not camouflaged or hidden in revetments, one fighter could take out five, six or even ten German airplanes.

I didn't go strafing because I enjoyed it. I did it because I felt it was the best way to destroy German planes.

The technique is to get as low as you possibly can, because it's more difficult for the flak to get a bead on you, and of course you have to stomp rudder and screw your plane around and never fly straight and level. However, towards the end of the war the German airfields had so much flak protecting them and they just threw up curtains of flak.

Fortunately, our planes, particularly the P-47, could take plenty of punishment. I once brought a Thunderbolt back from Kiel with three cylinders shot out of it. We were fortunate that the American planes were so solidly built. On a lot of my strafing missions I came back with holes in the plane.

Ironically, it was while strafing that Goodson was shot down and captured by the Germans. This happened during a June 20, 1944, mission to Politz, Germany.

Goodson was leading the squadron and after being relieved of escort duty for the bombers he flew ahead, looking for any German fighters that might be in the area. After dropping to 20,000 feet he was able to make out the thin shape of German fighters, well below him.

Rolling his Mustang over, Goodson went into a steep dive toward the Germans, the rest of the

squadron following. Closing on the rear German's plane, Goodson could see that it was an Me 109 and that it was throttling back to land at the airfield at Neubrandenburg.

Waiting until he was less than 200 yards behind the German plane Goodson then pressed the trigger. He described the action in *Tumult in the Clouds.*

The first burst scored hits all over him. I immediately pressed the trigger again. I was still hitting him when I had to stomp rudder and throw the stick forward and right to avoid ramming him. I looked back and saw him dive straight down to explode on the deck.

Now down to 2,000 feet Goodson fired at another 109 coming in to land as he flashed over the airfield. Putting the silver Mustang into a climbing turn, he looked back and noticed one of the new German rocket planes, an Me 163, hidden in a revetment on the edge of the airfield.

Deciding this would be a great opportunity to destroy one of the new enemy planes, Goodson came back across the field to strafe it. As he lined up his gun sights enemy flak burst all around him. He described the action that followed in *Tumult in the Clouds.*

The bright balls of fire came sailing up . . . [and] there were little clouds of heavier flak, with exploding flashes inside them. . . . Automatically I was taking evasive action . . . but always I kept my eye on the target and soon my shots were slamming into the prototype. . . . At the same moment I felt the plane shudder. . . . I felt a numbness in my right knee and knew I had been hit. . . . I gently eased the stick forward and let the plane down. . . . As we hit the ground I cut the switch, and bumped and skidded to a halt.

Goodson got out of the plane and walked to a nearby woods, with his hands in his pockets. After he was safely out of the way the rest of the squadron strafed his Mustang into junk.

Soon captured by the Germans Goodson was sent to a POW camp at Sagan. He was credited with fifteen victories in the air and thirteen on the ground at the time of his capture, and the Luftwaffe was glad to make him its guest.

Unfortunately for Goodson, he fell into the hands of the dreaded Gestapo immediately after his capture and was nearly executed. Taken to a Gestapo intelligence station, he was questioned and placed in solitary. Told he was to be shot, he did some fast talking and convinced the commanding officer he would be better off in the hands of the Luftwaffe.

Goodson remained a POW until early in 1945. Transferred to Mousburg near Dachau, he was liberated by advancing American infantry as the Third Reich he had fought so long crumbled into ruin.

Returning to the United States, Goodson underwent a brief period of rest and relaxation before going on a war bond selling tour. While on this tour he inadvertently embarked upon his postwar career.

I was giving a speech to workers at Goodyear Aircraft. They were making aircraft and news came through that the war was over. I'd just finished giving a speech, when the news regarding the end of the war came along—so they were in a rather enthusiastic mood. The chairman of Goodyear was standing next to me and he turned and said, "What are you going to do now, Colonel?" I said, "I'm going to get out of the Air Force and go to work."

He then asked me to come to work for Goodyear. "We have to build up our distribution in Europe," he said, "and you speak all of the European languages."

I wasn't married at the time, so I came to work for Goodyear in Europe, helping them to build factories in most of the European countries.

After working for Goodyear Goodson later went to work for ITT. He rose to an executive position with the corporation, at one time overseeing more than forty companies.

Because of his work in the international business community, Goodson began living in England. Still residing in England, he explained his decision to live overseas:

When I was with ITT a lot of our activities were in England and I had a company plane at Manston in England, and it was a good base to work from. When you have a lot of companies in different countries, the country you live in is only where you go on weekends if you're lucky.

I've always like England. I married an English wife and I found a very nice house in Sandwich in Kent. I have just sort of stayed on. I wish sometimes I had gone back to the States when I retired, but I just stayed in Europe.

The author of two books dealing with his participation in World War II, Goodson is planning to write a third book.

I think the next book I write will have to be fiction. A lot of people think that two I've written already are fiction, so I might as well write real fiction when I get time. I am pretty busy right now selling the books I've written so far.

More than fifty years have now passed since a young college student from New York named Jim

James Goodson receives an Air Force award in June 1986. Goodson chose to remain in England after the war, working for ITT and other American corporations. He remained in England and recently participated in ceremonies celebrating the 50th anniversary of the Battle of Britain. James Goodson

Goodson joined the RCAF. If the years have aged the body they have not dimmed his memory of those savage days of air battle in the skies over Europe. For Goodson and many others World War II was a great adventure and one they knew was worth the risks they took and will remember fondly as long as they live.

In the Second World War we had no doubts. We knew damn well what we were fighting for; everything was black and white.

We knew who the good guys were and who the bad guys were and we fought like hell. I look back upon those days with a great deal of fondness and pride.

You could question some things. Why did we bomb Dresden? Why did we bomb the churches in Germany?

One time I was asked to address a dinner honoring those who flew in the RAF Bomber Command. The bombers thought very highly of the fighter pilots because we protected them. I was at this annual dinner and I was sitting with Bomber [Sir Arthur] Harris, when somebody came in and said, "The press are here, which is unfortunate, but they say if you'll give them a 5 minute interview they'll leave."

Harris agreed to the interview and the reporters questioned him at length about why he had lost 45,000 or 50,000 air crew. Why had he bombed Dresden? Was it all worth it?

When the reporters had run out of steam, Harris said very quietly, "Well, gentlemen, we did not start the war, but we were asked to win it and I am reliably informed that is what we did!"

Chapter 8

David "Tex" Hill,
Legend in the Skies over China

"Tex Hill," wrote Robert Scott, "was the greatest fighter that I ever saw, the most loyal officer, and the best friend." David "Tex" Hill, a lean and lanky Texan, was a Navy pilot who became the second-leading ace of the legendary Flying Tigers. After the Flying Tigers were dissolved, he went on to command the 75th Fighter Squadron and the 23rd Fighter Group. Hill and Clinton D. "Casey" Vincent planned and executed the highly successful Thanksgiving Day, 1943, raid on a Japanese air base on Formosa. This raid marked the first time since the famous Doolittle raid that American planes had attacked the Japanese homeland. Hill left the Air Force after the war to follow other interests. Living in Texas, he has enjoyed travel and attending various veterans' reunions. Unless attributed to another source, all quotes are from a July 1989 interview with David "Tex" Hill.

Since the early thirties the empire of Japan had been repeatedly challenging the independence of China. In the face of this blatant aggression the United States had leveled moral condemnation on Japan or sent the suffering Chinese heartfelt expressions of sympathy.

Japanese aggression in Asia began with the occupation of Manchuria and attack on Shangai in 1931. The heavy Japanese bombing raids against Nanking and other Chinese cities in 1937 and 1938 received worldwide attention. Horrific newspaper headlines told of thousands of Chinese civilians killed in the terror bombings.

In the summer of 1940, encouraged by the successes of the German war machine, Japan made the moves that opened American eyes to its ambitions in Asia.

For three years Japan had been encountering stiffening resistance in China. To cut the supply lines to China, the Japanese in 1940 forced the Vichy government of France to allow them to occupy parts of Indochina and secured from Great Britain a promise to close the Burma Road, a main supply route to China. If successful here, the Japanese intended next to bring resource-rich Southeast Asia under their control.

President Franklin D. Roosevelt, increasingly alarmed by Japanese aggression, replied to these steps by placing a total embargo on steel and scrap iron shipments to Japan. Japan responded by signing the Tripartite Pact and joining Germany and Italy to form the Rome-Berlin-Tokyo Axis.

By 1941 the Japanese military faced two choices. One was to withdraw their troops from China, as America demanded, and then settle back to take economic profit from the war in Europe, just as Japan had done in World War I. The other was to continue the war in China and risk eventual conflict with the United States and Britain. The first course was obviously more sensible and it was the one advocated by the moderates in the Japanese government. But to withdraw from China would cause Japan to "lose face" in Asia and would indict the policy of the militarists as a failure, and this, of course, the militarists would not allow. A Japan that had won limited wars in China was quite certain it would do the same against an America that seemed to be a large but spineless playboy.

On April 15, 1941, President Roosevelt, convinced that something had to be done to keep China from surrendering to the Japanese, signed a secret executive order that allowed officers and enlisted people in the armed forces to resign their commissions without prejudice to their careers and to join a volunteer air force to defend the Burma Road.

Although the recruiting of pilots and ground crews was done in a clandestine manner, the news media were soon aware of the group's existence and mission, as shown by the article below, which appeared in the June 1941 issue of *Time* magazine:

> For the past few months tall, bronzed American airmen have been quietly slipping away from east and west coast ports making their way to Asia. Pilots to fly the P-40's and ground crews to maintain them will soon be scattered over Southwest China from the Burma Road to Chungking. These pilots were not just a crew of barnstormers turned war-stormers. They had been, until recently crack US Army Air Corps pilots. To take on this combat job they had been allowed to resign their Air Corps posts and enlist in the Chinese Air Force on the understanding that their US Army seniority would not be [a]ffected.

One of those tall, bronzed Americans who had quietly made his way to Asia to serve with the AVG was David "Tex" Hill. The son of a chaplain of the

Tex Hill at Loiwing, China, in 1942. "David Lee Hill was to many a one-man cross section of the AVG," wrote Robert Scott in *God Is My Co-Pilot. "He was the son of the Texas Rangers, but he was to return as a fighter to the Orient . . . and he was not to come back to America until three years later . . . [and] then in his twenty-ninth year, he had begun to feel the combat fatigue at last. The responsibility of commanding . . . had caught up with him."* Tex Hill

Texas Rangers, Hill would become a legendary figure of the China air war. To Gen. Robert Scott, author of *God Is My Co-Pilot,* Hill's character was straight out of the Wild West.

> He was a blue-eyed Texan, lean and lanky, six-feet-two of fighting blood. I imagine if he had lived in the frontier days of the American West, he would have been a gunman over there around the Pecos River—but a gunman on the side of the law. . . . He was the greatest fighter that I ever saw, the most loyal officer, and the best friend.

David "Tex" Hill was born in Kwangju, Korea, on July 13, 1915. When he was two years old his father, Paul, a Presbyterian minister, took the family back home to Texas. There missionary Paul Hill became Chaplain Paul Hill of the Texas Rangers.

Young David Hill's interest in aviation began when he took his first ride in a plane, an incident he later recalled:

> I took my first ride out at Winburn Field. I slipped off from Sunday school and paid a guy a dollar to take a ride; I couldn't have been very old at the time. It was an old plane of the type built by Travel Air. After the ride my conscience kind of bothered me because it was on a Sunday and I played hooky from church.

In 1933 Hill entered the University of Texas and then after two years he went on to graduate from Austin College in Sherman, Texas. Shortly after graduation from college he saw a poster on a post office bulletin board that read, "The US Navy offers you a career in flying," and he knew that was for him.

Hill was sent to Obalaka, Florida, which was an old Marine base. Here he qualified for what was called elimination flight training.

> We were given 10 hours [recalled Hill] and if you could solo and meet other requirements they selected you to go to Pensacola. At Pensacola I was what you would call an aviation cadet. We had almost a year's training and at that time the Navy training, I guess, was the best in the world.

The training was intensive and many would-be pilots washed out. Hill described some of the elements that made up the course:

> In Squadron 5 we received our instrument training and our fighter training. Of course the instrument training was very rudimentary in those days. You would make one letdown, needle ball and air speed over the mobile range, to qualify and receive your wings. In the meantime you had to qualify yourself in dive-bombing, gunnery, torpedo drops, horizontal bombing, everything that you do when you go to the fleet.

After graduation Hill was assigned to the US carrier *Saratoga* as an ensign. From there he went to the *Ranger,* assigned to VB-4. While serving on the *Ranger* he met some of the other men who would someday fly with him in the skies of China: Ed Rector, Gil Bright and Bob Neale.

The carrier pilots were the elite of the Navy, and although the training was intensely competitive, Hill felt it was "the finest training in the world and it was a lot of fun." He added:

I can't think of anything better than getting up every day and competing. The Navy is highly competitive from the individuals right up to the carrier level because everybody is trying to get that big *E* on the side of their airplane. If you reached a certain proficiency you got an *E* on the side of your plane. You competed against individuals, squadrons against squadrons, air group against air group and on up to carriers.

Then one afternoon, after Hill came down from a training flight, fate took a hand in changing his life. Along with Ed Rector and Bert Christman he walked into the office of the base executive and was introduced for the first time to Comdr. Rutledge Irvine.

Without preliminaries Irvine opened the conversation by saying, "We're looking for men to fight in China with Chennault."

Irvine had a map at hand, recalled Hill,

and it showed Burma, and this was the Burma Road, and he said they were looking for pilots to patrol this area. That sounded real good to us, and adventurous, you know, so we said we would like to go. It was just a fast deal. He explained it real fast, saying, "You'll get $600 a month; all you'll be doing is patrolling the Burma Road." This was in about March of 1941.

The decision to return to the Orient was a natural one for Hill, partly because of his family connection with Korea.

I'd always had a desire to go back. I'd sought to get an exchange from the carrier to one of the ships in the Far East. I was glad I didn't effect a change here, because a friend who was on the *Houston* wanted to change with me. We could do that in the Navy; if we could find somebody that wanted a spot

Second Pursuit Squadron, AVG: Buster Keeton, Frank Lawler, Rick Rickets, Frank Layher, Hank Gesebracht, Tom Jones and Frank Shield—back row, left to right; Ed Rector, Pappy Paxton, Peter Wright, Jack Newkirk, Tex Hill, Gil Bright and Francis Conant—front row, left to right. The 2nd Pursuit Squadron was commanded by Newkirk and nicknamed the Panda Bears. Tex Hill

on our ship, and we wanted one on his, we could effect that change. Of course, the *Houston* was sunk, so I was glad that didn't happen.

But the thing that motivated me to go to China was, more or less, adventure. I had no particular dedication to anything.

After receiving his discharge from the Navy Hill had orders to report to the Belmont Hotel in San Francisco. As the pilots and ground crews received their discharges they signed contracts with the Central Aircraft Manufacturing Corporation (CAMCO). They were provided with travel expenses and dispatched to the West Coast for the journey across the Pacific.

In June 1941 the first members of the AVG sailed on board the *President Pierce*. After brief stopovers at Hawaii and the Philippines they arrived at Hong Kong and boarded a Dutch packet boat for the trip to Rangoon. The first contingent consisted of ground personnel with instructions to prepare a training base at Toungoo, Burma, for those to follow.

Hill sailed from San Francisco on the Dutch ship the *Bloomfontein*. It was an unusual contingent of passengers, remembered Hill: "The passengers were half missionaries and half AVG people. I don't know who converted who on that trip—but the missionaries had a tough row to hoe, I'll tell you."

From July until late November AVG ground personnel and pilots continued to arrive in Rangoon. Their journeys varied, but most were in the vicinity of six weeks at sea.

Hill's contingent landed in Rangoon in July. As he stepped down the gangplank of the *Bloomfontein* he encountered a man who was to have a marked influence on his life, the legendary Claire Chennault, commander of the AVG.

We were met at the dock by Chennault and Skip Adair. I was very impressed by the old man when I first met him. His presence just seemed to instill a lot of confidence in you. He seemed like a guy that knew what in the hell he was doing.

I think anyone meeting Chennault for the first time would very definitely get the impression that he was a man who was a very dynamic person, and would have every confidence in him.

With the arrival of the pilots and ground personnel in Burma the human resource problem had been solved, but fighter airplanes were another and vexing matter. Finally, the Curtiss-Wright Aircraft Company in Buffalo came up with a scheme to procure some of the badly needed fighter planes. Curtiss-Wright said that if the British would waive their priority on 100 P-40C aircraft currently in production, the company would produce 100 later-model P-40s for them. Working under this agreement, the first contingent of P-40s

Skip Adair, Doc Prevo, Tex Hill, Arvid Olsen and Ken Jernstedt, left to right, in front of a C-47. "They wore," wrote Robert Holtz in With General Chennault, *"a motley assortment of clothes, from civvies to leather jackets to cover all flying suits and Chinese garrison caps. They were the mysterious American Volunteers who had come to defend the Burma Road." Tex Hill*

arrived in Rangoon barely in time to permit training operations to begin under Chennault's careful guidance. By September training was under way.

To train his volunteer pilots—who included bomber and transport pilots without any fighter experience—into shape, Chennault needed time and help from the British. The RAF provided this help by sharing with the AVG its Kyedaw training field at Toungoo, some 175 miles north of Rangoon. Kyedaw Airfield gave the AVG a training base well back from the reach of the Japanese fighters operating against Chinese targets.

Once stationed at Toungoo, Hill and the other AVG members participated in Chennault's training course. In *Way of a Fighter,* Chennault wrote,

> We began at Toungoo with a kindergarten for teaching bomber pilots how to fly fighters. Some learned fast and well. Bob Neale and David "Tex" Hill, both Navy dive-bomber pilots, had the best combat records in the A.V.G. . . . For others it was a long, tedious, and unsatisfactory process. Many multi-engine pilots had trouble getting used to the hundred-mile-per-hour landing speed and violent maneuvers of the P-40.

Part of the kindergarten course included 72 hours of lectures. Hill remembered Chennault

> using blackboards and chalk. He exhibited the type of formation that we would fly and the tactics that we would use against the Japs. It was a two-ship element, the basic element, and that was the first time I had ever heard of that. In the Navy we flew three ships. He felt that with the basic element being two ships, he could build it on up—four, six— and you work in pairs, all the time.

Chennault's training course also consisted of 60 hours of familiarization flying and mock combat with the P-40. The P-40 and Chennault's tactics were new to the fledgling AVG pilots, but familiarity brought confidence to Hill.

> The P-40s worked real well for us. It really was a dog of an airplane; it didn't come off well in the Pacific, but they didn't use it properly.
> But most fighter pilots are trained in the classical dogfight, trying to get on a guy's tail. Chennault knew the Japanese had very maneuverable airplanes with light wing loading that could turn inside of us. So he used the P-40's best features against the weaknesses of theirs.
> For one thing, we had the speed advantage and we could dive and get away from the Japanese. So you would just turn it over and dive and come back up and try to find another guy asleep.

From the middle of November on Chennault spent the hours of dusk and dawn in the control tower on alert. His one fear was that the Japanese would destroy his volunteer group on the ground with a surprise attack. He wrote in *Way of a Fighter:*

> My watch in the control tower ended at 11 A.M. on the morning of Dec. 8 [wrote Chennault]. Since we

were on the far side of the International Date Line our calendar read one day in advance of those in Hawaii and the United States. As I walked across the field, one of our radio men dashed across the turf waving a message frantically. It was the news of Pearl Harbor intercepted from an American radio news flash. The rising tide of the Pacific war had at last engulfed the United States and overtaken our American Volunteer Group.

The AVG's primary duty would be to help protect Chiang Kai-shek's supply routes through Burma. "It was immediately evident," wrote Chennault in *Way of a Fighter,* "that both ends of the Burma Road would have to be defended from heavy air assaults." Japanese air raids that would destroy Rangoon, the entry port, and Kunming, the main depository point in China, would be a cheap and effective means of blockading China without draining the far-flung offensives in the South Pacific. Rangoon was the only port through which supplies could still come into China. "Kunming was the vital

Bob Keeton, Ed Rector and Freeman "Rick" Rickets, left to right. Keeton attended Colorado College and played against football great Byron Wizzen White. Rector would command the 23rd FG later in the war. Keeton was credited with 2.5 victories, Rector with 6.5 and Rickets with 1.125 while flying with the AVG. Bob Keeton

valve," in Chennault's opinion, "that controlled distribution of supplies to the Chinese armies in the field."

The AVG—it had not yet earned the title of Flying Tigers—was ready for action. Chennault had given his volunteers the benefit of his own four years' experience fighting the Japanese in China. The training was over and Chennault's unorthodox band of adventurers was to lock horns with a veteran, combat-wise adversary. The AVG were still unruly civilians in the eyes of many and untried in combat, but it was now or never. No one, not even the AVG members, had any idea of how they would fare against the Japanese.

Once launched, the Japanese offensive rolled over all opposition. Everywhere the Japanese struck they scored stunning victories. They advanced from Thailand into the British Malay states, sliced into the Malay Peninsula to isolate British airfields and began their relentless advance toward the British bastion of Singapore. Early in December Japanese troops thrust out of Thailand and began to advance into lower Burma—and decided the pattern of battle for the AVG.

At the request of the British high command Chennault assigned the AVG 3rd Pursuit Squadron, "Hell's Angels," led by Arvid Olsen, Jr., to Mingaladon Airdrome to join the RAF in the defense of Rangoon. Twenty-one P-40B Tomahawks

Col. Robert Scott, Jr., with an ammo belt around his shoulders, helps R. Fuller and J. Teague load his guns in the wing of his P-40. "Bob Scott," recalled Tex Hill, "was a good pilot and a damn good commander." Fourteenth Air Force Association

were to assist the Brewster Buffaloes and Hawker Hurricanes of the British forces.

The 1st Squadron, "Adam and Eve," and 2nd Squadron, "Panda Bears," of the AVG were transferred en masse by Chennault to Kunming. Kunming, at the eastern end of the Burma Road, was situated in a mountain valley 6,000 feet above sea level.

On December 20 came warning of ten Japanese Sally bombers approaching Kunming from Indochina. The Chinese early warning system was active and working with great effectiveness. Chennault fired a red flare, sending the 1st and 2nd squadrons into the air, and drove to the combat-operations shelter and made ready for battle by the radio and phone communication equipment. Years later he wrote in *Way of a Fighter:*

> This was the decisive moment I had been awaiting for more than four years—American pilots in American fighter planes aided by a Chinese ground warning net about to tackle a formation of the Imperial Japanese Air Force, which was then sweeping the Pacific skies victorious everywhere. I felt that the fate of China was riding in the P-40 cockpits through the wintery sky over Yunnan.

Time magazine in December 1941 gave this account of the AVG's first battle with the Japanese:

> Last week ten Japanese bombers came winging their carefree way up into Yunnan, heading directly for Kunming, the terminus of the Burma Road. Thirty miles south of Kunming the Flying Tigers swooped, let the Japanese have it. Of the ten bombers, said Chungking reports, four plummeted to earth in flames, the rest turned tail and fled. Tiger casualties: none.

Although the Japanese bomber crews were brave, Hill felt the rigidity of their tactics often led to their downfall.

> The Japanese bomber crews, when they would go on a mission, were so regimented they would never break formation. They came in a damn big V and they [would] never break it. You could go right in on the back of them and eat them right up. They'll never break formation and you can go right down the line.
>
> The weakness of the Japanese pilots was that they were so regimented, they could not adjust to new situations. They had no capacity for ingenuity. Pearl Harbor was a good example of this. If a Japanese mission is not intercepted it will be very successful, it will come off just like clockwork, but once you break up their formations, they couldn't adjust to any kind of new situations.

On December 23, after the first bloodletting in the China skies, the Hell's Angels squadron in Burma took to the air with the British to stop a large Japanese formation of fighters and bombers heading for Rangoon. An AVG war diary report found in Robert Holt's *With General Chennault* gave this account of the battle:

No air raid alarm signal was given at [Mingaladon]. All ships were suddenly ordered off the airdrome. . . . Fourteen P-40's and sixteen Brewsters (R.A.F.) joined the fight. The enemy flew a very close formation—large V of V's. They were attacked by P-40's and Brewsters before they dropped their bombs. . . . When individual enemy bombers were shot down, the remaining bombers quickly filled in the key positions by means of fast executed cross-overs. Bombers put out a strong cross-fire from top turrets, and the air was filled with white tracers.

The AVG shot down twenty-five enemy planes in the battle and the British pilots blasted another seven out of the sky. Three of the P-40s went down before the Japanese guns, but one of the pilots made it home that night.

Although the AVG tasted its first combat over China, it was the bitter air battles over Rangoon that, according to Chennault, writing in *Way of a Fighter,*

stamped the hallmark on its fame as the Flying Tigers. The cold statistics for the ten weeks the AVG served at Rangoon show its strength varied between twenty and five serviceable P-40s. This tiny force met a total of 1,000 odd Japanese aircraft over southern Burma and Thailand. In thirty-one encounters they destroyed 217 enemy planes and probably destroyed forty-three. Our losses in combat were four pilots killed in the air, one killed while strafing and one taken prisoner. Sixteen P-40s were destroyed.

The Japanese were surprised at the AVG opposition over Rangoon, admitting for the first time significant losses. Heavy Japanese attacks against Rangoon were expected to continue and the 3rd Squadron had only eleven serviceable P-40s left, so Chennault sent the 2nd Squadron, led by Jack Newkirk, to relieve the 3rd.

As the Japanese regrouped to organize a massive attack to finish off Rangoon, the AVG took the offensive. On January 3, 1942, Newkirk and Hill of the 2nd Squadron led a strafing attack on the airfields in nearby Thailand to catch Japanese planes on the ground. It was Hill's first encounter in combat. He later reminisced about it:

The first combat that I was engaged in involved a raid on a place called Meshod, over in Thailand. Jack Newkirk was my squadron leader, and there was Jim Howard, Bert Christman and myself.
We took off early one morning. . . . Christman developed engine trouble and had to come back. . . . We dropped down on this airdrome. We could see planes parked there. . . .
Well, the first thing I saw when we pulled up, there was a Jap coming towards Newkirk. He just turned into him head-on, just as Newkirk pulled off his first strafing pass. He [the Japanese plane] just disintegrated. . . . Then I looked around, and here was this Jap on Jim Howard's tail, just sitting back there. . . . Well, I shot the Jap off his tail. . . . I was so

excited, hell I wasn't even looking through the gun sight. I was just looking through the windshield. Of course, we had tracer bullets. You might say it was just like putting a hose on a man. I just flew right up in the guy's tail and brought [my guns] around on him.

After saving Howard, Hill found himself in deep trouble as a Japanese fighter positioned itself on his tail.

This guy did an overhead on me and shot thirty-three holes in my plane. But for some reason, I don't know whether it was the way his guns were bore sighted, it was just the critical point where they intersected and began to spread, but the hits were on either side of my wings. Thirty-three of them. I didn't realize to what extent they had shot me up until I got back.

After evading the rear end attack by the Japanese fighter Hill found another Japanese plane coming at him head-on. "Of course, we had heavier firepower and soon broke the Japanese pilots from doing that," remembered Hill. "But some of those bullets stuck in the prop and threw the damn prop out of balance and the prop almost went through the side of the airplane."

Hill, 150 miles from base, throttled back "and kept one leg over the side ready to jump out." Landing at his home base, he realized how fortunate he had been during his first combat encounter.

A painter paints the finishing touches on the China Air Task Force insignia onto a P-40. "The China Air Task Force," wrote Claire Chennault in Way of a Fighter, *"was patched together in the midst of combat from whatever happened to be available in China during the gloomy summer of 1942."* National Archives

He felt lucky to be alive. "But," he commented, "I began learning fast from that time on, and I think my neck size increased about an inch—you know, keeping your head on a swivel, looking around."

On January 23 Hill and the AVG lost a good friend when Bert Christman was shot down over Rangoon. The death of Christman, an old shipmate and friend, brought home the ferocity of the war to Hill. He recalled Christman's death and funeral:

> He was killed in his parachute. He had holes in his chute but there was one bullet that hit him in the face on the side of the neck, that could have caused his death. Ed Rector and I went out to bury him. Of course, you know we had no way of embalming people and he was our very closest friend. It was terrible, you know. Here's your friend lying in a box and you can hardly stay around it.

It was not a gentleman's war in the skies over China. It was kill or be killed, and Christman was not the only flier to be machine-gunned while floating to earth in a parachute.

> If [the Japanese] ever caught you in a parachute they were almost sure to strafe you. I think our people did the same. I remember one guy came back from a mission, not in the AVG, but the Fourteenth Air Force, and his gun camera film had this Jap in the chute there and he had parachute shroud all over his airplane; he ran right through it; he must have had his gun switches on.

The first two Japanese planes Hill shot down while flying with the AVG were Nakajima I-97 fighters. These little Japanese planes were the first low-wing monoplane design. They closely resembled the early Japanese Navy Claud (A5M) in appearance. They were also the first to have an enclosed cockpit. Speed, firepower and armor received low priority, as everything was sacrificed for good visibility and maneuverability. These were the most maneuverable aircraft of the day and possibly in all of aviation history.

Hill's combat encounter with the I-97s left him with a great deal of respect for the Japanese plane.

> Toward the later part of the AVG days we ran into some Zeros. They were a very good airplane, but so were the I-97s. Those damn things! I mean, the Japanese pilots could wrap that thing up in front of your face.

Hill had a chance to fly the I-97 when he was hospitalized in North China. The Chinese had captured one and offered Hill a chance to take it up for a test flight. After finding out he couldn't fit his large frame in the cockpit with his parachute on, Hill managed to taxi down the runway, attempting to take off.

> The throttle opened backwards and it didn't have any brakes or a tail wheel; the rudder bar was just a bar; there were little trim tabs. Sitting in the cockpit, I had my knees up to my chin like a grasshopper.
>
> I taxied out, working the throttle a little bit to get the plane moving. Then, when I started to move, I threw the throttle wide open and, hell, I was airborne in 100 yards. I wrestled that thing around and was finally able to get familiar with it. It was trimmed so you could fly hands off at 15,000 feet at three-quarter power. It was quite a thrill flying the 97.

Between January 23 and 27 the Japanese made six major attacks against the AVG forces defending Rangoon. The Japanese ground forces were also slowly advancing and it was increasingly apparent that the British did not have the men, the equip-

Flight line of P-40s. "The P-40 worked real well for us," recalled Tex Hill. "It really was a dog of an airplane. It didn't come off well in the Pacific, but [USAAF pilots] didn't use it properly." Smithsonian Institution

ment or the leadership to stop the Japanese. It was only a matter of time before the Japanese ground forces would capture Rangoon.

Early news dispatches to the wire services had made the American pilots fighting the Japanese over Burma and China famous as the Flying Tigers. Chennault later wondered in *Way of a Fighter* "How the term Flying Tigers was derived from the shark-nosed P-40 I will never know." He gave credit for the first use of the shark's teeth to the British in North Africa and before them to the Germans in World War I.

> The insignia we made famous was by no means original with the AVG. Our pilots copied the shark-tooth design on their P-40s' noses from a colored illustration in the *Indian Illustrated Weekly* depicting an RAF squadron in the Libyan desert with shark-nosed P-40s.

Regardless of the origin of the name, few people came to know the AVG by anything other than their now legendary name, the Flying Tigers.

The fall of Rangoon on March 9 ended the battle of southern Burma. The Japanese won the city despite the heroic resistance of the Flying Tigers and the RAF allies.

After only a brief lull the bitter battle between the Japanese and the AVG-RAF combination continued over northern Burma. The Japanese had considerable forces at their disposal, wrote Chennault in his book *Way of a Fighter.*

> The enemy now had 14 air regiments based in southern Burma and Thailand with a strength of 420 to 500 planes. This compared with 30 serviceable fighters and a dozen Blenheim bombers of the Allied force. Over northern Burma the character of the battle shifted to continual attempts to catch opposition on the ground and shooting sitting ducks. This later became a characteristic of the Pacific war; the most decisive air battles were fought when attackers caught the enemy by surprise on the ground.

It was during the battle of northern Burma that the Loiwing "revolt" took place. The protest was precipitated by orders from Chennault to fly low-level escort missions for RAF Blenheim bombers far into heavily defended enemy territory. The AVG pilots balked at this and in mid-April the pilots at Loiwing decided to hold a meeting to protest the missions.

During the meeting, the pilots claimed they had signed up to fight and didn't mind defending airfields or flying other high-altitude missions where they had a chance against enemy fighters, but they felt they were being sacrificed on the low-level strafing runs. A petition of resignation was drawn up. Chennault attended the meeting and one by one the pilots let him know their feelings. Chennault heard them out and then voiced his feelings:

[He] carefully reminded them that their action—in the face of the enemy—could be considered desertion. There was silence in the room while he talked. He told them that under the Articles of War the punishment for desertion was death. (He did not add that they were all civilians and did not fall under the same rules as the military.)

Once Chennault left the room Hill rose to his feet and said he had a few things to say. All eyes now turned to the lanky blonde-haired 2nd Squadron commander. What followed was one of Hill's finest moments and stamped him forever as a great combat leader. "He wanted them all to know that he was

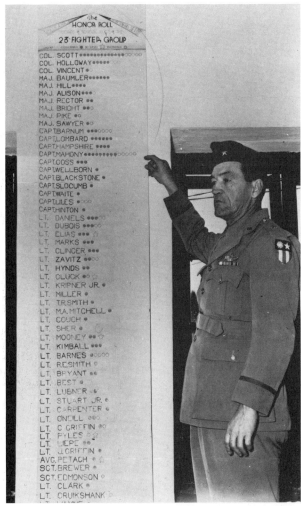

Gen. Claire Chennault points to a listing of the number of Japanese planes shot down by 23rd FG pilots. Winston Churchill saw the square-jawed Chennault sitting in a room and said to his aide, "'Who is that man?' The aide replied, 'That's Chennault, the Flying Tiger on China.' Then Churchill replied, 'What a face! What a face! Thank God he's on our side!'" according to Robert H. Schuler in Your Future Is Your Friend. *Smithsonian Institution*

not in favor of the resignation. He had not signed the protest."

Hill then told the assembled pilots the reason he would not sign.

> I said, "Hell, we're not a bunch of mercenaries over here. Hell, since we've arrived here our country's involved in war and this is part of our war. It's not just like a cold-blooded job or something like that, and whatever has to be done, we've got to do it. We've got a man who's our leader, who says this is the way it should be done. . . . We have to advise him of all the facts and our thinking on the thing, but if he makes up his mind and says it's still necessary, we've got to do it."

Hill had said his piece and to give meaning to his words he volunteered to lead a low-level mission to Chiengmai. Four others said they would go with him: Duke Hedman, Frank Schiel, R. J. "Catfish" Raines and Ed Rector.

The escort mission to Chiengmai was scheduled for the following day, but the British bombers never showed up at the rendezvous point with Hill's flight. It was fortunate the mission did not proceed as planned; none of Hill's flight might have made it back. Two of the P-40s had oil trouble and a third had not been filled with sufficient fuel. Another plane had a burned-out generator—none of its guns would have been able to fire.

In a few days the revolt was over. The pilots at Kunming were not involved in the petition and Bob Neale sent a wire down from Kunming to Chennault saying, "If those guys don't want to go, bring us down there. We'll go." In the end twenty-three pilots left their resignations on the petition, but Chennault never took any action to accept them. Cooler heads prevailed and they were back to flying by April 28.

Years later Hill reflected on the brief revolt:

> But many of these boys, and I've had it happen to several of them, when we were drinking, and everything, it's still on their conscience. They would give a lot of money not to have put their names on that paper. A lot of real good boys had their name on that thing and I'm sure they wish they never had signed it.

The popular image of the Flying Tigers later promoted by the newspapers, magazines and movies depicted them as wholesome, clear-eyed, lovable all-American boys fighting for God, country and apple pie. Claire Boothe Luce, in an article for July 20, 1942, issue of *Life* magazine detailing the end of the AVG, wrote the following honeyed words:

> In the autumn and early winter of 1941, there were 100 young American pursuit pilots stationed at Toungoo, Burma. They wore the uniform of the Chinese Air Force. . . . Madame Chiang Kai-shek smilingly called them "my angels with—or without—wings." . . . They were . . . nearly all blonde and more than half of them were 6 feet tall. They hailed from 39 of the 40 states of the Union. The names of their home towns made music such as Walt Whitman sang and Carl Sandburg sings now: Waseca . . . Marshall, Otis, Yanhill. . . .

> For a congeries of motives carried them to Burma: a little money to buy their girls pretty rings, or the folks a car, to marry on, or just to laugh and play on; a burning belief in China's cause, the love of high adventure in an alien land; in the sheer thrill of air combat. Each of them knew when he left our own peaceful land he might face a winged doom in the skies of Cathay.

In reality, however, the AVG was no bunch of angels. One US Army General described it as "the most underdisciplined outfit I've ever seen." The British troops stationed near an AVG base in Rangoon called the AVG members ruffians and roughnecks.

In May the Japanese Army advanced into southern China. The situation was perilous. The Japanese controlled all the seaports, and now they were advancing up the Burma Road, meaning that the only way of supplying China was by air from India, over the Hump to Kunming. Kunming had to be saved from capture, for if it fell, the only alternative route was an overland trek from the Soviet Union. Most experts agreed that if the city fell, the Chinese would be forced out of the war and the Japanese could turn their full military might toward India, Australia and, ultimately, the United States.

Only two things stood in the way of a rapid and overwhelming Japanese victory: the mile-deep Salween River gorge and Chennault's AVG. On May 5 the Japanese reached the western edge of the gorge, pushing the fleeing Chinese soldiers and civilians ahead of them along the Burma Road.

A reconnaissance flight reported that a Japanese motorized column was moving up the center of the road between swarms of unarmed Chinese soldiers and civilians on both sides. "This was one of the few times during the war that I became greatly alarmed," wrote Chennault in *Way of a Fighter*. If the Japanese could cut China off from Allied aid, "China's resistance would collapse like a punctured lung."

A Japanese engineering regiment soon arrived at the Salween River and began building a pontoon bridge. To prevent completion of the bridge Chennault decided to attack it with dive-bombers. It was a decisive moment of the war, wrote Chennault in *Way of a Fighter*.

> Tex Hill, Ed Rector, Tom Jones, Frank Lawler, Lewis Bishop, Link Laughlin, Frank Schiel, and Bob Little volunteered for the bombing missions. Just after dawn on May 7, a handful of AVG pilots took off to stop the victorious Japanese Army on the brink of the Salween—a task at which the combined British and Chinese armies in Burma had failed dismally.

Tex Hill led a flight of four P-40s loaded with fragmentation bombs in the wing racks and a big Russian demolition bomb under the belly. Four P-40s led by Arvid Olsen flew top cover.

As the eight P-40s approached the Paosham Plateau they found the way blocked by a particularly dark and threatening storm front, composed of many cells along the line, each identifiable by a flat base and rising warm air, which sent billowing white clouds thousands of feet into the air. Hill studied the front and decided to thread the flight as nearly as possible between the cells, hoping to avoid any dangerous ice and hail.

After a half-hour of turbulent flying through severe up- and downdrafts the P-40s broke through into a clear, cloudless sky with the muddy Salween River dead ahead.

No longer hidden by the jungle of lower Burma, the Japanese column now lay exposed and strung out along the road. The line of armored and artillery vehicles not only extended up the face of the western bank but ran for miles along the narrow road on the higher plateau. With a rock wall on one side and sheer bluffs on the other, the Japanese column would be trapped by any air attack.

With Hill leading the way the P-40s dove to the attack. Repeatedly, the dive-bombers plastered the rock cliffs above the convoy, bringing down landslides to block any retreat. After they dropped their bombs Hill led his flight in machine-gunning the column until all their ammunition was spent. All eight planes returned to Kunming after the attack.

For the next four days Chennault hurled everything he had, even antiquated 5B-3 Russian twin-engine bombers borrowed from the Chinese Air Force, against the Japanese in the Salween Gorge. By May 11 enemy traffic was heading not north but south on the Burma Road. As Chennault later

Claire Chennault talks to Fourteenth Air Force pilots in front of a P-51 Mustang. "Chennault was one of the greatest tacticians that has ever been around," claimed Tex Hill. "Some of these wienies in recent years are just now, as time goes on, beginning to appreciate more and more what a great man he was." Fourteenth Air Force Association wrote, "The AVG had staved off China's collapse on the Salween."

As early as December 30, 1941, plans had existed for the induction of the AVG into the USAAF. However, nothing was done about the proposition until March 29, 1942, when Claire Chennault was suddenly called to Chungking for a conference with Gen. Joseph Stilwell and Clayton Bissell.

Chennault vigorously opposed induction. "The AVG," wrote Chennault in *Way of a Fighter*, "had a combat record that was never equalled by a regular Army or Navy fighter group of similar size. I felt it was criminal to sacrifice the spirit and experience of the group for a mere change in uniform."

The USAAF pushed for induction, claiming that the paper work involved in supplying a non-regulation organization was difficult. Bissell and Stilwell made it clear to Chennault during the March 29 conference in Chungking that the AVG would be refused further supplies if it refused induction. Chennault was personally unwilling to stop fighting the Japanese under any circumstances and agreed to accept a return to active duty. He told Stilwell that the men of the AVG would make their own decision regarding induction.

Many of the AVG pilots were weary of combat and tired of overseas duty. Many were also bitter and upset over the offhand manner with which they were treated by USAAF officers, and it was this action as much as any other that soured the pilots and ground personnel on the idea of joining the USAAF.

The insulting manner of the regular Army officers toward the members of the AVG was exemplified by one colonel, the commander of a fighter group with the Tenth Air Force, who while in China sneered at the AVG pilots as plain mercenaries. The good colonel, standing with AVG members at a bar one night, also stated plainly that he could take on the best AVG pilot in aerial combat and beat him.

At this statement there was a blur of hands and $5,000 suddenly appeared on the table before the startled colonel—"who was invited immediately to match the bet by flying against the worst pilot for the AVG. The colonel managed to laughingly wriggle his way out of what had suddenly become a damnably embarrassing situation."

The cumulative damage had been done, however. Of 250 men in the AVG, only five pilots and twenty-two ground crewmen accepted induction into the USAAF.

Hill was one of the five pilots who agreed to stay. "I saw the old man [Chennault] in Chungking," he told Ed Rector. "He told me everybody's going home, but someone with know-how has to stay to activate new units. He wanted me to talk to you and some of the other fellows."

"I'm planning to go home," Rector said.

"So was I," Hill said, "but if all of us leave, this whole thing will fold up."

After talking with Tex Hill, Ed Rector agreed to stay, along with Charlie Sawyer, Frank Schiel and Gil Bright.

July 4 was the final day of the AVG, and the group celebrated it in fine style by knocking down five Japanese fighters over Hengyang.

In his memoirs, *Way of a Fighter*, Chennault recalled the combat record of his beloved AVG:

The group that military experts predicted would not last three weeks in combat had fought for seven months over Burma, China, Thailand and French Indochina, destroying 299 Japanese planes with another 153 probably destroyed. All of this with a loss of twelve P-40's in combat and sixty one on the ground.... Four pilots were killed in air combat; six were killed by antiaircraft fire; three by enemy bombs on the ground; and three were taken prisoner. Ten more died as a result of flying accidents.

With his induction into the USAAF Hill ended his memorable career with the AVG. His satisfaction in serving with the Flying Tigers was evident as he recently recalled the role of the AVG:

The thing that made the AVG effective over there was the fact that we wanted to be there in the first place and in the second place we had an objective and it wasn't money. Money is the last thing you think about once you get up there and you're coming to grips with the enemy and your life's on the line. I mean those 500 dollar bills disappear and you don't even think about them. We were soon in the war and we felt like we were making a hell of a contribution—that was the thing I'm proud of!

Despite the formidable obstacles that confronted them in China, the AVG pilots carved a niche in aviation history. Bob Neale led by shooting down sixteen planes and Tex Hill racked up a score of twelve to become the second-leading AVG ace. So many other pilots shot down five or more Japanese planes in combat that the Flying Tigers could well have been described as the Group of Aces.

Chennault wrote in his book *Way of a Fighter* that the AVG cost China about $8 million. He later wrote to Dr. T. V. Soong his regrets that the cost of the AVG had exceeded his original estimates. Soong replied, "The AVG was the soundest investment China ever made."

Perhaps Winston Churchill summed up the exploits of the legendary Flying Tigers best when he said,

The victories of these Americans over the rice paddies of Burma are comparable in character if not in scope with those won by the RAF over the hop fields of Kent in the Battle of Britain.

After the Flying Tigers were dissolved, Hill found himself a squadron commander in a motley, makeshift and make-do organization called the China Air Task Force (CATF). General Chennault, according to Duane Schultz in *The Maverick War,* wrote that the CATF was "patched together in the midst of combat from whatever happened to be available in China during the gloomy summer of 1942."

The CATF was less formidable than its name would indicate. At first it could muster no more than seven B-25 medium bombers and just thirty-one P-40Bs and twenty P-40Es from the AVG, and only twenty-nine of the P-40s were flyable. Ten additional P-43 Lancers were borrowed from the Chinese Air Force, but these planes were antiquated deathtraps; they had no armor plating or self-sealing gas tanks.

The fledgling CATF organized its fighter planes into three squadrons—the 74th, 75th and 76th—which formed the 23rd FG under the interim command of Bob Neale. Tex Hill assumed command of the 75th Squadron, Ed Rector led the 76th and Frank Schiel converted the 74th into an operational training unit.

For Hill the change from the AVG to the USAAF was a relatively easy one. "I had just come down off a flight and they had a table set up there and a guy just swore me in and said, 'You're now Major Hill of the 75th Fighter Squadron.'"

The 23rd FG had no holiday, even though it was activated on the Fourth of July. On the night of July 3 Radio Tokyo warned the new American fighter group that the Japanese would quickly annihilate the newcomers, for it was common knowledge that the experienced AVG personnel were leaving for the United States.

The Japanese promptly threw a large force of bombers and fighters at the group in an attempt to destroy the "newly arrived" units.

Instead of finding green and inexperienced fighter pilots, the Japanese encountered AVG veterans who had agreed to stay behind for two weeks to help during the transition phase.

The Japanese came in over Kweilin doing "arrogant acrobatics, expecting to strafe the Chinese civilians in the city without opposition." General Chennault, wrote Bob Scott in *God Is My Co-Pilot,* watched the approaching Japanese planes with field glasses and called directions to Neale, Rector and Hill, who were "sitting with their ships in the sun high overhead at 21,000." At Chennault's radio order of "Take 'em," the 23rd with the AVG attached dove out of the sun and tore into the startled Japanese. Soon thirteen Zeros and new twin-engine Nakajima I-45 fighters were wrecked and burning on the ground.

On July 10 Hill led four P-40s on a mission to Hankow. The prime objective was to escort five B-25 bombers against the docks of Hankow.

After the B-25s had released their bombs and headed home Hill called for an attack by the fighters on the enemy shipping in the Yangtze River.

Robert Scott described the attack in his wartime book *God Is My Co-Pilot:*

> One of the bomber pilots said that Tex rolled his ship over from sixteen thousand feet and streaked down for the Japanese gunboats below. The little gunboats were shooting everything they had at the American fighter—but that I've learned since, was what Hill liked. Tex Hill's guns were firing even as he pulled out right on the water, and they swept the decks of the enemy gunboats. The bomber pilot said that as the fighter ships would turn low to the water, and come in, each concentrating on one of the little Jap warships, he could see the six lines of fifty-calibre tracers cutting across the water. . . . On the second attack one of these gunboats was sinking and on fire. Hill's four fighters sank all four of the little metal gunboats.

The next day Hill led eight fighters, four with wing bombs, on a mission to Nanchang. While four

American and Chinese ground crew men work together to install a machine gun. Ground crews in China found out rapidly that ingenuity was not a lost art. They usually kept the aircraft flying even though they often worked without the spare parts, specialists—such as electrical, propeller and hydraulic experts—and shops or special equipment normally needed in support of aircraft. National Archives

P-40s went down to bomb, Hill flew top cover with the other four planes just in case Japanese Zeros tried to surprise the dive-bombers.

John Petach, one of the AVG veterans who had extended for two weeks to help the transition from AVG to 23rd FG, lost his life on this mission. "Petach dove for his target, one of the gunboats on the lake, but as his bomb hit the boat the P-40 was seen to explode, evidently hit by ground fire."

Petach's death was a shock to Hill because he had talked to Petach about extending at Chennault's request.

Petach had his suitcase packed and was telling everybody good-bye. I came out of the old man's office and told him what Chennault had asked and Petach said, "Sure, I'll stay."
He was killed on a mission I didn't think would be that difficult.

On July 28 Hill led five P-40s on a dawn mission to dive-bomb Canton. Turned back because of bad weather, his flight was nearing Hengyang when the Chinese warning net reported heavy engine noise to the north and an estimated seventy Japanese fighters heading for Hengyang. Hill, wrote Scott in *God Is My Co-Pilot,* parried this attack with

nothing more lethal than a microphone [wrote Chennault]. Aware that the Japanese generally monitored the American combat radio frequency, "Tex" began giving orders for the deployment of imaginary fighter squadrons. His mates quickly sensed his intentions and responded with acknowledgements indicating at least forty American fighters in the air. The Japanese didn't like the sound of things and headed back toward Hankow.

On July 19 Bob Neale had been succeeded by Col. Robert Scott, a commander of the 23rd FG. Scott was a native of Georgia who had flown several combat missions with the AVG.

Scott's admiration for Hill was unqualified. He vividly described Hill in his wartime book, *God Is My Co-Pilot:*

I'd seen Tex shoot down Japs in the sky and I had followed on his wing to learn the tactics of the AVG. I know that if there is any man I owe my life to during the months I fought in China, it is Major Tex Hill: seeing what he did in combat, and how he handled his ship; seeing his coolness on the alert, and his keen desire for action. I can hear Tex now, after he had studied the plotting board that the interpreters were covering with little red flags showing the positions of the approaching Jap fighter ships. I can hear him saying, "Well, gentlemen, I think we'll take off." And he would smile as he pulled on his helmet and goggles.

An October 25 raid on Hong Kong gave Hill and Scott their first chance to fly together as members of the 23rd FG. The objective of the mission was to attack a Japanese task force that was believed to be anchored in Victoria Harbor.

"We had the great sum of seven P-40s," recalled Colonel Scott, "and our mission was to escort twelve B-25s to bomb the task force." Taking off from Kunming, the American strike force flew 500 miles to Kweilin. After arrival they gassed and bombed up and took off just after noon for Hong Kong. "When we got there the task force had gone, so the bombers turned to the secondary target," said Scott. The secondary target was the Kowloon docks. "Just as I finished taking pictures of the bombs hitting the docks, I said to myself, 'This is a soft job. No Zeroes.'"

Scott and his formation were at 18,000 feet and he soon found that he was badly mistaken about the presence of Zeros. He talked about the air battle in a 1990 interview with the author:

Down below us was Victoria Harbor and of course Kaitak Air Base.
Tex Hill was in my right wing and I was leading the formation. This great formation representing the United States of America, the greatest country in the world, and all we had were seven P-40s.
We began to see flashes of light down below from Kaitak airfield and they were from the square windshields of the Japanese airplanes.
I began counting the Japanese planes out loud over the radio, and when I got to twelve my voice was very strained, but when I got to twenty-four I suddenly realized we were outnumbered twenty-four to seven.
I figured we had to go down and get them. The way you do that is to push forward on the stick. I never will forget: as we dove Tex Hill didn't push forward on the stick, he did what is known as a split-S. That's when you half-roll the ship and pull the stick back so you go down about 500 mph.
So I saw the number 155 on the bottom of Tex's ship. I had already pushed my nose down, so he beat me to the first Japanese plane and shot it down. I got the second one. But what Tex said, as he dove, was what impressed me. Remember now, we're outnumbered twenty-four to seven and Tex says, "Hell, we outnumber them today—let's go get 'em!"

The P-40s shot down nineteen Zeros and Scott and Hill strafed the main street of Kowloon and White Cloud Airdrome. American losses were listed as two P-40s.

Under Colonel Scott's command the 23rd FG consisted of three fighter squadrons and one headquarters squadron. Hill had one squadron at Hengyang and with him were such deputy leaders as Maj. Gil Bright, Maj. Johnny Alison and Capt. Ajax Baumler.

Hill's 75th Fighter Squadron at Hengyang was surrounded by Japanese air bases. Hankow to the north on the Yangtze River was the main Japanese staging point for the bombing raids on Hengyang. At first the Japanese had tried to bomb Hengyang during the day, but when that proved too costly they switched to a period of constant night attacks.

To counter the harassing Japanese night attacks Hill prepared his men for a night interception. This would be a new tactic for the 23rd FG, since the P-40 had no equipment for night fighting.

Hill had taken his idea for a night interception to Chennault.

> I discussed it with Chennault. He said, "Tex, I'll tell you, the only target is the field at Hengyang. There's nothing else there. At some point in time the Japanese will be directly above that field. The only thing you have to figure out now is the direction they're coming from and what altitude."

During the day, Hill and his men prepared for the night mission. They estimated the Japanese bombers had come in at around 8,000 feet, at about 0200 hours. Hill couldn't be sure the Japanese would return that night or duplicate the time and altitude, but it was a starting point. If the Japanese did return, Hill wanted his planes to be at about 12,000 feet to have a little altitude advantage.

Hill had decided to send Alison and Baumler up for the interception. Alison was a superior fighter pilot and combat leader. "He knew the P-40 better than anyone I have ever seen," wrote Colonel Scott in *God Is My Co-Pilot.* "He had instructed the British in their use in the United Kingdom and then gone over to show the Russians how to fly and repair them near Moscow."

Scott, writing in *God Is My Co-Pilot,* felt that Captain Baumler "was the best operation officer [he] ever saw. He could go out and shoot down Japs all day, then come in and read the combat reports of twenty pilots, digest them all, and write out the most comprehensive report in the world."

Hill had faith that Alison and Baumler could pull off a successful night interception. He and his men were ready. They could only hope the Japanese bombers would keep the appointment.

At about 0230 hours on July 29 Hill received word that Japanese bombers were approaching Hengyang.

> So I jumped out of bed. I just had on one of those Burmese loincloths, just a little wraparound thing. I ran down to the field and Alison and Ajax took off and I had a radio off the edge of the field in a little slit trench. I was talking to them; I believe I had

The 23rd FG started to receive its first P-51Bs in February 1944, although Claire Chennault had managed to "divert" a few as early as November 1943. "The P-51 was the best airplane produced," wrote Tex Hill. "The Navy guys swear by that Corsair, but I'll take the P-51 any day. It had all the performance you'd want. God, you had speed, altitude, firepower, dive . . . you had it all." Smithsonian Institution

them fly to 8,000 and 10,000 feet. I had them separated by 2,000 feet.

Alison found that visibility was not as good as he had hoped. He couldn't spot the bombers, so he had to rely on Hill's instructions over the radio until he made visual contact. He listened intently to the crackling noise in the headset as he looked for Baumler's P-40. "It was a nice moonlit night," remembered Hill, "and in those days the Japanese came in with their running lights on, because usually there was no opposition, no ground fire or anything."

Hill picked up the bombers and radioed to Alison, "Okay, they're coming in from north to south," wrote Cornelius and Short in *Ding Hao.*

Good [thought Alison]. *They've made a practice run, not anticipating what we have in store for them.* Alison rubbernecked all around as he crossed the field from east to west. He should have been able to see them to his left, but he could not see anything. Then the thought struck him—maybe they were not below him at all, maybe they were above at a higher altitude. He looked up, and sure enough, there they were.

Hill, waiting below "for what seemed like eternity," was hopeful that Alison would be able to make visual contact. Alison's radio message came through loud and clear to a relieved Hill. "I got them in sight. Watch the fireworks!"

Hill observed a little string of tracers come from the bomber back toward Alison's plane. "And then all of a sudden those six .50s of his just lit up the sky, and I thought, *Oh, Christ, what's happening?*"

Suddenly the Japanese bomber burst into flame and slowly turned on its back and spun crazily toward Hengyang. Hill watched Alison continue his attack on a second bomber.

He moved over, there was a second bomber, you could see it from the flash of the first bomber, and he moved over on that and got that one—it burned too. The first one hit about 100 yards from me. The third one turned north and there was a big burst of flame

Japanese planes on fire after the surprise raid on Shinchiku on Thanksgiving Day, 1943. Within 12

minutes the attack destroyed or severely damaged more than 40 Japanese planes. Luke Kissick

in the night sky about 10 miles north of the field. Ajax had picked that one up and got it.

Hill soon noticed that something was wrong with Alison's plane. He could see it and it was not flying normally. Every now and then it would stream fire that was more than just backfire. He could hear the engine missing badly.

Alison called in that he was hit, but he would try to land his ship on the field. Hill watched him attempt to land.

He came in high and I could see him silhouetted and he couldn't get it down. The field at Hengyang was very short, only 900 meters, so he poured the coal to it, and when he did the engine quit, so I thought that was the end of the line for John Alison.

Just as Alison was attempting to land Hill was informed that another wave of Japanese planes was coming in. "So I ran and jumped into an airplane, and I still had that damn Burmese loincloth on, and I take off and I just clear the field and a big stick of bombs explode[s] across the runway behind me."

Turning north, after his narrow escape, Hill began to climb, looking for the enemy bombers. Not being able to locate the Japanese planes, he decided to return to the field at Hengyang.

Hill made his approach and had just put his landing gear down.

And a stick of bombs explodes across the runway right in front of me, and I almost spun in. I pulled up and poured the coal on. They informed me over the radio that the Japanese bombs had knocked out some of the runway. So what I did was lean it back as much as I could and circled around until I could see what in the hell I was doing.

Finally, at 0600 hours, Hill felt it was light enough to land. After touchdown he gathered with Colonel Scott and other pilots to discuss the battle. "I remember Tex Hill shaking his head," wrote Scott, "and saying, 'I'm afraid Johnny didn't make it. Dog-gone, he was a good boy.'"

Scott sent Captain Wang, the salvage man, out to see if he could get any news of Major Alison. Hill and Scott wrote out their reports and kept waiting on the alert. They had just about given Alison up for dead, wrote Bob Scott in *God Is My Co-Pilot.*

we heard the sound of sharp explosions. All of us ran to the alert shack, to see the strangest sight that we ever saw in China.

A procession had entered the field. The Chinese sentry had passed the crowd of people and was himself holding his thumb in the air calling, "Ding-hao-ding-hao." In the midst of the procession and surrounded by children shooting Chinese fire-crackers in celebration was a sedan chair carried on the backs of the villagers of Hengyang. And Johnny Alison was in the sedan chair—smiling.

Alison had a couple of burns on his hands and legs from Japanese explosive bullets and was a bit worse for wear. His plane had hit the river as if it were landing on a featherbed, and he had swum ashore. The Chinese had picked him up and treated him as the hero of the town.

Hill—relieved that his good friend was still in the land of the living—sat down to have a relaxing cup of tea, "and here [came] another alert; the Japanese [had] this big fighter sweep coming in."

The Japanese dove to the attack with thirty-five Oscars in a widespread, loose V-formation. From the opposite direction came Hill with ten P-40s behind him. General Chennault, in his book *Way of a Fighter,* wrote of the battle that followed:

Tex singled out the Japanese formation leader and then ensued one of the strangest sights ever seen in air combat. "Tex" headed for the Jap leader in a head-on pass with both of them shooting and closing the range at better than 600 miles an hour. It was like a pair of old-fashioned Western gunmen shooting it out on the main street of some cow town. Watching from the ground a collision seemed certain. Neither would give an inch.

At the last second before the crash, the Jap pushed over into a steep dive. "Tex" barely brushed over his cockpit. The Jap trailed a thin plume of smoke. He must have been badly hit, for he circled over the field and then deliberately pushed over into a vertical dive, holding it until he crashed into a row of bamboo dummy P-40's parked on the field. It was the first Kamikaze on record.

Years later Hill recalled his head-to-head duel over Hengyang:

If I had not hit him we probably would have run into each other, but those heavy six .50s were just devastating.

But he hit right on the end of the damn runway— so I came in and landed, but boy I'll tell you, that was a long day.

Hill put in a good number of long days during the defense of Hengyang. "Tex flew himself to a frazzle during those critical days," wrote Chennault. "He stayed on only because somebody ha[d] to finish the dirty job."

During the Japanese blitz against Hengyang, Hill flew alone to Hankow one night to dive-bomb the airdrome and give the other pilots a rest from the enemy raids that interrupted their sleep. Hankow was then the most heavily defended target in China. Hill's raid kept the Japanese too busy to bomb Hengyang that night.

To Hill this daring one-man mission was nothing special.

I was just testing the feasibility of dive-bombing at night. It was a bright, moonlit night and I just followed the river that led straight up to Hankow.

I just felt that I could do it and I tried it. I kept a few of them up at night and made them know we could get at them.

For his solo mission Hill was awarded the Silver Star.

On September 2 Hill and Scott led a flight of sixteen P-40s on a mission to Lake Puyang Hu, near Nanchang. The object of that mission was to attack river craft hauling rice to the front and evacuating troops on the return trip.

Hill's flight opened the attack by diving on a fleet of Japanese sailboats and junks. His flight of P-40s found twenty-six junks and steel barges. "They sank some and saw others with their sails on fire, floating for shore where the hungry Chinese coolies would salvage the rice."

During the air battle that followed the attack, Lt. Henry Elias, a popular pilot of the group, was lost.

"Through the four passes at the Japanese, Elias was right on Tex's wing, but on the fourth pullout he dropped behind the formation." Elias was intercepted by three Japanese planes and shot one down before his plane was heavily damaged, forcing him to bail out. As Elias floated to earth the remaining two Japanese planes machine-gunned him to death.

After Elias' death, "all of us watched for Japs bailing out," wrote Colonel Scott, "so that we could shoot one or two down for Elias, but we didn't get the chance."

During all of this time, the CATF was under-supplied. "P-40s were flying on oil that had been refiltered until it was barely usable. Tail wheel tires were also in short supply and pilots flew combat missions with rags stuck inside their casings." By early September the CATF was down to thirty-eight pilots and thirty-four flyable P-40s distributed among four fighter squadrons.

Yet newspaper stories being released in the United States made it sound as though a large American air force was operating in China. The September 27, 1942, *New York Times* carried the following story:

With the American Air Forces in China, September 27 (AP)

Resuming their air offensive against the Japanese after a lapse of nearly a month, the American Air Force in China strafed troop columns in Southwest Yunnan Province yesterday after having made another of their attacks on Hanoi in French Indochina the day before, Lieut. General Joseph W. Stilwell's headquarters announced today.

Hill flew like a man possessed during those critical days. He carried out mission after mission when he should have been in a hospital sickbed.

I had chronic malaria. I was carrying around a high fever, I felt like hell all the time. I didn't even know what it was until a little old Chinese gal took a blood sample—took it out of my ear. She opened a book and showed me what I had, what she saw

P-40 with rocket launchers at Kweilin, China. With these launchers the P-40 could carry six rockets weighing 50 pounds each. Luke Kissick

under the microscope. I was down to 147 pounds and at 6 feet 2 inches I was pretty thin.

It was clearly time for Tex Hill to return to the United States for rest. He had been in continuous combat for a year. However, Clayton Bissell, the commander of all the American air units in China, delayed Hill's return home, according to Chennault in *Way of a Fighter*.

> Bissell bluntly informed me that he sitting in Delhi, was a better judge of a CATF fighter pilot's condition than I was, and he forced AVG veterans Tex Hill and Ed Rector to stay in China an extra month after they were both ill with malaria and dysentery.

On November 30 Major Hill left the CATF to return home to the United States. After eighteen months overseas with the AVG and USAAF, he was in need of a well-deserved rest. He called his squadron together for a final talk before returning home, "and those who knew him knew he was not a man to waste words. He said what every man who worked for him hoped he would say—'If possible, I would like to return to the 75th after my leave.'"

Major Hill returned to the United States in December and was assigned to Eglin Field, Florida, as a proving ground group commander.

This choice assignment lasted until General Chennault called Hill one night from China and asked him to return, this time as commander of the 23rd FG. At Chennault's request Hill was released to return to China for a second tour of duty.

In early November 1943 twenty-eight-year-old Lt. Col. David "Tex" Hill assumed command of the 23rd FG from Lt. Col. Norval C. Bonawitz. At this stage of his life Hill had proven himself as both a pilot and a squadron commander with the AVG and CATF; now he would be subjected to the pressures and responsibilities of commanding the many flights and squadrons that make up a fighter group.

At 6 feet 2 inches the new group commander was an imposing figure. "He was tall and lanky," recalled Sam Palmer, who flew P-38s in Sicily and China. "He was blonde, good-looking, handsome." Luther C. "Luke" Kissick, the 74th Squadron intelligence officer, said Hill was "long and tall, with a shallow face; he was a slow, deliberate type who was always thinking. He looked you straight in the eye and shot from the shoulder very definitely."

To the men of the 23rd FG Hill was something of a legend. He was the AVG and US Air Force all rolled into one. "The pilots respected Tex Hill very highly," wrote Kissick. "They had explicit faith in him. He was an easy-going type, really down to earth; he was not after glory for himself, he was just interested in doing the job."

Hill's presence inspired confidence. It could be said of him that which was written of Union general Winfield Scott Hancock during the Civil War: "One

felt safe to be near him."

"He took care of you even on the ground," recalled Gen. Wiltz Segura, who flew with the 75th Squadron in World War II. "If you flew and fought you were a member of the team and he never forgot that. I don't think he ever forgot a man who flew with him or worked for him. . . . I've served thirty years in the Air Force under many commanders—he was the best! . . . Some guys you have confidence in, some you don't."

Hill had come to China seeking adventure and now, in November 1943, he would find responsibility and the stress of command. He was ready for command, however, even if the last two tours of duty in China had taken a physical and mental toll. His poise, courage, common sense and intensity of purpose gave him an abundance of the quality of leadership, and officers and crew members turned to him instinctively.

Don Lopez, in his classic book of the China air war *Into the Teeth of the Tiger*, wrote of his first meeting with Hill as 23rd Group commander:

> I had read about Tex Hill in *God Is My Co-Pilot*. He was one of my heroes, so I was somewhat over-awed at the prospect of meeting him. He put one at ease immediately. I entered his office, came to attention in front of his desk, and started to salute when a long arm snaked out, grabbed my hand, and shook it before I could complete the salute. He was a tall, lean man who looked like a Texan. His office was stark. Two chairs and a desk with an in-basket and an out-basket made up the whole complement. There were no papers in sight—the in-basket was full of peanuts, and the out-basket full of empty shells. China was a most informal theater. Tex Hill was obviously one who led by example and not by the trappings of military rank or by paper work. . . . His air of quiet confidence was infectious.

Charlie Cook, who flew more than 100 combat missions in China, recalled with amazement a premission briefing held by Hill that may have been the shortest of World War II.

> One time we were preparing for a mission with about forty-five P-40s and sixteen B-25s, and that was a major mission for China. You have seen the movies and read about the wonderful lengthy briefings that took place in Europe. Tex Hill called us into the alert shack and said, "Follow me, fellows!" That was the briefing.

The 23rd FG was part of the Fourteenth Air Force, the forgotten air force of World War II. Conceived in adversity, fighting an air war largely ignored by the media, and overshadowed by the air battles in Europe and the Pacific, the Fourteenth Air Force helped to achieve America's strategy of keeping China in the war.

Though it was numerically small, the Fourteenth Air Force had a large responsibility. It covered southeastern and central China, the South

China Sea, Haenan, Formosa, North Burma and Thailand. It assisted the Tenth Air Force in guarding the air supply route over the Himalayas, aided the Chinese ground operations, and attacked the Japanese Air Force and shipping in accordance with the primary mission of preserving Chinese territory as a base for possible future attacks on Japan itself.

While planning missions in China, Hill and his superiors had to consider the ever-present problem of supply. Japanese ground advances virtually sealed off China from sources of supply by land during the war. The only route for supplies was across the rugged Himalayas, whose peaks scratched the top of the sky at altitudes of up to 18,000 feet.

The Burma Hump fooled everyone, including Henry "Hap" Arnold, chief of the Army Air Corps. He thought a heavy bomber, like the B-24, could fly a combat mission after four transport trips back to India for gasoline. Experience proved him wrong. It usually took nine or ten trips back to India to store up enough gas for one bomber, like the B-24, to fly one mission against enemy targets in China. A 4 inch pipeline was eventually laid from India along the Burma Road and completed as far as Kunming—by the summer of 1945—but by that time the war was almost over.

The men who flew the Hump to haul personnel and supplies to the air squadrons in China were mostly from the Air Transport Command and several combat cargo squadrons. These men were fighting a war just as hazardous as that of the bomber crews and fighter pilots in China.

Maj. Pappy Herbst in his P-51, Tommy's Dad. *Herbst commanded the 74th Squadron, 23rd FG. He had flown with the RAF against the Germans and shot down one German plane. Herbst became the leading ace of the Fourteenth Air Force with 18 victories.* Luke Kissick

During the three years of Hump operations, the Air Transport Command delivered 736,374 tons of war materials to China. This operation cost 594 airplanes of all types that crashed into the mountains, were shot down or were forced down by bad weather. This was nearly as many aircraft as the Fourteenth Air Force lost in its three years of combat. The cost in lives was also staggering: 910 crewmen and 130 passengers. Of those who went down on a Hump flight, only seventy-five were ever rescued.

Because of the difficulty in transporting materials and supplies over the Hump, the Fourteenth was primarily a low-level air force. Supplies were always lacking, and when a bridge had to be knocked out, the Fourteenth couldn't afford the European practice of assigning a group of heavy bombers to plaster it from high levels with hundreds of tons of bombs. It had to send a single B-25 to ram home a pair of 1,000 pound bombs from 200 feet, where it would be hard to miss.

Receiving adequate supplies was not the only concern facing Tex Hill when he assumed command of the 23rd FG. He and Col. Casey Vincent, commander of the 68th Composite Wing, began planning a deep-penetration, surprise raid against Formosa's Shinchiku Airdrome, in the northwest part of the island of Formosa (now Taiwan). Shinchiku was one of the largest Japanese air bases on the island.

Hill recalled the planning that went into the mission:

> We had been flying recon missions over Formosa for six months prior to the raid. We tried to figure out how we could get to Formosa because it was such a lucrative target.
>
> We knew the Japanese had some 100 fighter aircraft on the field, and there were close to 100 bombers stationed there.
>
> There was extreme secrecy attached to the mission because we were planning to make the long trip across the straits of Formosa on the deck to avoid detection by Japanese radar.
>
> Everything depended on surprise, and had the Japanese gotten any early detection we would have been caught down on the deck and been easy game for them.

The raid on Shinchiku would be a typical Fourteenth Air Force mission. A small group of fighters and bombers would fly a daring hit-and-run operation against a superior force. The Americans would rely on surprise and tactics to defeat the Japanese.

The dangers involved in attacking the large and well-defended island of Formosa were well known. Formosa was the key to the inner defense circle of the Japanese Empire, second only in importance to Japan itself. It was the main transshipping point in the Japanese supply chain to the Southwest Pacific. If the daring attack failed, precious planes and highly skilled personnel—all irreplaceable—would be lost. But Colonel Vincent believed that with Hill commanding the mission his pilots could pull it off.

Hill would lead the strike with an American force consisting of fourteen B-25s, eight P-38s and eight P-51As. The plan was for the P-38s to go in first, followed by the B-25s, which were to approach the target dropping fragmentation clusters, the most effective bombs against aircraft on the ground. The P-51s would come in last to "mop up" anything still not smoking—or still flying in the traffic pattern—that the others had missed.

Hill and his men jumped into high gear when they received a report from the weather forecasters that Thanksgiving Day would be clear. On November 22 and 24 reconnaissance planes brought back pictures of Shinchiku, revealing more than eighty aircraft, mostly medium bombers, on the field.

On Thanksgiving Day, 1943, the men who would participate in the mission were awakened at 0315 hours. Not until the briefing at 0830 hours was the target revealed to the air crews.

The briefing was handled by Captain Nichols, Lieutenant Colonel Wells, Lieutenant Colonel Hill, Lieutenant Colonel Branch and Lieutenant Colonel McMillan. As part of the briefing all bomber crews and fighter pilots were shown maps and recon photos of the target. The pilots and crews were also informed that it was 424 miles to the target, including a 94 mile sweep on the deck over the Formosa Straits.

Famed war correspondent Theodore H. White, who would cover the mission from a B-25, attended the premission briefing, and wrote in his book *In Search of History:*

> The men shifted uneasily as they learned that there was just enough gas to reach the Japanese base and get back to refuel at Kweilin. Success, said the briefing officer, depended on three things: surprise above all, for if the Japanese had 5 minutes warning they could rise from their fields to overwhelm us; next, weather—a cold front and clouds were coming down from the north; and last, pinpoint navigation—Shinchiku lay by the shore, and we must make landfall directly on target, for an error of navigation of even 1 degree would let the Japanese get their fighters aloft.

The raid was launched from Suichwan, 250 miles east of Kweilin, in east central China. Making good time, the American strike force crossed the China coast shortly before noon.

All three squadrons crossed the straits of Formosa on the deck to avoid detection by Japanese radar. Hill remembered the trip across the straits:

> The B-25s were to do the navigation. It was a pretty hairy trip in retrospect because there was 100 miles of water there that we crossed in single-engine airplanes, with no Mae West, to hit a target, and

then 100 miles back. That's a pretty good little risk. However, at the time we never thought anything of it because we never had any Mae Wests and it's only in retrospect that I kind of break out in a sweat thinking about it.

As soon as the coast was sighted, all aircraft began to climb from the deck to at least an altitude of 500 feet. In spite of strong northerly winds over the straits, which made navigation difficult, the American strike force hit the target area right on the nose and achieved complete tactical surprise.

Maj. Sam Palmer and his P-38 group hit the target area first, flying 30 seconds ahead of the other American planes. The P-38s, now flying up at 1,500 feet, were in luck as they arrived over Shinchiku. Palmer recalled the sweep over the target in an interview with the author:

> We hit the target right on time, as the Japanese were in the landing pattern . . . but I never saw so many damn airplanes in my whole life. The Japanese didn't land like the Americans did—they would string out and then make the turn in. Those planes were strung out 15 miles, I guess, one behind the other, and you had all kinds of targets.
> I just cut back speed because the Japanese planes were going rather slow, and a lot of them had their landing gear down.
> We just dropped right over and we had a little

Gen. Casey Vincent and Tex Hill at Kweilin, China, in 1944. "Casey Vincent," wrote Tex Hill, "was the kind of guy that would have made a hell of a Chief of Staff of the United States Air Force. He had everything going for him, and has never gotten the proper recognition he deserves. The entire weight of that Chinese war was on his shoulders at the age of 29." Tex Hill

altitude on them and we just started right down the line firing.

The first two I hit went right on down. One Jap even stuck his head out of the airplane and was looking back. . . . I was on his left coming in and I saw the damn window of the Betty open and I saw his head. He was so damn amazed. After I hit it, the bomber went down in flames.

Then we split up into twos and we went right down on the deck and I could see the fighters trying to take off and I was strafing the bombers that were lined up until I was almost out of ammunition.

The P-38s were followed by the B-25s, which were spread out fourteen abreast as they swept across the field. The B-25s plastered the hangars and parked aircraft with string after string of fragmentation bombs, destroying and damaging aircraft and facilities and causing innumerable casualties to personnel, still trying to take cover.

Theodore H. White, a correspondent for *Time* magazine, was a passenger in the B-25 piloted by Wells. White, who would later write the famed Making of the President series of books, viewed the sweep across Shinchiku out of the side blister of the bomber and described the scene in his book *In Search of History.* "The P-38s had preceded us over the airport by a matter of seconds, diving to strafe the field. . . . I counted fourteen Jap planes burning, bursting outward like brilliant rosebuds and then flowering into orange and black coronas."

Col. Tex Hill greets Gen. Claire Chennault on the latter's arrival in New Orleans in 1945. Chennault was not invited to the Japanese surrender. Of this intentional oversight he wrote in Way of a Fighter: *"I left China full of anger and disappointment. For eight long years my sole ambition was to defeat the Japanese and now I was deprived of participation in that final victory."* Tex Hill

John Stewart, flying a P-51, gave this description of the surprise attack:

This was my first mission in a P-51A. Of course we carried drop tanks under each wing and were still on the drop tanks when we reached the Formosa coast. As we climbed to 500 feet I dropped my tanks along with the others but failed to switch the external tanks and made my strafing run on a dead engine. So I'm going across Shinchiku on a windmilling prop. If you want to know how long it takes to hit all the switches in a P-51 cockpit, it takes 11 seconds because I hit all of them and the engine caught just as I fired at a Betty bomber parked on the field and blew it up, killing the surprised crew chief who was sitting on top of the fuselage.

Hill, flying a P-51A, shot down an olive-drab Oscar Mk 11 during the sweep across the field. He recalled that it was an easy kill.

We hit the airfield right on the nose. Sam Palmer was leading the P-38s and Preacher Wells was leading the B-25s. I remember, there was a Japanese transport plane coming north down the coast and I dispatched a P-38 over there to shoot it down, which it did.

Then we came in on the deck and the B-25s were equipped with fragmentation bombs and they pulled up to 1,000 feet and released them. It was an ideal situation. The Japanese bombers had apparently been on a mission and they were in a landing pattern coming in, so they had the gasoline trucks and personnel out on the field to receive the bombers.

God O'Mighty, the devastation was something!

The Japanese got seven fighters off during the raid and we shot all seven down.

The one I shot down had just taken off and pulled up on a steep left climbing turn and all I had to do was raise the nose of the P-51 and fire. I hit him and the plane just exploded.

Within 12 minutes the American strike force had destroyed between fifty and sixty aircraft in the air and on the ground and damaged others. Hundreds of the enemy were killed or wounded on the ground as the American planes shot up the field.

The strike force then regrouped and headed back out across the straits of Formosa, leaving Shinchiku in flames behind. It was not an entirely uneventful return flight for Hill, however.

I had a little trouble on the way back that scared me. During the raid I had a gun jam, and my guns were very hot from all the shooting. Of course, we were right on the deck going back, and I breathed a sigh of relief that the mission was accomplished, when I had a round of ammunition cook off in the hot barrel and I made a fast maneuver and almost went into the water.

Back in Kweilin Colonel Vincent was waiting for news of the mission. He had devised a code: if the mission was a failure, Hill was to call, "New York"; if it was a success, the code word was San Antonio,

Hill's hometown. Whoops went up in Kweilin as the Texas drawl of Colonel Hill came over the radio: "San Antonio—in a big way."

The Shinchiku raid was a huge tactical success that was accomplished without the loss of a single Fourteenth Air Force aircraft and with only minor damage to four B-25s and one P-38.

Because Formosa was considered part of the Japanese homeland, the success of the mission made the Japanese aware that they were vulnerable. "It was the first time," recalled Hill, "except for the Doolittle raid, that American air forces were able to bomb part of the Japanese homeland."

Robert Lee Scott in an interview with the author felt that the Shinchiku mission "was the greatest mission ever flown in China. It has never gotten the recognition it deserves."

Two Japanese versions of the raid were broadcast. One newscaster reported an attempted strike on the Shinchiku Airdrome in which the Japanese forced the raiders to turn back before reaching the field, shooting down two American aircraft. Another broadcaster reported that the American bombers were forced to jettison their bombs before reaching the target and all except one were shot down. To the Americans who monitored the Japanese broadcasts such exaggerated claims were additional proof that the Japanese had been severely jolted.

By leading the Shinchiku mission Hill displayed the type of leadership that made him popular among the pilots of the 23rd FG. He did not delegate authority or ask others to fly tough missions for him. "My theory on leadership was that you had to be the number 1 guy. Most people will tell you I didn't tell my men to do something—I said, "Let's go!" And guys liked that. If there was any kind of a tough mission I wanted to lead it."

On May 6, 1944, Hill took off in a P-51 from Kweilin. After staging at Lingling he joined Mustangs of the 76th Fighter Squadron to escort American bombers to Hankow. Hankow was the site of one of the main Japanese air bases in China and a heavily defended target. As the American strike force neared the target ten Oscars and Hamps were sighted. In the air battle that followed, Hill shot down one Japanese plane. This victory was one of the few he would claim while serving as the group commander. Although we would have enjoyed trying to add to his score of Japanese planes, Hill now found few opportunities for aerial combat.

You're restricted when you're a group commander. You have a lot of knowledge of future plans and you just can't fly anywhere. In the later days of the war we had to go into enemy territory to find the Japanese; they weren't coming over like they did earlier.

We knew that if anyone was captured, they would probably talk. As a matter of fact, our people were briefed to tell the Japanese what they wanted to know if captured. We knew the Japanese would use methods that would break anybody.

On May 22 Hill led eleven P-51s on a dive-bombing mission to Anking to attack a military storage area. The mission was successful, with a large fire bellowing up from the target. Twelve Japanese fighters were sighted east of the target but the Japanese chose not to attack, and, as night was setting in, the American planes returned to formation and headed home.

Sam Palmer, who led the P-38s on the Shinchiku mission, came to know Hill well while serving in China. Palmer flew with the 449th Fighter Squadron, which was formed from planes and pilots who volunteered to fly in from North Africa in July 1943.

After a tour of duty with the 449th Palmer left the squadron and moved to Kweilin, where he served as an operations officer under Tex Hill and Casey Vincent.

One major target of the Fourteenth Air Force was Hong Kong. Palmer and Hill spent many long hours working out the details of the air raids on this lucrative target. "Tex and I would plan. We would get information [about] which Japanese boats were in the harbor through the Chinese intelligence net. We were also getting information from John Birch."

Skip bombing was one technique used by Fourteenth Air Force planes against Japanese shipping in Hong Kong Harbor. This technique was not always effective, however, according to Palmer.

We thought skip bombing would be an effective technique. . . . We would strafe with the P-40s and P-51s—one from one side and one from the other—crisscrossing from the front of the boat to the back of the boat, then we'd come in from the side, skip bombing with the P-38s with 500 pound bombs.

We first started using 1 second fuses in the first missions and the damn bomb would skip and go right on through the damn big boat, come out the other side and be chasing us, then explode. We got down to a 1/10 second fuse that would explode as soon as it hit. We had to use a different diving angle to do this and a few of the bombs would skip right over the ship.

Going back to the drawing board, Palmer and Hill worked on the skipping and timing skills until they thought they had the technique down. They ended up using a modification of the attack method Palmer had practiced in North Africa. The Japanese were averse to having their ships sunk by low-flying planes, however, and they countered with a novel defense described by Palmer: "The Japanese would fire a mortar shell with cables and they'd fire those up and have a parachute attached and the cables would dangle and you'd run right into them, so you would have to break off your attack right quick or the cables would cut your wings off."

Despite the strong Japanese defenses around Hong Kong, it was an important Fourteenth Air

Force target. General Chennault described the campaign that laid siege to Hong Kong in his book *Way of a Fighter*.

> For three years we pounded it with an ever-increasing weight of bombs. We mined the harbor, skip and dive bombed shipping in the roadstead, pounded the docks, oil storage tank farms, and shipyards from high altitudes and strafed Kaitak and Sanclair Island airdromes. When Major General Festing led the British occupation forces into Hong Kong in the summer of 1945 he found the harbor clogged with sunken ships and all but one of the five major dock areas knocked out by our long campaign against the port.

Much of the work Palmer did with Vincent and Hill took place at Kweilin, China. Even though Kweilin was the headquarters of Vincent's 68th Composite Wing, it was not immune from Japanese attack. Palmer remembered many of the Japanese raids on Kweilin:

> The Japanese would come over at night on harassment raids. They would drop those saki bottles. They would dump out cases and cases of empty bottles; the bottles would fall and they'd whistle like hell; they just made a mournful goddamn whistle. Then maybe in the midst of it they'd drop a bomb with a delayed fuse on it. Damn thing might have a 5 second, 30 second, minute or hour delayed fuse mixed up with all those damn bottles.

A Fourteenth Air Force reunion in Chinatown, New York City, October 1957: Luther C. Kissick (intelligence officer, 74th Fighter Squadron), Mrs. Clinton D. Vincent (wife of 68th Composite Wing commander), Paul Frillman (AVG chaplain and intelligence officer)—bottom, left to right; Lt. Col. Michael Lucky, Col. Ed Rector and Col. David Lee "Tex" Hill—top, left to right.

> Then in 15 minutes a bomb would go off, 30 minutes later another would go off, and they just had the damn ground crews sleepless, tired. We just couldn't get maintenance or anything else. The guys were right on the edge—they damn near destroyed us mentally.

If the night raids on Kweilin were an annoyance to Hill, the well-planned Japanese Ichigo Campaign proved to be a major headache.

This Japanese offensive began in April 1944. Its main goals, which were to be achieved in five months, were to force the Fourteenth Air Force to withdraw from its air bases in eastern China and to open secure land communications to the Japanese Southern Army located in French Indochina.

An estimated 80,000 well-equipped Japanese veterans began the offensive, and as the campaign progressed, reserves totaling 120,000 were committed, making it the largest Japanese offensive since the Sino-Japanese War began.

In the early stages of the offensive the Japanese advanced down waterways in powered landing barges, sampans, double- and triple-decked river steamers supported by gunboats, and light destroyers. On land, along the eastern flank of the offensive, cavalry spearheads led the advance, supplied by motor convoys and packhorse trains.

During the first months, the weather was so bad that the Japanese relied upon it for protection against air attack and moved openly during the daylight hours. The Japanese commanders expected the poor weather conditions to ground the USAAF.

Ignoring the dreary weather conditions, the fighter-bombers of Hill's group launched an all-out aerial attack against the advancing Japanese. The casualties suffered by the Japanese during this part of the campaign were immense. A mission flown by Don Lopez on June 26, 1944, is described in his book *Into the Teeth of the Tiger*:

> In the morning, I took part in an eight-plane offensive reconnaissance mission . . . where a large movement had been reported by Chinese intelligence. The weather was marginal, which gave us a better chance of finding the troops on the move. They usually stayed under cover during daylight in good weather. Sure enough, we surprised a force of more than a thousand infantry soldiers leading hundreds of supply-laden horses. They were in the worst possible location—in a deep, several mile-long railroad cut, with steep, almost vertical sides. We were carrying the ideal bomb load for this situation—parafrags. The first flight dropped its frags at the front end of the column, and the second flight dropped theirs in the rear, temporarily stopping either forward or rearward movement . . . all eight planes strafed at once. The troops were so tightly packed in the narrow cut that it was virtually impossible to miss them. We flew up and down that cut, strafing until the two flights expended all of their 10,000 rounds of ammunition,

leaving a mountain of dead and dying men and horses. . . . Two flights from another squadron were diverted to the railroad cut. They arrived soon afterwards and continued the slaughter. Probably because of our deep enmity toward the Japs, no one ever expressed anything but satisfaction at the success of a mission like this, except that the pilots regretted having to kill the horses. Killing the men bothered no one.

As August began the tension and strain from weeks of continuous combat were reflected in the faces of Hill and his commanding general, Vincent. "There was no question of finding targets," remembered Luke Kissick in an interview with the author. "Many pilots were flying five to six missions per day, burning up gun barrels; we were just slaughtering them as fast as we could, but we couldn't do it fast enough to stall the drive."

After a forty-nine-day battle Hengyang fell to the Japanese. The fall of Hengyang simplified the task of the Japanese. The northern Japanese armies could now launch an attack toward Lingling and the main American air bases at Kweilin and Liuchow.

At the American bases, built at a great expense of time, money and human power, American GIs and Chinese coolies dug holes in the runways and planted 500 and 1,000 pound bombs and tramped down the earth over them. These would be used to deny the bases to the advancing Japanese.

On September 14 generals Stilwell and Chennault came to Kweilin for a last conference with General Vincent. After much discussion Stilwell approved the decision to blow the airfield and retreat.

Early on September 15 demolition teams began blowing up the airstrips at Kweilin. The demolition experts left one airstrip temporarily untouched so that the two American planes that remained at Kweilin could take off.

As the early morning sun began to creep over the horizon Vincent and Hill finished packing. A last-minute check turned up a stock of six bottles of bourbon, which, after an extremely short discussion, they decided to bring along. The bourbon, which had undoubtedly been used for medicinal purposes, was felt to be too valuable to leave for the Japanese.

As Vincent and Hill walked to the flight line they were rocked by concussions from the exploding bombs planted earlier by the American demolition teams. The early morning sky was bright red from the roaring flames and burning buildings; it was a scene of destruction that could have been used as a backdrop for Dante's *Inferno*.

Arriving at the waiting B-25, Vincent took the pilot's seat, with Hill crouching down behind him. Also aboard was *Time* correspondent Teddy White, who, after witnessing the destruction of the air base, wrote, "That night was a wild and wonderful thunder-popping, flame-streaked, explosion-rocked orgy of destruction that is the most scarlet and brilliant night of my memory." At 0530 hours the B-25 lifted up off the one remaining airstrip, and Vincent and Hill left Kweilin for the last time.

The Japanese offensive had forced Hill and his pilots out of Kweilin. Eventually the Japanese would capture all the East China airfields, but only at a tremendous cost. Driven from East China, the Fourteenth Air Force would continue air attacks on Japanese troops and shipping from other Chinese bases until the end of the war.

One of Hill's last combat missions in China was flown in a P-51B. This was the first time that he had flown the P-51B in combat and he expected great things from the Mustang.

I remember we had this fight over Hong Kong because I figured we were really going to eat them up down there in our P-51s. . . .

We arrived down in the Hong Kong area and the first thing I know I see three enemy aircraft up there I couldn't identify. I knew they were Japs, but I'd never seen that type [of plane] before. We called them out and turned into them, and as we pulled up into them, why, they went straight up and I could see we were going to stall out and so I bent it over. These guys came right down on top of us and shot down the three guys who were with me, and they chased me all the way down to 8,000 feet, which was the altitude I needed to get back over some hills.

I swear I believe this Jap was trying to overrun me in a dive. His tracers were really going by my head. When I got back I talked to the old man [Chennault], telling him about this new type of Japanese fighter, which was later identified as a Zeke 52, or Tojo. . . . I told him, "Well, I don't know, there's a new type here. I don't know if we're going to be able to beat these guys in the air." And Chennault thought awhile and very characteristically . . . said, "Well, Tex, don't worry about that. Get them on the ground; then you don't have to fight them in the air."

On October 18, 1944, after flying more than 150 missions as a member of the AVG and 23rd FG, Hill left China, for the last time, to return to the United States. "I was unhappy to come home the second time," Hill recalled, "because I wanted to be in on the final assault against the Japanese."

The Ichigo Campaign had taken its toll on Hill. He had suffered many sleepless nights and unbearable tension as he and his men labored to stop the Japanese. Robert Scott, who had preceded Hill as a commander of the group, described Hill's appearance upon his return to the United States in his book *God Is My Co-Pilot:*

His hair had thinned in those two bitter years. His body was now tense and coiled like a spring. . . . He had used up his reserve of energy, as well as his reserve of healthy flesh. Both of them had drained away from him until he was so tired and thin that he appeared gaunt. His eyes were too bright; a kind of fire of tiredness glowed in them, the weariness of a man who has seen too much and felt too much and endured too much for one person.

Upon return to the United States Hill was assigned to the 412th FG, the first jet group in the USAAF, where he became group commander. He left the USAAF in July 1946 and joined the Air National Guard. He was appointed brigadier general and was the youngest one-star general in the history of the Guard. He was decorated by the Chinese government seven times and was awarded the British Flying Cross by Lord Edward Halifax. Hill's American decorations included three Distinguished Flying Crosses, two Air Medals, the Silver Star, the Legion of Merit and the Presidential Unit Citation.

Hill has been portrayed in several movies dealing with the air war in China. Perhaps the most famous of these is *Flying Tigers* with John Wayne.

David "Tex" Hill holds a painting of AVG P-40s downing Zeros over China. "Toward the later part of the AVG days we ran into Zeros. They were good airplanes, "but so were the I-97s. Those damn things, I mean the Jap pilots could wrap that thing in front of your face."

The movie was the brainchild of two members of the AVG who were dishonorably discharged: Larry Moore and Ken Sanger. "John Wayne didn't use my actual name in the movie," remembered Hill, "but his character was based on me. It's a terrible movie, but it will play forever. I still enjoy watching the movie; it's corny as hell!"

Even though he put his life on the line many times in actual combat and watched many good friends die in battle, Hill harbored no ill feelings toward the Japanese.

I never had any personal animosity towards the Germans or the Japanese. I was president of the American Aces Fighter Association and I invited all those guys over here. And, hell, we get to drinking whiskey and telling war stories and it's been wonderful.

Those Japanese pilots were just targets. Saburo Sakai, the great Japanese ace, gave me a damn Zero that I wear on my sport coat, a Zero pin that has a little diamond in it, a little stainless-steel Zero.

His daughter was here and I took care of her while she was visiting. I had a little shindig when Saburo came down to visit his daughter. I got some of the local fighter aces together and he got up and made a speech and said, "There ought to be a better way for us to settle our differences than by killing each other."

I just couldn't agree with him more!

Hill went to China in 1941 as an obscure former Navy dive-bomber pilot. He returned home to the United States for the last time in October 1944, a much-decorated veteran of 150 combat missions. Though he fought in a forgotten theater of the war, his courage, patriotism and sense of duty have not been forgotten by those who knew and served with him. Gen. Robert Lee Scott took the measure of Hill when he said, "Tex Hill, to my mind, is one of the greatest Americans that ever lived, not only a great fighter pilot, but one of the great Americans."

Hill never sought greatness; he only strived to do his duty. That he achieved greatness was because of his fierce devotion to those he led and the cause of freedom. May America always be so fortunate in times of war or danger as to have people like Hill to defend it.

Chapter 9

Jim Howard, the One-Man Air Force

On January 11, 1944, Maj. James Howard of the 354th Fighter Group stood off thirty German fighters that were attacking B-17s of the 401st Bomb Group. For this incredible feat of bravery Howard won the Medal of Honor. He was the only fighter pilot in Europe to win this award during World War II. Before the war he left the Navy to join Claire Chennault's AVG and flew fifty-six missions in China while shooting down six Japanese planes. Later, while serving as squadron and group commander with the 354th FG, he downed six German planes. He left the Air Force after the war for civilian business interests. A brigadier general in the Air Force Reserve, he retired in Florida. Unless attributed to another source, all quotes are from a July 1991 interview with Jim Howard.

On January 11, 1944, bombers of the Eighth Air Force took off from their bases in England to attack the twin targets of Halberstadt and Oschersleben located in central Germany. The attack force consisted of 663 B-17 Flying Fortresses and B-24 Liberators, with a fighter escort of Spitfires, P-47 Thunderbolts, P-38 Lightnings and P-51 Mustangs.

As the bombers climbed for altitude and began to assemble into battle formation, Eighth Air Force Command watched the weather with growing concern. As the bombers began to fly toward the target area the weather worsened and the B-17s of the 3rd Bombardment Division and the B-24s of the 2nd Division were ordered to return to their bases in England. The 1st Division, at this time less than 100 miles from the target, was allowed to proceed.

Unfortunately for the attacking force, weather conditions over central Germany were good enough for the Germans to assemble a large force of defending fighters. The air battle that was about to be fought would be one of epic proportions. More than 200 German fighters, Me 109s, FW 190s and Me 110s (armed with rockets) would savagely attack the bombers and their fighter escort. The bomber formations would be subjected to some of the most concentrated rocket attacks by twin-engine aircraft so far experienced in the European air war.

As the leading elements of the bomber formation reached the target area the German fighters began their fierce attacks. P-51s of the 354th FG led by Maj. James Howard raced in to defend the bombers against the attacks. "When we started up the bomber stream they were extended for miles and miles," recalled Howard.

In the initial fighting Howard quickly became separated from the rest of his flight and found himself alone defending B-17s of the 401st BG from a vicious attack by German fighters. He gave the following description of his efforts to defend the bombers in his combat report found in Bill Hess and Tom Ivie's, *Fighters of the Mighty Eighth:*

> I discovered I was alone and in the vicinity of the forward boxes of bombers. There was one box of B-17s in particular that seemed to be under attack by six single and twenty twin-engined enemy fighters.
>
> . . . The first plane I got was a two-engined German night fighter. I went down after him, gave him several squirts and watched him crash. . . .
>
> After that a Focke-Wulf came cruising along beneath me. He pulled up into the sun where he saw me. I gave him a squirt and almost ran into his canopy when he threw it off to get out. He bailed out.
>
> . . . I saw an Me-109 just underneath and a few hundred yards ahead of me. He saw me at the same time and dropped his throttle, hoping my speed would carry me ahead of him. It's an old trick. I chopped throttle . . . and we went into a circle dogfight. . . .
>
> I dumped 20 degree flaps and began cutting inside him, so he quit and went into a dive with me

Jim Howard flew 56 combat missions and shot down six Japanese planes while flying with Claire Chennault's AVG in China. He became a member of the Ninth Air Force's 354th FG, which became the first outfit in England to be equipped with the North American P-51B Mustang. Smithsonian Institution

after him. I got on his tail and got in some long distance squirts from 300 or 400 yards. I got some strikes on him but I didn't see him hit the ground.

. . . Back up with the bombers again, I saw an Me-110. I shot at him and got strikes all over him. He flipped over on his back and I could see gas and smoke coming out—

I saw an Me-109 tooling up for an attack on the bombers. They often slip in sideways, the way this one was doing. We were pretty close to the bombers and I was close to him. I gave him a squirt and he headed down with black smoke pouring out.

I saw an Me-109 over on the starboard side getting in position to attack the bombers. I dived on him from where I was and got strikes all over him with my one gun. He turned over on his back and skidded out. He thought that he had lost me with the skid and he pulled into a 45 degree dive. I followed him down and kept on shooting.

I'd been with the bombers for more than an hour altogether by then and just before I left I saw a Dornier 217 coming alongside the bombers, probably to fire rockets. I dived on him and he left, but I never did fire a shot at him.

After breaking off the fight with the German aircraft Major Howard returned to his base. Upon landing and after inspecting his Mustang he found only one bullet hole, through the left wing.

Despite Howard's heroics, German fighter attacks relentlessly lashed the bombers of the 401st BG. More than 400 individual attacks were re-

ported by the 1st Division in 3½ hours. More than sixty bombers were lost in the battle.

As the air crews of the 401st BG returned to their base in England they began to talk about the courage and daring of a lone, unidentified P-51 pilot they had observed battling against the German fighters. The *401st Bomb Group History* published in 1946 gave the following account of the crew's comments:

The Mustang pilot was all by himself when one of the wing formations was attacked by a swarm of 30 to 40 German fighters. Instead of turning tail and abandoning the wing in the face of impossible odds the P-51 pilot sent his plane right into the midst of the Jerries. And for the next 20 minutes the Fortress crews were treated to one of the greatest exhibitions of sheer courage they have ever witnessed.

". . . It was a case of one lone American against what seemed like the entire Luftwaffe," said Lt. Col. Allison C. Brooks, who led the wing the Mustang pilot defended.

Singlehanded against those terrific odds he covered the wing all by himself. He was all over the wing, across and around it, and my gunners tell me he definitely shot down two of the enemy fighters while they were watching him. . . . For sheer determination and guts it was the greatest exhibition I've ever seen. They can't give that boy a big enough reward.

Lt. Col. Edwin W. Brown, pilot and squadron commander was equally lavish in his praise.

We don't know who he was [said Brown], but there isn't a one of us who wouldn't like to shake his hand. He's my idea of a hero.

The sight of him out there, all alone, surrounded by all those Jerries, trading punches right and left is something I'll never forget.

High-ranking Fighter Command officials were at first unsure of the identity of the lone pilot. It was only after they scoured the records that they were able to identify him as Howard.

The modest Howard played down his heroism, remarking in a July 1991 interview, "I'd seen my duty and I done it. I never saw thirty fighters all at once the way the bomber people tell it." After a thorough investigation of the battle Howard was given three confirmed kills for the day and awarded the Medal of Honor.

Word of Howard's exploits soon spread to the United States, and *Time* magazine for January 31, 1944, carried this account of his daring:

The bomber men who saw the beginning of the combat lost sight of the Mustang in a dive. It seemed little better than a 1-100 chance that such gallantry could have survived such odds. . . .

Correspondents who interviewed Major Howard found no daredevil youngster, but a lanky, quiet spoken, 30-year-old veteran air fighter with thinning reddish hair, a slow smile.

. . . Modest Howard's combat report last week claimed only two planes destroyed, two probables and one damaged. But the Confirmation Board which passes on his report may have the unusual duty of revising a victory claim upward. Shoptalking airmen in London this week understood Major Howard was being recommended for the Congressional Medal of Honor.

James Howard was born in Canton, China, and spent the first fourteen years of his life there; his father had been professor of ophthalmology at the Peking Union Medical College. After their long stay in China the Howards returned to the United States, where Doctor Howard was assigned to the Washington University Medical School in St. Louis, as head of the eye department.

Upon graduation from high school in St. Louis young Howard traveled west to enter college in Pomona, California. While he was attending Pomona College a recruiter came in to talk to any young men who might be interested in joining the service. Howard remembered the occasion:

There was an announcement made that this naval aviator would give us a talk in the small dining room. There were a group of us that went over and listened to him. Following his talk, I went

and took the physical exam and passed it. That put me on the list to go through what they call elimination flight training.

They had then what they called elimination flight training, where they would test these fellas and find out if they could really fly or not. If not they would bust them out and those that passed would go on to Pensacola.

After graduating from Pomona College Howard entered the Navy, receiving his wings in January 1939. After serving with a number of fighter squadrons he found himself assigned to the USS *Enterprise*, on which he served for over two years.

While fulfilling his duty on the *Enterprise* Howard decided to join the AVG, which was seeking volunteers to help defend the Burma Road. Duane Schultz, in his book *The Maverick War,* details Howard's reasons.

The chance of returning to my boyhood home in China, while defending the interests of America at the same time, was the opportunity of a lifetime. I couldn't have been in a better position at a better time. The nostalgia of going to China would be a strong incentive, but the overriding reason was my yearning for adventure and action.

A P-51B of the 353rd Squadron, 354th FG, is looked over by crewmen of the 401st Bomb Group in December 1943. The P-51 could outdive the German Me 109 and FW 190. Thus, for the first time in the war, the *Germans could no longer break off aerial combat at will with the familiar split-S and dive. The Mustangs forced them to fight and often followed them to their airfields.* Smithsonian Institution

In October 1941 Howard arrived in Rangoon to serve with Claire Chennault and the AVG. He recalled his first meeting with Chennault:

> He was a very gentle individual. He gave the appearance that he wasn't, but he was. He impressed us that here was a man who was able to take over, take charge. He had our problems at first but things started ironing out.
>
> We got rid of many of the malingerers who decided to come over and get the hell out of the service. Once they went all that was left were the pilots who were eager to get into combat and to do the job.

Chennault was well aware that the AVG would be facing heavy odds when it encountered the Japanese. To be prepared for this upcoming ordeal he instituted a vigorous two-month training period at Toungoo, north of Rangoon, that went far toward molding the inexperienced group into a first-class combat organization.

Chennault had been in China for years fighting the Japanese. He knew they were a worthy foe, but he also knew their weaknesses. To defeat the Japanese Chennault based his tactics on three elements: his men, his planes and the enemy. "His planes were obsolete by all American and European standards," wrote Robert Holtz in *With General Chennault.* "Only in the Orient were they fit for combat."

The P-40B Tomahawk was powered by a 1,150 hp Allison engine. The strong point of the aircraft was its six machine guns. Two heavy .50 caliber guns were mounted on the nose and synchronized to fire through the propeller blades. Four .30 caliber guns were mounted on the leading edges of the wings. The P-40D would have even more impressive firepower with six .50 caliber wing-mounted machine guns. "You just aimed it at a Jap plane and it just blew up," claimed Howard.

The P-40 could also take tremendous punishment and keep flying. The cockpit had two heavy slabs of steel armor, which covered the back of the pilot's head and the pilot's back. The self-sealing gas tanks were designed to take machine gun bullets without causing fire or excessive damage. "The P-40 was not a spectacular performer," wrote Bruce Holloway, a Fourteenth Air Force ace; "it was a rugged, simple, reliable craft which could take more punishment and get home more often than any other fighter of its era except perhaps the P-47."

Although the Japanese Zero was a superb combat aircraft, the principal advantage of the P-40 lay in its heavier firepower, additional protection for pilot and fuel, rugged construction and much higher diving speed. In his book *With General Chennault,* Holtz described the diving ability of the P-40:

> This incredible speed in a dive, which saved the skin of many an AVG pilot, resulted from the heavy engine and the addition of more than half a ton of armor, guns and equipment to the original P-40 design without altering the design to accommodate the added weight. With its nose down the Tomahawk picked up speed at an unbelievable rate. The additional weight which made this possible, however, cut down performance on climb and ceiling. The lighter Japanese planes had a rate of climb more than twice that of the Tomahawk. They could turn twice as fast and enjoyed the advantage of a higher ceiling.

As part of his training program, Chennault instructed the AVG pilots on the tactics and maneuvers used by the Japanese. He told his combat pilots, according to Holtz's *With General Chennault:*

> You will face Japanese pilots superbly trained in mechanical flying. They have been drilled for hundreds of hours in flying precise formations and rehearsing set tactics for each situation they may encounter. Japanese pilots fly by the book. They have plenty of guts but lack initiative and judgment.
>
> Their pursuits always pull the same tricks. God help the American pilot who tries to fight them according to their plans.

Chennault had organized the AVG into three squadrons. After the Japanese attack on Pearl Harbor he sent the 3rd Squadron, "Hell's Angels," to Rangoon to assist the RAF, and on December 19, 1941, the other two squadrons were ordered to Kunming.

During its first week in action the AVG began to build the extraordinary record that gave it fame. Its pilots destroyed fifty-five Japanese bombers and fighters while losing only five P-40s. This marked the first defeat of the war for the Imperial Japanese Air Force.

On January 1, 1942, the 2nd Squadron, "Panda Bears," was sent by Chennault to Rangoon to relieve the Hell's Angels. Howard was a member of the 2nd Squadron and the transfer to Rangoon gave him ample opportunity to see combat against the Japanese.

On January 3 Jim Howard and two other pilots, Jack Newkirk and Tex Hill, took off for a mission to attack Japanese airfields in Thailand.

The objective of the mission was TAK Airdrome on the Mae Nom Ping River, 300 miles to the east. Arriving over the enemy airfield, the three pilots could see rows of Japanese planes lined up neatly on the runway. Ground crews were busy servicing the planes for another raid. It was a lucrative target and the Japanese appeared to be caught off guard.

Diving to the attack, the three P-40s flashed across the field. "Newkirk, in the lead, wheeled just before the edge of the field to pick off a circling Nakajima." Howard, following, lined up his guns on a Japanese fighter that was taxiing for takeoff. He wrote in *Roar of the Tiger* "[I] gave it a 5-second burst of .30 and .50 caliber fire," he recalled. "A sudden billow of orange flame swallowed the plane."

One of the Nakajimas latched onto Howard's tail and started firing. Hill maneuvered behind the Japanese fighter and "shot the plane to pieces with a stream of machine gun fire." As Hill flew through the falling debris of the plane he found himself approaching another Japanese fighter head-on. Hill began firing and his six machine guns shot the lightly armored Japanese plane out of the sky.

As Howard flew over the field he noticed movement to his left. He relates the scene in his book *Roar of the Tiger:*

> A comic scene suddenly appeared. . . . Crowds of people on a grandstand were scrambling over themselves in a kind of wave to get out of the line of fire.
> I roared down the line of idling aircraft with my thumb on the firing button all the way. The machine guns left a wonderful line of destruction the length of that array of fighters.

Hauling back on the stick, Howard began to race away from the field. As the nose of the P-40 came up, a Japanese bullet smashed into his engine. "Smoke poured from the cowling and the screaming Allison went dead," wrote Howard in *Roar of the Tiger.* "My prop idled down until it was just a windmill."

In the distance Howard could see Hill and Newkirk dashing for home. Alone and with his air speed down to 90 mph, Howard, according to *Roar of the Tiger,* prepared to make a crash landing.

> I rolled back my canopy and tried to project my descent so that I would wind up at the far end of the field near the woods. If it worked out I could make a run for it into the trees.
> My hand was on the flap control when the Allison gave a tentative cough.
> I advanced the throttle a notch. She caught again! COME ON! . . . The engine picked up momentum and the prop started spinning faster.

Closing his canopy, Howard began the race for home. Looking around, he was startled to observe Japanese Nakajima fighters on either side of him. With his heart in his throat he flew alongside the Japanese several moments, wondering why they

Jim Howard, third from right, and other pilots of the 354th FG at Boxted. "The 354th Fighter Group called itself the Pioneer Mustang Fighter Group," recalled Howard, "and we developed a real fighting organization that ended the war with the greatest number of aerial victories of all the fighter groups in Europe." US Air Force

didn't attack. It suddenly dawned on him, he related in *Roar of the Tiger*, that the Japanese pilots "had their gaze fixed on the ground, engrossed in the confusion and disaster that had befallen their fellow pilots."

Applying maximum throttle, Howard set a course for Rangoon and soon left the Japanese planes far behind. Back at the air base Hill climbed from his P-40 and walked over to Howard. Hill related the conversation that followed in a 1989 interview:

"Good thing I shot that Jap off your tail, Jim," he said.

"Whose tail?" Howard asked. "There was nobody on my tail."

"Take a look at your plane, Jim. It's full of holes."

A close inspection of Howard's P-40 revealed eleven bullet holes. Walking over to check Hill's P-40, they counted thirty-three. It had been a close thing for both of them.

The Japanese made a sustained effort to wipe out the AVG and the RAF so that they could attack Rangoon unopposed. Using a number of tactics, including false orders broadcast in English over the AVG radio frequency and low-level formations of fighters slipping in to strafe the airfields, the Japanese attempted to wear down the morale of the AVG pilots.

During another Japanese attack on Rangoon, Howard and Newkirk led their flights against a big formation of Japanese bombers and fighters. Climbing to 12,000 feet, the Americans awaited the arrival of the enemy. As the Japanese approached, they split into two groups, one formation heading for Rangoon, the other for Mingaladon. Newkirk radioed Howard to take his formation and attack the Japanese headed for Mingaladon; Newkirk and his formation would defend Rangoon.

Howard related the action in his book *Roar of the Tiger*:

> I could see that a swarm of Nakajima fighters was flying top cover above and behind the bombers. As the huge formation advanced unrelentingly toward us it seemed an act of folly for our eight fighters to challenge it. It was an awesome sight. The twin-engine planes flew in fight formation and were camouflaged brown and green, the red ball of the Rising Sun blazoned on the upper and lower wing tips.
>
> . . . I banked and picked out three bombers on the lower left edge of the formation. As I closed at an estimated combined speed of about 500 mph I knew I would have only a few seconds in which to fire before passing the target. I threw on my gun switch and pressed the firing tit for a 3 second burst. My plane shuddered as I saw my tracers crisscross 300 yards ahead. The strikes showed as flashes, but I had failed to allow enough lead and most of my shots were above the planes. I pulled up in a steep chandelle. My speed had put me above the waiting enemy fighters. The other P-40s attacked head-on and two bombers started smoking on their way to fiery crashes.

After the first pass Howard and the rest of his formation found themselves above the Japanese fighters, which had gone into a protective Lufbery circle below. Howard put his P-40 into a steep dive and dove into the tail of one of the enemy fighters. Pressing home the attack, he gave the Japanese plane a long burst from behind, and it went down in a spiral.

The attack over, the AVG pilots returned to the field to tally up their score. The Japanese had lost six bombers and eight fighters. The AVG had suffered no losses and the bombing results were limited.

On another occasion Howard and his formation took off from Mingaladon and rendezvoused west of the field at 14,000 feet. Looking off in the distance, Howard could see about thirty Japanese bombers approaching the field and the glint from the sun on the protecting fighters above.

Like any good fighter pilot Howard had his neck on a swivel and looking down he was startled to see Japanese fighters strafing the Mingaladon field. He called to Newkirk over the radio and a

Col. Jim Howard being congratulated by Mr. R. M. Lovett after receiving the Medal of Honor for his heroics in defending B-17s of the 401st BG on January 11, 1944. One American bomber crewman described Howard in the 401st Bomb Group History as "one lone American taking on the entire Luftwaffe." Single-handed, Howard had fought off more than 30 German planes as they attempted to attack the American bombers. Smithsonian Institution

hasty strategy was devised. "Instantly," wrote Howard in *Roar of the Tiger*, "Jack responded over his radio, 'This is Newkirk. The 2nd Squadron will engage Jap fighters that are strafing our field. Let's dive and give 'em a dose of lead poisoning.'"

Diving from 10,000 feet, the P-40s roared to the attack. The Japanese—unaware of approaching disaster—continued to work over the field, having set fire to a Blenheim bomber and a parked truck.

As Howard approached the unsuspecting Japanese he saw that their planes were a different model than he had encountered before. He describes the action in *Roar of the Tiger*.

As I got closer to the ground I noticed that some of the planes were sleeker than the fixed-landing-gear Nakajimas. They were Zeros! As I continued my dive I approached a Zero from the rear and at 300 yards fired a long burst, causing the Zero to cartwheel into the ground, where it exploded. My closing speed was so great I had to haul back on the stick to avoid flying into the ground myself. As I did so another P-40 crossed in front of me on the tail of an already smoking Nakajima.

I heard Tex Hill yell, "I got one!"

Just then another Zero headed straight for the ground. The impact at the edge of the field caused a gigantic plume of flame. Planes were swirling all over. . . . The Japanese were no longer strafing—they were heading straight for the border.

Chasing a retreating Nakajima, Howard maneuvered behind his tail. Just as Howard was about to press the trigger the pilot pulled up in a half-loop and roll designed to bring him on Howard's tail. Countering the sudden Japanese maneuver, Howard nosed his plane down in a right spiral, his speed taking the P-40 far away from the Nakajima.

After landing, Howard found that the AVG pilots had accounted for two bombers and ten fighters, including two Zeros. Once again the Japanese had been foiled in their attempt to wipe up the AVG.

Flying and other duties forced Howard into a series of 20-hour days, so he was unable to drive to Rangoon and witness firsthand the destruction done to the city by the relentless Japanese bombing attacks.

As July 4 neared, the AVG was scheduled to go out of existence; the air war was slated to be taken over by the USAAF. A few AVG members would remain in China to serve as a replacement unit.

For Howard it was a difficult time: he had reached the end of his rope physically. He had come down with a mysterious ailment that caused him to be hospitalized. "It was some kind of skin disorder; I could press any place on my skin and water would squirt out." The doctor in charge of Howard's case ordered him to the hospital and after a few days of treatment the condition cleared up. To this day Howard is unsure of what the illness was.

Maj. Glen Eagleston of the 354th FG taxies his P-47D to the runway with a ground crewman on the wing guiding him. Jim Howard called Eagleston "a terrific character, and one of the great fighter pilots of all time." Eagleston finished World War II with 18.5 aerial victories. Smithsonian Institution

Jim Howard's contract with the AVG expired in July 1942 and he decided to return to the United States. Claire Chennault had wanted him to stay in China and had offered him the rank of major and command of his own squadron. "But I turned it down," recalled Howard, "because I was sick with a fever and wanted to return to the States."

Returning to the United States, Howard found letters from both the Army and the Navy offering him a set rank if he would join their respective services. After a short period of indecision Howard chose the USAAF and was sent out to Santa Ana and the Orange County Airport. There he was designated to take over a squadron of the newly formed 354th FG.

The 354th was the first group to join the newly formed Ninth Air Force. Commanded by Col. Ken Martin and trained on P-39s, the group was sent over to England on a troopship carrying more than 6,000 soldiers and airmen.

The group arrived in England on November 4, 1943, and soon learned it was to be the first fighter group to receive the highly touted North American P-51B Mustang, which it was to introduce into combat in Europe. Because of this the group later adopted the name The Pioneer Mustang Group.

The 354th FG was scheduled to fly its first mission on December 1. It was to be commanded by Lt. Col. Don Blakeslee, famous leader of the 4th FG. During the premission briefing Blakeslee was all business, wrote Grover Hall in *1,000 Destroyed*.

He explained we had three tactics to use against the enemy: (1) shoot down the enemy plane (or be shot down), (2) make the enemy fighter break off an attack first, (3) if the enemy fighter fails to break off, continue on a collision course.

We were stunned. Did he mean we should deliberately ram the enemy head-on?

Blakeslee hesitated for emphasis and then said, "We never turn away from a head-on attack. If we do, the word will get back to Luftwaffe pilots that the Americans break first in a head-on pass. They will then have a psychological advantage of knowing beforehand what we will do."

A young pilot in the front row asked what would happen if the German pilot followed the same orders. Blakeslee looked down at the young man with a contemptuous smile and said, "In that case you've earned your flight pay the hard way!"

Because of the Mustang's tremendous range and the need for fighter escort for the B-17s and B-24s of the Eighth Air Force, the 354th was assigned to long-range escort duty. The first mission of impact saw the Mustangs escort the heavy bombers 490 miles to Kiel, a new record for fighter escort.

On December 20 Howard's squadron provided support for an attack on Bremen, Germany. Flying at 24,000 feet, Howard spotted three Me 110s gearing up to attack the bombers. Jettisoning his belly tanks, he dove to the attack. One of the Me 110s turned into him and the two planes flashed toward each other head-on. Firing short bursts, Howard caused the German pilot to split-S away. Not wanting to leave the bombers, Howard broke off the attack.

Climbing back to the bombers, Howard and his wingman sighted an Me 109 flying below. Howard once again put his P-51, *Ding Hao!,* into a dive and pulled up on the unsuspecting German from dead astern. He related the action that followed in his combat report of December 29, 1945:

I noticed he carried what appeared to be a belly tank. It was a center tank, mounted on the fuselage and not the wings. This was the first Me 109 that I had seen, so I pulled up alongside to make positive identification. I was about 50 feet off to his right and about the same time I saw his markings and determined him to be a 109. He looked in my direction and saw me. He immediately rolled over in a diving turn to the left. I followed him and pulled inside his turn, gave him a burst of approximately 3 seconds, when he rolled over and went down in a dive. I did not follow him but returned to my position with the bomber.

When I returned to the bombers I observed two B-17s go down, evidently hit by flak. One was a direct hit, the effects of which caused the bomber to explode in the air and disintegrate into little pieces. The other one was on fire but stayed in formation for a time.

Flying with the bombers, Howard drove off three Me 109s that were making passes at the formation. Latching onto the tail of one of the 109s, he followed it through the bomber formation. Now above and slightly behind the German fighter, he closed in for the kill. He describes the action in his combat report.

I was positioned almost dead astern and gave him about four 2 to 3 second bursts, very little deflection. My hits seemed to be in the fuselage center and large clouds of black smoke began to pour out of his ship. I continued to fire until I passed through the smoke. Lieutenant Smith, who was flying my wing, saw pieces fly off the 109 and then the ship exploded. Smith flew right through the debris and his vision was obscured by the oil from the Me 109 covering his wind screen. The Me 109 went into a vertical dive and was last seen going straight down.

On January 5, 1944, the group escorted the bombers to Kiel. While over Haligoland the fighter pilots watched helplessly as a B-24 on fire exploded and disintegrated. Over the target they also observed a B-17 explode and three chutes open, all of which appeared to be on fire.

During the bombing run, the P-51s were busy thwarting rocket-firing Me 110s. One of these was downed by Lieutenant Hunt of the 354th. The pilots reported in a January 5, 1944, combat report the enemy as being extremely aggressive in their attacks, often approaching the bombers head-on "and using the strategy of attacking singly, rolling over on their backs and breaking down through on their attack." The pilots of the 354th were able to down sixteen enemy fighters during this mission without loss to themselves.

On February 11, during a support mission to Frankfurt, group commander Col. Ken Martin began a head-on attack on a German Me 109. Never wavering as he pressed home his attack, Colonel Martin's P-51 collided with the German 109 in a devastating head-on collision. The colonel managed to bail out but was captured by the Germans and became a POW for the rest of the war. On February 12 Col. Jim Howard was named the new group commander.

During March 1944, Howard had the opportunity to meet Gen. Dwight D. Eisenhower, the Supreme Commander of the Allied armies. Howard's version of the meeting was typically prosaic:

Why sure, in fact, I met Eisenhower and I have a picture of me shaking hands with him just before D-day. We had a display of planes that were to support the invasion. He requested along with many other fine muckamucks to inspect and view what we had. I had my P-51 there and I sat back and he came by and I was introduced as the holder of the Medal of Honor. We had quite a chat and he made some remark about the fact that in his early days he wished he could have been a fighter pilot.

Howard downed an FW 190 during an April 8 escort mission. The 354th was heavily engaged while defending the bombers. The group's intelligence report detailed the action:

Bombers hounded by 60 plus FW 190s and 15 plus Me 109s at 1320 in Vie of Wittiggen. When E/A [enemy aircraft] made their first pass on the bombers three bombers were seen to explode and three others seen spinning out of formation, many chutes were observed. Most E/A carried rocket guns and were very aggressive. All our combat took place north of Brunswick. Barrage type flak thought to be rockets was encountered over Celle and Heldesheim, no smoke seen, just hundreds of flashes, extremely accurate as to height over both places. One B-24 straggler escorted from T/6 area

Flak-damaged B-17 of the 398th BG; the bombardier was killed. Despite the fighter protection offered by the escorting Allied fighters, flak remained a danger to the bombers throughout the war. Smithsonian Institution

to Oldenburg, where heavy accurate flak was encountered, B-24 blew up, five men seen to jump, 3 chutes opened, 2 failed to open.

Slightly before D-day Jim Howard left the 354th FG to join Gen. "Pete" Quesada at Ninth Air France Headquarters to help plan invasion operations. Howard at first resisted General Quesada's invitation to join his staff but finally gave in to his pleadings. Howard later felt, "This was a big mistake, and although I went back to fly with the group several times, it just wasn't the same."

In September Howard returned to the United States. During his tenure with the 354th FG he had managed to shoot down six German planes.

Once back in the USA Howard, after a series of assignments, decided to leave the USAAF. The war was almost over and he was anxious to get on with his life. "I spent something like a long seven years in the service away from home and I wanted to get married, along with other things."

Once home in St. Louis, Howard was honored with a parade and reception. At the reception the main speaker was Gen. Omar Bradley. While listening to Bradley's speech the mayor of St. Louis leaned over to Howard, who later recounted the conversation that followed:

> [The major] said, "Now that you're out of the service what do you plan to do?" I said, "Well, I don't have a thing definite but I would like something that offered a challenge."
>
> The mayor thought for a moment and said, "How would you like to drop into my office on Monday. I'd like to talk to you."
>
> So I did and he offered me the job of director of sanitation for the city of St. Louis, which I took, naturally, although I shouldn't have.

The city government job offered to Howard was a bureaucratic nightmare and he left the position after one year. The next few years were a long struggle for Howard, fighter ace and holder of the Medal of Honor.

> Well, after I left city government I got into various things, and this and that failed and led to a flame-proofing company which also failed. I searched around and I wrote dozens and dozens of letters to people applying for jobs, very little of which ever came to anything.
>
> Yah, I was really in pretty bad shape and then for a while I was living at the Missouri Athletic Corporation in St. Louis and I swallowed a chicken bone which stuck in my throat and I went down to the hospital to have them fix it. While trying to extract it they ruptured my esophagus.

Only quick action by his father, who was a doctor and who called a friend who administered penicillin, which had just been discovered, saved Howard's life. A ruptured esophagus at that time was usually fatal.

Howard's father then asked him to come down to Clearwater, Florida, "and recover from [his] problems and live in the garage apartment behind [his father's] house in Belair."

After recovering, Howard moved to Washington, D.C., where he started the Howard Research Corporation. After moving to Arlington, Virginia, the corporation grew to more than 350 engineers and was eventually bought out by Control Data Corporation. Howard came out of this in a financially secure position.

> What happened was that there was a one-for-one exchange of our shares for theirs and the price at the time was $35. A month later it was up to $44 and then it started climbing all the way up to $164 and of the 80,000 shares that were exchanged—you can figure it out for yourself how I did.

Now retired and living in Florida, Howard has written a book dealing with his career as a fighter pilot in the AVG and the USAAF. Titled *Roar of the Tiger,* the book was released in August of 1991.

In 1982 Stewart Howze, a member of the 401st BG, met Jim Howard on a golf course in Tampa. Howard Bowman, group commander of the wartime 401st, received Howard's address from Howze and

Lt. Bruce Carr of the 354th FG standing beside his P-51D, Angel's Playmate. *Carr was another of the great aces of the 354th, scoring 14 victories in the air and 11.5 on the ground.* Smithsonian Institution

156

invited him to a 401st Group reunion. Howard accepted the invitation, recalled Bowman in *Roar of the Tiger*:

> and was guest of honor and speaker at our reunion in Little Rock. Following the banquet, a long line formed to shake his hand. Ted Brown, with tears in his eyes, said, "If it hadn't been for you, a lot of us wouldn't be here tonight." Jim is now an honorary member of the 401st Bomb Group Association.

Howard's career has been one of valor, excellence and glory. His exploits are the things legends are made of. Pappy Boyington, another AVG pilot and Medal of Honor winner, once wrote, "Just name me a hero and I'll prove he's a bum." In the case of Howard, many members of the 401st BG would argue that Boyington was wrong.

B-17s of the 381st BG en route to their target. Although a superior pilot, Jim Howard realized that his main role as a squadron and group commander was to afford the bombers protection from the fierce German fighter attacks. Howard downed six German planes in aerial combat, but his men considered him more valuable as an air commander. "He flies into enemy territory," recalled a 354th Fighter Group pilot, "waits until enemy aircraft come to attack the bombers, looks the situation over and then dispatches flights from his group where they will do the most good." Smithsonian Institution

Chapter 10

Charles MacDonald: He Led by Example

Charles Henry MacDonald graduated from Louisiana State University in 1938. After winning his wings at Kelly Field in 1939 he was assigned to the 20th Pursuit Group. In February 1941 he was assigned to duty in Hawaii and he was a witness to the infamous December 7 sneak attack. In October 1943 he was assigned to the 475th FG and soon scored his first aerial victories, becoming an ace on February 9, 1944. Named group commander, he felt the primary job of a group leader was to lead and he lived up to his philosophy by personally leading the group on many of the major missions to Rabaul and the Philippines. With twenty-seven victories he was the leading surviving P-38 ace of World War II in 1991. His record is all the more remarkable because he scored most of these victories while serving as squadron or group commander. He retired in Florida. Unless attributed to another source, all quotes are from a July 1989 interview with Charles MacDonald.

It was early Sunday morning, December 7, 1941, and Charles Henry MacDonald was catching some needed sleep at his North Beach home on the Hawaiian island of Oahu. MacDonald, a major, flew with the 20th Pursuit Group stationed at Wheeler Field.

A series of loud, abrupt knocks broke the quiet and forced MacDonald out of bed. Going to the door, he noticed his neighbor obviously in a state of great excitement. "Turn your radio on," shouted the neighbor. "The Japanese have launched an attack." Hurrying to the radio, MacDonald found the airwaves full of "hysterical stuff, [saying] the Japanese were attacking all over."

Dressing hurriedly, MacDonald thought he had better report to Wheeler Field, where his squadron was stationed.

I jumped into my car and started for Wheeler. There was mass confusion that day—rumors flying about.

When I drove by Haleiwa Airstrip a Japanese Zero strafed the field.

There was a little emergency airstrip there; he just made a fast pass and left; I'm not even sure he hit anything.

Wheeler Field was the Army fighter base located at the center of the Islands. Lined up on the airfield were sixty-two of the Army's brand-new P-40s in neat rows. At 0802 hours Pfc. Arthur Fusco, on guard duty with his rifle, froze in his tracks as the first Japanese dive-bomber peeled off. Fusco recognized the red balls on the wings and rushed into the hangar for a machine gun. He couldn't break the lock of the armament shack, but it made little difference, as the Japanese dive-bombers and strafers were already at work.

Arriving at Wheeler, MacDonald found mass confusion.

The field was a mess; we lost almost everything we had. All the hangars were bombed out, most of the aircraft were burned up.

We wheeled some airplanes that were still serviceable out to one end of the field and flew a mission that afternoon, but the Japanese were long gone.

After an apprehensive 1½ hours aloft MacDonald and his fellow pilots flew back to Honolulu, and there they ran into a veritable hornet's nest. The trouble came not from the long-gone Japanese fliers but from the jittery American gunners on the ground. A fierce hail of flak rose to meet the American planes. With gas low, MacDonald had no option but to run the gauntlet, landing back safely at Wheeler Field.

The Japanese were gone from the skies over Pearl Harbor, but MacDonald would encounter them many times again in the air over the Southwest Pacific and the Philippine Islands. He would fly more than 200 combat missions and end World War II as America's fifth-leading USAAF ace with twenty-seven Japanese planes to his credit.

Charles Henry MacDonald was born in DuBois, Pennsylvania, and graduated from Overbrook High School in Philadelphia in 1933. He attended Louisiana State University from 1935 until 1938, graduating with a B.A. degree in journalism.

The transition from college senior to Army pilot was an easy one for MacDonald.

I was always interested in flying and when I was a senior at LSU the Navy flight team from Pensacola and the Army flight team from Randolph Field came through. They were mainly medical people, but they were proselytizing for flying cadets, so I took both those exams. I passed them both but I decided to go with the Army because its school started first. I graduated in May and then went right to flight training in July at Randolph and Kelly fields in Texas.

After finishing at Kelly in 1939 he was assigned to the 20th Pursuit Group at Barksdale Field in Louisiana, flying P-36s.

MacDonald became a second lieutenant during his training when he easily passed the test for a commission in the regular Army. By the time his new commission came through he moved to California in preparation for his group to be assigned to Hawaii. In February 1941 forty P-36s were loaded aboard the aircraft carrier *Enterprise* and MacDonald's group sailed to Hawaii. MacDonald subsequently had a rare experience for an Army pilot: flying off the deck of an aircraft carrier to land his plane in Hawaii.

After the debacle at Pearl Harbor MacDonald remained in Hawaii until early 1943 when he was sent back to the United States to train a P-47 squadron in Massachusetts.

While training the new P-47 pilots MacDonald was under the command of Neal Kearby. Kearby would win the Medal of Honor for shooting down six Japanese planes in one engagement and run his score to twenty-two before being killed on a mission to Wewak.

In their P-47s Kearby and MacDonald would often test their flying skills against one another.

Kearby and I engaged in several mock dogfights in Massachusetts while we were training the P-47 squadrons. He was the group commander and I was one of the squadron commanders.

I did well against Kearby. I remember one dogfight. It wasn't a fair dogfight as far as turning or anything because we had set up this point to meet—he would be with his wingman and I would be covered by my wingman—but I had managed to come in on a point where I knew the sun would be behind me, so I had the initial advantage.

June 1943 found Major MacDonald stationed with the 348th FG at Port Moresby, New Guinea. The assignment proved uneventful as he flew missions in his P-47 for several months, covering transports in the Marilinan area.

If the assignment to the 348th was discouraging to MacDonald, he got his chance in October 1943 when he was assigned to the 475th FG.

The 475th was Gen. George Kenney's dream unit, the first all-P-38-Lightning-equipped group in the Fifth Air Force. Under an agreement with Gen. Henry "Hap" Arnold, Kenney supplied the personnel for the 475th and Arnold provided the aircraft.

Kenney had scoured the 11th Air Replacement Depot for promising fighter pilots and the existing Fifth Fighter Command squadrons were told early in the spring of 1943 to assign some of their best pilots for duty in the new group.

The names of the pilots who transferred to the 475th would in many cases become synonymous with fierce combat action in P-38s. George Prentice, who commanded the first P-38 squadron in New Guinea, was chosen to command the new group. Harry Brown, Jack Mankin and Frank Nichols

Charles MacDonald, the fifth leading army ace of World War II with 27 victories. Dennis Cooper

159

came from the 49th FG to help form the new 431st Squadron. From the 80th Squadron came Danny Roberts and James Ince to help form the nucleus of the 432nd Squadron. General Kenney expected great things from the 475th FG and they would not disappoint him. Many would become aces.

By May 14, 1943, the 475th came into existence at Amberly Field, Australia. The group spent three months preparing for combat and early in August started out for New Guinea by C-47 transport planes and, for the ground echelon, Liberty ships.

On August 16 the group made its first contact with the enemy. While escorting transports to Tsili Tsili the pilots of the 431st Squadron ran into two dozen Japanese fighters and bombers. In their first combat the Lightning pilots shot down twelve Japanese planes for a loss of two P-38s—an auspicious 6 to 1 margin of victory and a forecast of the great things that were to follow.

Untested as yet in combat, MacDonald joined the 475th at Dobodura, New Guinea.

Conditions were not too bad [recalled MacDonald]. We had a couple of good airstrips. Most everyone lived in tents. The food was terrible because at that time we were on Australian rations —and they were horrible, so most of us were living on peanut butter and moldy bread.

On October 15 the controller at Oro Bay, New Guinea, flashed a radar warning report that a large force of enemy aircraft was moving toward the Allied base at Dobodura. The warning blared across the field. Pilots quickly ran toward the P-38s, strapped in, closed the canopies and thundered down the runway into the air. Behind them the field was controlled pandemonium. Other pilots were coming from all directions, racing in anything that had wheels to get to the airfield.

MacDonald had just driven up to group headquarters when the air raid alert sounded. This attack would afford him his first and nearly last opportunity for action against the Japanese.

Dennis Cooper, left, the intelligence officer of the 475th FG, and Lt. Col. Charles MacDonald stand by

MacDonald's P-38, Putt-Putt Maru. Pete Madison, 475th Fighter Group

Capt. Bill Ivy came running out of group headquarters and said, "There's a bunch of Jap bombers coming in—let's go!" So we jumped in my jeep and drove down to the airstrip and found two P-38s that were serviceable and we jumped in and took off.

I no sooner got the gear up on takeoff when I saw the Jap bombers coming down on their runs on the ships in the harbor. That's when we split; I never saw Ivy until later on.

MacDonald's plane and fifty other P-38s of the 475th managed to take off before the Japanese—now identified as a force of sixty planes—came into contact. The Lightnings were still climbing, pilots pounding their twin throttles, as the battle was joined over the Oro Bay area.

MacDonald managed to race ahead and attack a force of seven Vals. One Val that he assaulted from the rear hit the water and exploded. In the wild melee that followed, MacDonald shot at another dive-bomber from the rear and watched it explode just as he passed ahead of it. During a subsequent attack on a third Val, MacDonald's luck changed.

I was closing in on a Val bomber and not paying attention to what was behind me, and what was behind me was a little Jap Zero, just shooting the hell out of me.

As soon as I heard the bullets hitting my plane I broke left as hard as I could. It was a purely instinctive action; you just jerk everything as hard as you can and pull. I had no fear at all. I did what I thought I had to do. Fortunately for me he didn't follow around, because he had shot me up pretty badly. My plane wasn't on fire but it must have thrown a lot of fumes out back of me to make the Jap pilot think I was.

I hoped I could make it back to the airfield. The Val had been right on the water and I had no altitude, one engine was shot out and I couldn't feather the prop because the electrical system was shot out. The other engine was overheating because he had shot up the coolant. I thought, *If I can get up high enough I'll bail out,* but I couldn't. I was about 30 or 40 miles from base and over water.

I got back to the strip but had no hydraulic pressure and had to belly in. I wasn't hit but some of those bullets came mighty close. That was the closest I ever came and it sure taught me a lesson.

Charles MacDonald, left, and Charles Lindbergh in front of MacDonald's P-38. "It didn't make a damn bit of difference to me about Lindbergh flying with us," recalled MacDonald. "I couldn't have cared less whether he was a civilian or a general or whatever. If he wanted to fly and live with us that was fine. We treated him just like anyone else." Dennis Cooper

The business end of Charles MacDonald's P-38,
Putt-Putt Maru, *in 1944.* Glen Brewin

Despite MacDonald's close call, the 475th managed to shoot down thirty-six Japanese fighters and bombers without the loss of a single American plane. Two Lightnings were damaged, but all landed safely.

For MacDonald it was a memorable mission: he had shot down two Japanese aircraft. But most important, he learned the value of checking his rear and the need for the protection of a wingman. These were lessons he would never forget.

Not long after MacDonald arrived at the 475th he was named group commander to replace George Prentice, who was being sent home.

As group commander, MacDonald found himself in charge of approximately 1,000 people. It was an awesome responsibility, recalled MacDonald.

> A group commander has three squadrons and he does everything. He has a staff that does the planning for the movements, training, et cetera. In a wartime situation we would get all the operation orders.
>
> I was the kind of fellow like Ronald Reagan: I delegate. I had a very fine group executive officer who was not a pilot, named Maxwell Stubbs. All the housekeeping I put on his shoulders and he did a bang-up job. That gave me more time to fly because I felt the primary job of a group commander was to lead.

An October 25 mission to Rabaul illustrated MacDonald's leadership at its best and most daring. On this morning B-24s had formed up for another strike on Rabaul. MacDonald was leading all the squadrons assigned to cover the big bombers, including an 80th Group squadron and a 49th Group squadron, as well as eight P-38s of the 432nd Squadron. He recalled the approach to the target:

> The weather was stinko and everyone turned back except my flight, and we went in over Rabaul with the B-24s. The B-24s were hollering over the

radio, "Where in the hell's the fighter cover, there are Zeros coming in."

The weather to the east of the target was bad, noted MacDonald.

> Rather than let the bombers go on alone, I took my seven men very high and covered the lead bomb squadron of the 90th Group, so that the enemy seeing us would be discouraged and perhaps figure there were lots more of us. We figured to be mostly moral support.
>
> Off Cape Gazelle the lead bombers were intercepted. We made a dive and scared them [the Japanese] off. Then all the squadrons began talking at once that they were being hit. We helped them out mostly through scaring the enemy who weren't too eager. Over Vunakaman I shot a Zeke who burst into flames. Flak was terrific over the harbor. We stayed over the target 45 minutes.

Although the mission to Rabaul was a success, lack of adequate fighter cover could have led to disaster had the Japanese been more aggressive in their attacks. MacDonald thought the bomber crews were partly to blame for being without fighter cover.

> They were so dumb, the damn bombers. They should have been listening on the fighter [radio] frequency anyway. Then when they hear one squadron say, "We can't take this, we're in clouds and we're turning back," and another squadron say, "It's getting worse, we're turning back"—if they would have been listening on the fighter frequency they would have known what was happening.
>
> But the bombers didn't until they got to the target, then they said over the fighter frequency, "Where in the hell are the fighters?"

The aggressive action of MacDonald and his squadron undoubtedly saved many of the B-24s from being shot down by Japanese fighters.

> That's the kind of leadership that MacDonald exhibited [remarked Maj. Dennis Cooper, former intelligence officer of the 475th Fighter Group]. He felt that this is why we're fighting the war and we've got to go through with the mission. When he returned from the Rabaul raid there was no braggadocio; he just very quietly filled out his reports and said little about the mission.

For his courage and leadership in escorting the B-24s to Rabaul on October 25, Lieutenant Colonel MacDonald was awarded the Distinguished Service Cross, one of two he was to win during the war.

On January 9, 1944, Colonel MacDonald led a six-plane sweep to Wewak and the Lightning pilots found forty Japanese fighters swarming into the air against them. Against these odds MacDonald shot down a Tony, for his tenth kill, on the way out of the area.

Although he claimed only one Japanese plane over Wewak, the mission was still vivid in his mind after almost forty-five years:

A nearly intact Oscar. The Oscar was produced in greater quantities than any other Japanese fighter during the war years. It was the preferred plane of many Japanese fighter aces. Charles MacDonald counted two Oscars among his 27 victories. Dennis Cooper

The Jap fighters didn't even see us. There was an overcast and they were assembling and the leader was taking them up through the overcast. Well, I just tacked onto the rear end of the formation. Actually, I got two that day but I only claimed one.

I only claimed one—it was really funny. I go over that in my mind a lot because Neal Kearby saw the gun film and he said, "Hey, good going, you got two up there."

But I only claimed one because the poor bastards were forming up on the rear end of the formation, and the front end of the formation was going up through the clouds and in the excitement I closed in on the first one and blasted him and then I moved over to the second guy who was still concentrating on his formation flying and I got the back of his head in my sights and I don't know what the hell came over me and I thought, "Holy shit, he doesn't know I'm here—this is murder!" So I moved the sight off the back of his head down to the wing root and then I fired. I just had a momentary emotional blockage about hitting that guy.

I got him because the film shows the bullets hitting the wing root. Later I kicked myself in the pants for being so chicken shit—that's why I only claimed one.

The P-38 shot down more Japanese aircraft in World War II than any other fighter plane. Although conceived as a high-altitude interceptor, it was called upon to fill a number of roles with varying degrees of success. It should be remembered that as an escort fighter, the P-38 was a twin-engine aircraft competing with single-engine aircraft and that few twin-engine fighters achieved its record.

At this writing, Charles MacDonald is the top-scoring P-38 ace to survive World War II. He survived the war owing to luck, his incredible flying skills and the P-38. He described the big twin-engine fighter with these words of praise:

It was a marvelous aircraft! It was the best aircraft I flew in the war, by far. I never flew the P-51—it's been one of my life's regrets—but I flew just about everything else there was.

I liked the P-38's rate of climb, its speed, the way it handled and its firepower—directly out the nose.

The P-38 would turn with almost anything—in fact, it would outturn the P-47, outclimb it and outmaneuver it.

The P-38 was one of the great aircraft of World War II. Our thought was that those guys in Europe didn't know how to use it right, and I still think that.

The main Japanese fighter in the Pacific was the Zero, a highly maneuverable aircraft. MacDonald admired some aspects of the Zero.

The Zero had maneuverability and the capacity to get altitude, because usually they were higher than us when we started—however, their firepower was quite weak and the Zero was flimsily built by American standards, but that's why they were so maneuverable.

You couldn't climb away from a Zero in a straight climb away. You had a speed advantage, but you had to make a turn.

I turned many times with a Zero. I didn't try to circle with one, but I certainly turned as hard as I could with one on my tail to keep it from hitting me. The Japanese pilots tended not to press their attacks like we did.

Japanese pilots also reflected on the relative merits of the P-38 and Zero. One great Japanese fighter ace, Saburo Sakai, as related in Lawrence Cortesi's *Pacific Siege*, told American interpreter Roger Pineau after the war:

On my first confrontation with the P-38 I was astonished to find an American aircraft that could outrun, outclimb and outdive our Zero, which we thought was the most superior fighter plane in the world. The Lightning's great speed, its sensational high-altitude performance, and especially its ability to dive and climb much faster than the Zero presented insuperable problems for our fliers. The P-38 pilots, flying at great height, chose when and where they wanted to fight, with disastrous results for our own men. The P-38 boded ill for the future and destroyed the morale of the Zero fighter pilot.

In 1944 Gen. George Kenney, commander of the Fifth Air Force, arranged for Charles A. Lindbergh to visit and fly with some of the P-38 groups. Kenney "had an important job for Lindbergh that would keep him busy every minute he could spare." Kenney's top priority was to have Lindbergh teach the P-38 pilots how to get more range out of their airplanes through careful cruise control of their engines.

Lindbergh spent most of his time with the 475th FG. "What started as an overnight visit," remembered MacDonald, "became a stay of nearly two months. During this time, the man who came to observe and learn gave us, from the store of his experience, knowledge which had a marked effect on the course of the war in the Pacific."

Lindbergh flew constantly with the 475th for several weeks and demonstrated his cruise-control techniques to the combat pilots. Lindbergh had promised to extend the radius of action of the P-38 nearly fifty percent. The P-38s were operating at a distance of about 400 miles from their airfields. If Lindbergh was right, they could stretch it to 600 miles. Before long, under Lindbergh's guidance, the P-38 pilots were talking enthusiastically of getting an 800 mile radius out of their airplanes.

Pilot standing by the tail boom of a P-38 with the Satan's Angels insignia of the 475th FG clearly showing. John Campbell

On July 28, 1944, operating from the 475th's airfield at Biak, Indonesia, Lindbergh went along with Colonel MacDonald and other pilots on a "milk run" escort mission to the island of Ceram. The flight became sticky when a Sonia-type Japanese plane and Lindbergh met head-on. Colonel Mac-Donald described the action that followed in a 1946 article for *Collier's* magazine:

As I continued my own steep bank I could see the Jap in a slight climb and Lindbergh in a slight dive, the distance between them lessening rapidly, their guns spitting bullets so fast the muzzles resembled so many acetylene torches.

For moments which seemed like years the antagonists came at each other. Lindbergh's cannon and machine gun bullets jolted into the Jap. A collision seemed unavoidable. Something had to be done, and quickly. His slight advantage in height prompted him to try to go over the Jap. He pulled back the stick with all his strength. The badly hurt enemy tried for a crash. As Lindbergh's plane started up, the Jap too pulled up violently. He was too late. Lindbergh's plane caught the shock of air as the two missed by a narrow margin. The Sonia, its mottled green camouflage contrasting with the

bright red of the Rising Sun insignia, rolled over like a broken toy and began a long dive that ended in the sea.

Headquarters finally found out about Lindbergh's combat missions and put an end to them. For his part in allowing civilian Lindbergh to fly into danger, MacDonald was sent home on "punitive leave" by Gen. Paul Wurtsmith, and the 475th was led for the next two months by Meryl Smith. "It was something Wurtsmith felt he had to do to make it look good," recalled MacDonald. "Actually, we did a little private laughing about it." MacDonald was sent home for a month, which gave him a chance to see his baby son and still allowed him plenty of time to add to his score of Japanese planes.

Lindbergh agreed to return home, feeling he had taught the P-38 pilots all he could. Kenney asked him "not to tell anyone back home about being in combat as long as the war lasted." Kenney told Lindbergh that if the story leaked out, he "would tell the newspapermen that there was no record of his having flown on a combat mission, let alone of having shot down a Jap airplane." Lindbergh told Kenney he had no intention of telling

A wrecked Sonia dive-bomber at Hollandia. This was the type of Japanese plane downed by Charles

Lindbergh while flying with the 475th FG. Dennis Cooper

the story, "as he too was anxious not to have any publicity in regard to his activities in the Pacific, particularly while the war was on."

MacDonald wrote an account of Lindbergh's combat activity with the 475th FG in an article that was published in 1946. Lindbergh had wanted MacDonald to have the article published in the *Reader's Digest*, but *Collier's* magazine offered more money and won the right to the article. "The magazine went defunct shortly after the article appeared," joked MacDonald when complimented on the fine writing style evident throughout the two-installment article.

In October 1944 American forces invaded the Philippines. To support the invasion fleet, fighter cover was needed, and the 475th FG moved into Dulag airstrip in the Philippines. MacDonald remembered this as a time of tremendous strain. "We were kind of groggy; we'd go to sleep at night, wake up and take off at dawn—day after day. You got so tired, days didn't mean much."

On December 6 Colonel MacDonald was leading the 475th FG flying fighter cover for an Allied convoy in Ormoc Bay. Flying his silver P-38 with the yellow spinners, nicknamed *Putt-Putt Maru*, he searched the sky for Japanese fighters and bombers he was certain would try to attack the American amphibian force.

As MacDonald's flight patroled the sky one of the pilots reported four aircraft, ahead and above. They were quickly identified as Japanese planes and MacDonald turned to the attack.

Pushing his throttle wide open, MacDonald began climbing toward the enemy. He described the action that followed:

There were four Japanese planes and they came down out of this big cumulus cloud. I turned into them and as they went by I tagged on to one and shot him down. Then I got on one's tail who was chasing Smith and I fired a burst at the Japanese plane and cut it in two. The tail section and part of

Charles MacDonald in the cockpit of his P-38. "The P-38," recalled MacDonald, "was just an all-around good airplane. It maneuvered, it climbed well, it performed, plus it sounded like the Cadillac of *airplanes on the ground. When taxiing it made its own peculiar sound; it was real smooth." Pete Madison, 475th Fighter Group*

the fuselage glided slowly off to the right and the front end with cockpit and wings tumbled forward.

The four Japanese planes had now dwindled to one. The Lightnings sped after it as it flew full speed to the west, heading for its base on Negros Island. MacDonald remembered the pursuit:

> We chased the one remaining Japanese plane back toward Negros Island. The Japanese pilot was watching me intently; every time I got close enough to take a shot he would yank his plane real hard to the left and then I would have to pull back up.
>
> After he did this a couple of times he was so intent on me that a kid named Les Blakley came right up behind him and shot him down.

With the last Japanese plane accounted for, MacDonald turned back toward the American convoy. Slightly below at about 8,000 feet he spotted a Zeke diving fast toward the American ships. It was one of the few encounters MacDonald was to have with a kamikaze plane. He described the incident:

> The kamikaze got through the fighter cover and through the naval antiaircraft fire and dove toward a cruiser—but the size of it must have awed him because he flew toward it and then pulled up and dove into a destroyer, which he damaged badly. A kid named Carol Anderson followed that Zero through the ack-ack but couldn't catch him before he dove into the Navy destroyer.

Fire and black, boiling smoke rose from the stricken destroyer. Anderson, lucky to be alive, pulled up, roaring over the warship just after the crash of the Japanese plane.

MacDonald soon learned that his wingman, Meryl Smith, was missing. "We started assembling and Smitty was gone. So we started searching all over the area but there wasn't an oil slick or anything. We went back and landed and took off again and searched until dark. None of us could figure out what happened to Smith."

Smith was never seen again. It was a hard loss for MacDonald to take, because Smith had been a close friend. Dennis Cooper remembered the impact of Smith's disappearance:

> Meryl was a very well liked man. It was a tragedy when he didn't come back.
>
> That is an awful thing, for a leader like MacDonald, when you live and die with these people all the time, every day almost—leadership can be very lonely.

Colonel MacDonald's last victory of World War II was one of his easiest.

> We flew across the China Sea, escorting some bombers to China. I shot down a Japanese DC-3 that looked like it was heading from Shanghai to Formosa. I just happened to run into it out over the middle of the China Sea.

MacDonald in 1989 looked back over the years and reflected on his service in World War II:

> In the light of the wars since then it seems to me that we were in the best war of all. Everyone really had a purpose. The fact that we were opposing regimes like Hitler's Nazis and Tojo's expansionist people in Japan made it a good war. I have a good feeling about my participation in World War II and I rather doubt that people who have been in the Korean conflict and Vietnam could have the same emotional rationale.

MacDonald retired to live the good life in Florida. His contribution to final victory in the Pacific in World War II was a large one. Shooting down twenty-seven Japanese planes was a significant achievement. That he did so while also commanding the 475th FG put him into the ranks of the few special people who were able to lead, command, teach and inspire at the same time.

Chapter 11

Tom McGuire and the Race to Beat Dick Bong

Thomas B. McGuire won his wings at Kelly Field in 1942. He was then assigned to duty in Alaska but was eventually transferred to the Fifth Air Force, 475th Fighter Group, in the Southwest Pacific. On his first combat mission he shot down three Japanese planes, setting the stage for a long string of victories. Flying the P-38 Lightning, he shot down three planes on five occasions, five times scored doubles and on December 26, 1944, downed four Zeros to bring his score to thirty-eight, only two behind the leading American ace, Dick Bong, who had returned to the United States. McGuire's dreams of passing Bong never materialized. On a January 7, 1945, mission he attempted a low, tight turn to save a fellow pilot under attack and crashed into the jungle. He was posthumously awarded the Medal of Honor for his heroism in the air war over the Philippines. Unless attributed to another source, all quotes are from a July 1991 interview with Doug Thropp, Jr.

During the last week of October 1944, the center of operations for the Fifth Air Force was the Philippine Islands. Fighters were needed desperately at Tacloban Airdrome on Leyte and now they were in sight. Twenty big Lockheed P-38s were coming in slowly to land on the pierced steel planking that made up the hurriedly improvised Tacloban strip.

All eyes on the ground were glued to the P-38 Lightnings as they approached the field; no one noticed the ten Japanese Zero fighters break through the cloud cover and dive toward the unsuspecting P-38s. The Japanese pilots had timed their attack perfectly—the Lightnings were set up like ducks for the slaughter.

Suddenly one P-38 came alive. The pilot rammed the throttle forward, hit the gear and flap levers and issued a warning by radio to the other

P-38 pilots. Surging ahead, the Lightning skidded crazily to the side even as a Zero's tracers flashed by where it had once been. Quickly the big Lightning turned around and rushed toward the Japanese planes, accelerating rapidly. The four machine guns and one cannon boomed out from the nose. The lead Japanese plane staggered in the air as the bullets hit home; a wing broke free and the Zero tumbled wildly into the trees and exploded.

What had begun as a Japanese ambush soon turned into a wild free-for-all. The P-38 rushed head-on into the remaining Japanese planes, catching them by surprise and forcing them to delay their attack. By the time the Japanese pilots regained their composure it was too late. The twenty P-38s were all over them.

Only four of the Japanese planes survived the dogfight that followed; six Japanese Zeros were left burning in the jungle. All twenty P-38s came into the landing pattern once again and eased down onto the steel planking. The pilot who had sounded the warning and gunned down the first Zero taxied away from the runway and cut his switches. The big P-38 came to a stop. Officers had men crowded around the P-38 named *Pudgy V*, staring at the rows of Japanese flags stenciled neatly on the nose.

Maj. Thomas B. McGuire, Jr., of the 475th FG, climbed down from *Pudgy V* and grinned. He had just shot down his twenty-fifth Japanese plane.

Shooting down Japanese planes was something that McGuire was an expert at. He was short, standing about 5 feet 7 inches tall, and gaunt, with steely gray eyes. He sported a big black mustache to make himself appear older than he was. "His face was narrow," recalled Carroll Anderson, a noted aviation historian, "with an undershot jaw that gave him a sharp, pugnacious look. He was aggressive as hell. He wanted to be number 1, to win the Congressional Medal of Honor and get a colonelcy before going home."

Tom McGuire by the front of his P-38, Pudgy V. *McGuire, with 38 victories, was the second-ranking* *American ace of World War II.* 475th Fighter Group Museum

169

McGuire was also a magnificent pilot, supremely confident and absolutely without fear. Once, over Wewak, a burning Japanese fighter had been closing at him head-on. Neither McGuire nor the Japanese pilot would give way. A jarring bang rocked the planes as they flashed by each other. McGuire pulled up and away, and the Japanese plane continued on to be shot down by another American pilot. After McGuire landed at his home base of Dobodura, the ground crew had to use steel wool to scrape the broad smear of Japanese paint from under the wing of his Lightning.

McGuire was the commander of the 431st Squadron of the 475th FG. The 475th was commanded by Col. Charles MacDonald, who finished the war with twenty-seven Japanese planes to his credit. MacDonald flew more than fifty missions with McGuire and remembered him as an excellent pilot. "He was an extremely ambitious man; he worked hard and that's why he got to be squadron commander. He was more a great leader of men in the air than on the ground."

The pilots of the 431st Squadron felt that McGuire could do things with a P-38 that were impossible. His skill with the heavy, twin-boomed P-38 was so extraordinary as to defy reality, and he had such faith in himself and his airplane that he never indicated any hesitation in turning to attack enemy fighters or to tangle with Japanese planes in swirling dogfights, in which he always managed to prevent the Japanese pilots from using the superb maneuverability of their planes to shoot him down.

Little is known about the life of Thomas B. McGuire, Jr., before World War II. He was born in Ridgewood, New Jersey, on August 1, 1920. His family later moved to Sebring, Florida, where he completed high school. After attending the Georgia Institute of Technology he enlisted as an aviation cadet, earning his pilot's wings and lieutenant's bars upon graduation in February 1942.

McGuire's early career as a fighter pilot was undistinguished. For a short period of time he served in the United States, fretting over the lack of action and badgering his superiors for overseas duty. Finally he received orders to ship out to Alaska.

McGuire's joy soon faded as he faced the reality of the biting cold, thick fog and fierce winds of the Aleutian Islands. Little combat flying was to be found in the Aleutians and McGuire once again began rocking the boat, asking, pleading and demanding to be sent to a combat zone. Finally, in

Francis Lent, Tom McGuire, Charles MacDonald and John Loisel, left to right, at Hollandia. All four of these 475th Fighter Group pilots became aces.

Final totals were Lent 11, McGuire 38, MacDonald 27 and Loisel 10. Dennis Cooper

March 1943, he was ordered to report to the Fifth Air Force in the Southwest Pacific.

When McGuire arrived in the Southwest Pacific the name on everyone's lips was that of Dick Bong, a brilliant P-38 pilot. Bong was knocking down Japanese planes with a persistence and skill that splashed his name across front pages throughout the United States.

Bong already had sixteen Japanese planes to his credit before McGuire made his first claims in August 1943. While others fell by the wayside McGuire—who made no secret of the fact that he wanted to be number 1—steadily closed the gap, raising his score with a series of multiple victories over the course of the year. By early December 1944, when Bong moved in with McGuire's 431st Squadron, the score stood at thirty-six Japanese planes shot down for Bong and twenty-eight for McGuire.

When Bong scored his fortieth victory and was rotated home, it seemed certain that McGuire would eventually catch and surpass him to become the Ace of Aces. It was said that when McGuire quickly began increasing his score in the Philippines he had the squadron painter apply miniature Japanese flags to his plane's nose area, which were then covered with tape; when he returned after a combat mission the necessary tape was removed as soon as his victories were confirmed. Gen. George Kenney even grounded McGuire until Bong had a chance to get home, feeling it would be unfair if McGuire dampened the event by breaking Bong's record.

That both Bong and McGuire were great pilots was undisputed; however, Carroll Anderson, who flew with the 433rd Squadron, noted that their combat roles and flying styles were different.

> McGuire was an earthy, brash type of guy who led by example. . . . McGuire could be abrasive and caustic but he fought and led, which Bong never did. Bong did not command. He was up at Fifth Fighter Headquarters, and when a good mission was forthcoming he dropped down . . . and flew with the boys. When you consider the Billy Bishop free-lance possibility of Bong's efforts against the necessity of running a squadron by the book, McGuire's record becomes all the more fantastic.

On Christmas Day, 1944, McGuire volunteered to lead a squadron of fifteen planes to provide protection for B-24s attacking Mabaldent Airdrome. As the formation crossed Luzon it was jumped by twenty Japanese fighters. In the battle that followed, McGuire shot down three Zeros.

The following day McGuire volunteered to lead a squadron to Clark Field. Over the target area one of the bombers was hit by flak. As the bomber left the formation it was rushed by Japanese fighters. McGuire had only a slim chance of helping, but he opened fire at long range, nearly 400 yards, with a 45 degree deflection shot. He hit the cockpit of the Zero, which burst into flames and fell toward the ground. It was fantastic shooting. McGuire made a diving turn to the left and got two more bursts into another Zero, which flamed and crashed. Then immediately three more Zeros joined the fight. McGuire singled out one and fired, his bullets shattering the cockpit and the pilot. The Japanese plane fell into a dry streambed. On the way out of the target area McGuire shot down another Japanese plane—his fourth for the day—bringing his total to thirty-eight.

On Thursday, January 18, 1945, the *New York Times* carried the following news release on its front page:

McGuire Pacific Air Ace, Killed; He Downed 38 Japanese Planes, San Antonio, Tex., Jan. 17
Major Thomas B. McGuire, Jr. of San Antonio and Ridgewood, N.J., the leading American ace with 38 Japanese planes to his credit, was shot down and killed in the Philippines Jan. 7, Lieut. Gen. George

Tom McGuire and Dick Bong at Hollandia. Bong and McGuire carried on a spirited, friendly rivalry to be the top-ranking American ace. McGuire was usually eight victories behind Bong and at one point in frustration remarked Gen. George Kenney in his book George Kenney Reports, *"I'm still eight behind. I'll bet when this war is over, they'll call me Eight Behind McGuire."* Dennis Cooper

C. Kenney, commanding the Allied Air Forces in the Pacific, informed Mrs. McGuire in a letter dated Jan. 8.

Mrs. McGuire received General Kenney's letter today. The Allied air chief said that the word Major McGuire had been shot down brought him the worst of a number of bad moments he had to face since the war began.

"I felt that he would make a name for command as well as for leadership and for great personal courage," the letter stated.

"The accident, which left him vulnerable on Jan. 7 and in which he met his death, was sheer chance as Major McGuire was one of the most capable fighter pilots I have ever known.

"Your husband was one of the men the Air Forces can never forget. We will find it more difficult to carry on without him," General Kenney added.

The letter indicated that Major McGuire's plane was in some way disabled in the air, making him an easy prey for defending enemy fighters.

Major McGuire became the leading ace when Maj. Richard I. Bong of Poplar, WI returned to the United States on leave. Major Bong is credited with downing 40 Japanese planes.

Since McGuire met his death many varying accounts of his last mission have appeared.

Gen. George C. Kenney, in his 1949 book *General Kenney Reports*, gave the following details concerning McGuire's last mission:

He [McGuire] said that the next morning he and [Maj. Jack B.] Rittmayer, a visiting P-38 pilot from the thirteenth Air Force, who had four [Japanese planes] to his credit, were planning to take a couple of youngsters, who had just arrived in the squadron, for a sweep over the Jap airdromes on Cebu and Negros to see if they could stir up something.

On the morning of the 7th McGuire and Rittmayer and the two new lads took off on the mission as scheduled. At 2000 feet altitude over Negros they sighted a lone Jap fighter plane, flying at about 200 feet off the ground. McGuire led his flight to the attack. The Nip turned sharply to the left and quickly maneuvered into position on Rittmayer's tail. Rittmayer called for help as the Jap fired a quick burst into him. McGuire pulled around in a frantic effort to get his guns on the Nip and save Rittmayer. He pulled his turn too tight in the attempt, and the airplane stalled and crashed to the ground. The Nip poured another burst into Rittmayer's already crippled P-38. Rittmayer went down in flames. The Nip ducked behind a hill and got away. The two youngsters, who had gone on the flight to get experience, in trying to stay with their two leaders had gotten out of position and couldn't catch him before he had disappeared from sight.

Martin Caidin, in his 1973 book *Fork-tailed Devil: The P-38*, had McGuire's flight of four bounced from above by one of Japan's greatest fighter pilots, Shoichi Sugita.

Sugita came down beautifully.

Only the combat experience of McGuire saved the moment as Sugita opened fire. Immediately, McGuire broke into a vertical bank, coming around in a steep turn. . . . The four P-38s slid into a lufberry circle, snaring Sugita inside.

Any other pilot would have been boxed in, caught, unable to escape. Sugita was no ordinary man at the controls. . . . The formation with the Zero in its midst dropped down to only 200 feet above the trees, with Sugita still trying to break free without being caught in a crossfire.

There was no going lower. The P-38 formation scattered, flashing low over the trees. It was a fatal mistake.

Before the American could counter the move, the Zero clawed around in an impossibly tight turn, Sugita . . . fastened onto the tail of a P-38. . . .

The P-38 pilot shouted for help, and McGuire, unthinking, responding to that plea, rushed to his aid. . . .

. . . Working hard rudder and full aileron, McGuire snapped the P-38 into a hard, vertical turn.

It was too tight and too steep for low speed, high drag and heavy weight. And there was no room below. The Lightning staggered suddenly as though it had rammed into an invisible wall in the sky. No Japanese plane was near McGuire. No Japanese gun or cannon fired at him. But he had been snared by the inviolable laws of aerodynamics. . . . Almost instantly the P-38 was into a high speed stall. . . .

The Lightning flipped lazily over on one wing, control wrested from its pilot. If he had altitude below him McGuire would have fallen, brought the fighter out of its plunge as he regained lift.

There wasn't room. The Lightning snapped over on her wing. Almost in the same instant it plunged into the jungle.

A blinding sheet of flame erupted through the trees.

Tommy McGuire was dead.

Carroll Anderson, a wartime pilot with the 475th FG, in an excellently written and researched article for *Air Force Magazine*, was the first writer to disclose that two Japanese planes were actually involved in the dogfight.

Anderson's article included a letter from flying sergeant Mizunori Fukuda, who entered the air battle after it began. Fukuda's letter disclosed the name of the first Japanese pilot, the fact that Fukuda was flying a Ki-84 Frank, and the fact that Fukuda was the pilot who shot down Major Rittmayer.

For nearly thirty years after the dogfight Douglas Thropp, Jr., and Edwin Weaver, who survived the flight, had thought their only adversary had been a lone Japanese pilot in a green Nakajima Ki-43 Oscar. Not until they were contacted by Anderson while writing his story were they aware that they had, in fact, engaged two Japanese planes on that fateful day. Thropp, who is now the only living member of McGuire's original flight of four, has since added new details concerning what really happened over Negros Island on January 7, 1945.

On the night of January 6 Thropp had joined a group of 431st Squadron pilots drinking and shooting the breeze in one of the squadron tents. During the conversation that followed, the pilots discussed various ways McGuire could get enough victories to pass Bong, who at that time was the ranking American ace with forty victories. McGuire had thirty-eight victories but was scheduled to go home in February.

In a 1991 interview Thropp recalled "that there was a Jap fleet off Mindoro, and by flying cover over that, the Japanese were bound to send somebody up." After further discussion, recalled Thropp, "it was decided to go out over those Jap ships and circle above them, until they requested Jap air protection from some of their remaining air bases. This seemed the most likely way to lure enough Japs to a fight."

Within minutes Captain Weaver and Major Rittmayer had volunteered to accompany McGuire on the mission. McGuire then turned to Thropp and said, "Do you want to go?"

"Hell, yes," answered Thropp.

"O.K., then," answered McGuire, "you tail-end Charlie, flying Rittmayer's wing."

After organizing the fighter sweep McGuire left the tent, saying "that he would make arrangements to have the planes equipped with drop tanks and was [to be] awakened in time for takeoff."

Even though the January 7 mission would be led by McGuire, the top-ranked active American ace, it was, according to Thropp, unauthorized.

It was not an ordered mission sent down from Fighter Command by TWX.

Pappy Cline was then C.O. [of the 431st Squadron]. McGuire had been relieved of command and was with the squadron on a visit with his friend Rittmayer. Mac had already moved out of the squadron area to keep him from flying any more combat.

I do not believe Pappy was with the unit that night—nor do I know who McGuire talked to, to have the planes ready and have us awakened for the flight.

Perhaps [Fred] Champlin, who was operations officer, knows how it was set up with no mission authorization prior to takeoff, because McGuire had been put on limited flight activity.

The flight of four would represent a formidable force to any Japanese planes they encountered on the mission. The pilots who had volunteered to fly with McGuire on his last mission were seasoned veterans.

Weaver, who would fly on McGuire's wing, had flown P-40s in North Africa. On April 18, 1943, while flying with the 65th Squadron, he had shot down two German Ju 52s.

Rittmayer, who would lead the second element, had flown with McGuire and Bong on several previous occasions. On December 7, 1944, he had shot down a Kate and two Tojos while flying with the 431st Squadron. On December 17, 1944, he had

Maj. Frank Nichols, Lieutenant Calhoun and Tom McGuire, left to right, discuss a wrecked Tony at Hollandia. McGuire's 38 victories included two Tonys, both shot down over Wewak. Dennis Cooper

Tom McGuire, left, and Charles Lindbergh, right, discuss a mission. After Lindbergh and McGuire flew a recon mission together, McGuire stepped out of the cockpit and said to his crew chief, Frank Kish: "Frank, this is just too good to be true. I never dreamed that I'd fly with Lindy!" Dennis Cooper

flown a fighter sweep with Bong to Mindoro beachhead, where each shot down an Oscar.

Thropp was twenty-one at the time of the mission. Although he would be flying tail-end Charlie, he was no stranger to aerial combat, having flown fifty-three missions and 133.5 combat hours. He had one victory to his credit when on December 7, 1944, he had shot down a Hamp. McGuire had also shot down two Japanese planes on this day.

As McGuire's flight prepared to take off, the following facts would appear to be evident, based on Thropp's recollections:

1. The mission was an unauthorized fighter sweep over Mindoro.

2. The mission was not a planned fighter sweep to Negros Island.

> If we took off for a fighter sweep of Negros [recalled Thropp] we would not have needed two 150 gallon wing tanks to accomplish that mission. We needed the gas to give [us] time to get to the Jap fleet and await their land-based fighters to be scrambled to clear the sky above their ships.

3. All four pilots were experienced combat veterans. They totaled forty-five victories between them.

The flight took off at dawn on January 7, the P-38s laden with full drop tanks. McGuire did not fly his P-38, *Pudgy*, which was grounded; instead he flew Fred Champlin's P-38, *L. No. 112*. According to a 1988 interview with McGuire's crew chief, Francis Kish, in *Aviation Heritage* magazine, McGuire was uncomfortable about the mission.

> The night before, when he told me that he wasn't taking his own plane up, but some other fellow's, I said to him, "Major, why change horses in the middle of the straight?" You know what he said to me then? He said that he thought that he'd pushed his luck in *Pudgy* and that his number might be up.

After takeoff McGuire leveled the flight off at 10,000 feet. Looking ahead, the pilots could see that the clouds were towering high above them. Thropp recalled the events that followed:

> Now, the weather is what caused us to come down in the vicinity of Negros.... The flight leader makes

the decision and McGuire decided, to hell with this, and he started down through the openings through various groups of clouds.

Once over Negros the flight became separated, according to Thropp.

I was flying Rittmayer's wing and we were separated from McGuire and his wingman by a mile or more. I can only attribute this to the fact that Rittmayer felt uncomfortable going down through the clouds and throttled back a bit. When we broke out, McGuire and his wingman were way out ahead.

McGuire said, "Close it up." He wanted the flight to get back intact.

Rittmayer said, "I'm having trouble with an engine."

McGuire said, "O.K., Thropp, move it up. You take the number 3 slot."

I then kicked up my rpm's and my gas power setting and closed the gap.

As Thropp began to close the gap Weaver announced over his radio that a Japanese plane was coming toward the flight 500 feet below and 1,000 yards ahead.

The Japanese plane was a Ki-43 Oscar piloted by Akira Sugimoto of the 54th Sentai, or 54th Squadron. Sugimoto had been ordered to fly a search mission in an attempt to locate a convoy of American ships headed for Mindoro or Lingayen. After a fruitless search he was heading back to his home air base at Fabrida.

At this point, recalled Thropp, he was still separated from McGuire and Weaver.

I was closing the gap and I'm still a considerable distance away when Weaver calls in—that he sighted a Jap low and to the front, coming towards them.

I'm still not up in a normal position; I'm still a couple of football fields back. But I'm coming in. Because of the Jap being called in I didn't keep track of Rittmayer; I don't know how close he was to me.

Because of the tremendous closing speed, Sugimoto flashed underneath McGuire's flight before either side could react. Thropp, now flying in the number 3 position, recalled what followed:

The Jap goes for McGuire and his wingman. They go into a Lufberry to the left. The Jap flies past them and he starts toward me, and I do what our normal routine is, to split the element.

I turned left (south), which made it easier for Rittmayer to come close, because when you're chasing after somebody if he will turn in front of you, you can get on the inside of the curve and catch up faster.

I split the element to the left with the Jap coming up after me. He started pulling up on me and now I'm the clay pigeon. The theory of the thing is that therefore McGuire and Weaver can break that Luf-

Charles Lindbergh, driving, Tom McGuire, center, and Charles MacDonald, right, at Hollandia. Lindbergh's lectures on cruise control helped P-38 pilots such as MacDonald and McGuire extend the range of the P-38. Dennis Cooper

berry and come up and shoot him off me. That was the concept—that you split the element and that allowed the other guy to shoot the guy off me.

As Sugimoto closed on Thropp he began to fire. Thropp, looking back and down at the climbing green-painted Oscar, could see the muzzle flashes of Sugimoto's machine guns. Sugimoto's bullets struck home, damaging one of Thropp's turbochargers. Sugimoto, an experienced pilot, closed for the kill. Thropp, wide-eyed and looking back, thought, *He's so close, I could hit him with a rock.*

Realizing he had to shake the Oscar off his tail, Thropp toggled his drop tank switches, ready to jettison his external fuel tanks. At that moment, according to Thropp, a command from McGuire came over the radio: "Daddy Flight! Save your tanks!"

Why McGuire would issue this command when engaged in low-level combat with an extremely maneuverable Japanese plane is still debated to this day. Ronald Yoshime, in his book *Lightning Strikes*, speculated on the reasons McGuire may have had:

Doubtless many factors came to bear on the major causing his decision. He was determined to beat Bong. The 475th unofficial historian Andy Anderson noted that Pudgy V, Mac's regular ship languishing in a Dulag repair bay, had four blank spaces reserved for McGuire's anticipated victories. Disposing of the tanks would force a premature return to Leyte and [a lost] chance at more kills over the lucrative Mindoro hunting grounds. Major Charles L. Brammeien, in a USAF Air Command and Staff College paper, agreed with Anderson that Mac's race to beat Bong "...clouded his judgement."

But Brammeien also conjectured an over confidence born of declining enemy skills and the four-to-one odds against Sugimoto.

Thropp realized he was in mortal danger, with his plane encumbered with heavy drop tanks and Sugimoto closing in on his tail. Thropp wondered where McGuire was, thinking to himself, *What in the hell are they still doing in the Lufberry down there!*

Rittmayer came to Thropp's rescue, firing a burst that drove Sugimoto off his tail. Thropp realized the Oscar had broken away.

[I] made a tight turn to the right to try and get behind the Jap.

McGuire and his wingman are still down on the deck in the Lufberry. The Jap, having broken away from me, goes diving down towards their Lufberry.

At this point Thropp, turning to the right, lost sight of Sugimoto's Oscar as he dove toward McGuire and Weaver below. Weaver, looking back, had watched Rittmayer force Sugimoto to break off the attack on Thropp. He now observed the Oscar turn inside and above him. Weaver's combat report (in which he called the Oscar a Zeke) detailed the action that followed:

That put the Zeke in range and inside of me, in #2 position. I radioed Major McGuire that I was being attacked and increased my turn, diving slightly. The enemy stayed with me, but I was now inside and a little below my leader. At this time Major McGuire attempting to get a shot at my attacker, increased his turn tremendously. His plane snap-rolled to the left and stopped in an inverted position with the nose down about 30°. Because of the altitude of my plane, I then lost sight of him momentarily. A second later I saw the explosion and fire of his wash. The Zeke broke off his attack just before Major McGuire's crash and climbed to the North. It is my opinion that the enemy did not at any time change his attack from me to my leader. I believe his crash was caused by his violent attempt to thwart my attacker, although it is possible the Major was hit by ground fire, which had now begun.

In his heroic attempt to come to Weaver's aid McGuire was, according to Martin Caidin in *Fork Tailed Devil*, "snared by the inviolable laws of aerodynamics." His Lightning, sluggish because of the weight of the drop tanks, and flying at a low speed, went into a stall and crashed. The combat career of McGuire had come to a tragic end.

Tom McGuire's P-38L, Pudgy IV, *was named after his wife, Marilynn.* Dennis Cooper

Thropp, maneuvering to gain the advantage on Sugimoto, dipped a wing, "and something caught [his] attention and [he] saw an explosion on the ground and a big fire." He now knew that either Weaver or McGuire had gone in, but in the confusion of the moment he didn't know who.

Sugimoto sped north, climbing for the base of the clouds and safety. Thropp, the closest pursuer, fired a 3 second burst as the Oscar entered the clouds. "The next thing I did," recalled Thropp, "was to work my aircraft up, flying in the same direction under the base of the clouds, so if he came back down I would see him come through and be slightly above him."

Sugimoto's plane had been badly damaged from Rittmayer's fire and Thropp's last, long burst. Flying below the cloud cover, he found a flat place to land the crippled Oscar. Unfortunately for Sugimoto, who had overcome tremendous odds to survive his combat against the four P-38s, his landing had been observed by Filipino guerrillas. The guerrillas closed in and shot Sugimoto to death. He was later found with six bullets in his chest.

Thropp, flying close to the base of the clouds, was completely unprepared for what happened next. "Through the clouds comes this big-ass propeller. I can see the propeller and I ducked because I was sure it would hit my canopy. The plane that came back through the clouds came right over my head."

The Japanese plane that appeared suddenly out of the clouds was a new Ki-84 Frank. Piloted by Mizunori Fukuda, it was a formidable opponent. Equipped with a radial engine fitted with fuel injection and having a top speed of 392 mph, the Frank was perhaps the best all-round fighter in the Japanese Army Air Force. Armament consisted of two 20 mm Ho-5 cannon in the wings and a 12.7 mm type 103 on the fuselage top. If the Frank could have been produced in quantity the Allies might have had a difficult time achieving air supremacy in the Pacific.

The sudden appearance of the Frank surprised and confused the Americans, who assumed that Sugimoto had returned to the fray.

Sergeant Fukuda, coming through the overcast, delivered a surprising head-on attack. Thropp turned to the left in a 180 degree turn, "using dive and maneuver flaps." "I realized the airplane was flying like a Mack truck," he recalled. "So I said, 'What the hell, I still got the belly tanks.' So I straightened out from my turn and dropped the tanks."

Weaver fired at the Frank and missed, and in the wild maneuvering that followed, Fukuda managed to get behind and above Rittmayer. Fukuda closed to almost pointblank range and fired. "His guns rumbled, sending a stream of slugs smashing into Rittmayer's plane, shattering the canopy, goug-

ing the wing root, and virtually destroying the center section." Closing to almost 33 feet, Fukuda broke away below Rittmayer's stricken P-38.

With Rittmayer probably dead at the controls the Lightning plunged to the ground, a huge explosion "covering the ground less than 2 miles from where McGuire had died moments before."

Thropp recalled, "The next thing I was totally aware of was that a second airplane hit the ground and blew up in one hell of a big fire. Again I don't know who it is."

In the dogfight that followed, Weaver and Thropp attempted to gain the advantage on Fukuda. Fukuda, a superior pilot, maneuvered into a position behind Thropp's damaged Lightning.

We play tag with this Jap; as it turns out he ends up behind me and again we're working two planes against one. I do the clay pigeon thing again. This guy is behind me—not real close but coming. I'm not immediately aware of where Weaver is. But I make a shallow climbing left turn and I'm waiting for Weaver to shoot him off me, being the clay pigeon. I'm sitting there looking in my rearview mirror, which is at the top of the canopy. I see his guns blink; each time I saw a burst I either dropped or pulled up quickly, 20 feet or so. In any case I went up and down, right and left to evade the shooting. It seemed a lifetime while the Jap was shooting at me.

Weaver, according to Thropp, came to the rescue in the nick of time and "shot Fukuda up." Thropp continued to climb and reached the overcast and safety, his P-38 smoking in one engine.

Once in the clouds, Thropp called on the radio: "McGuire, you are alone, I have left the fight. Do you understand?" Getting no answer, Thropp repeated the message. Suddenly Weaver came on and said: "Thropp, this is Weaver. I'm up above the clouds."

Thropp attempted to find Weaver but was unsuccessful and turned for home. It had to be a lonely and terrifying moment for him. He knew he was alone over Japanese territory in a damaged P-38. He also probably thought that McGuire and Rittmayer were both dead and that the Japanese plane was still somewhere in the vicinity.

Fukuda, however, had problems of his own. Weaver had shot well and the Frank was badly damaged. Fukuda brought the stricken aircraft back to his base at Manapala and attempted to land.

In the landing pattern only one of the plane's main gear locked in the down position. The aircraft cartwheeled onto its back in a cloud of dust. Fukuda half-crawled and was half-dragged from the wreckage. His ground crew later counted twenty-three bullet holes in the aircraft.

Heading home, Thropp had time to think about the tragic events that had just transpired.

On the flight back what you're thinking about is how in the hell are you going to explain this. One

Jap came up, took on four P-38s and knocked down two, including the squadron commander. What I knew was that one Jap had killed McGuire and Rittmayer, had damaged my airplane and wounded our watch. There wasn't a hell of a lot to be happy about.

Thropp landed his damaged P-38, *Evelynn*, at 0755, followed by Weaver 10 minutes later. The unauthorized mission to help McGuire break Bong's record was finally over.

For some reason Weaver and Thropp never met to discuss the mission. Weaver declined to discuss the mission with anyone after he filed his combat report on January 9, 1945. "All he would ever say," recalled Thropp, "was, 'Get a copy of my combat report, it's all in there.'"

Thropp and Weaver would never meet again, even after the war. They were both invited to the dedication of McGuire AFB, but neither could attend. "I tried to get there but couldn't arrange transportation," remembered Thropp, "and Weaver declined to attend. He was working for the telephone company at the time and maybe couldn't get off."

Shortly after the mission was over, Thropp was summoned to the tent of the commander of the 475th FG, Charles MacDonald. Present with Mac-Donald were the three squadron commanders. Thropp was questioned by MacDonald about the mission, with MacDonald's first question being, "What in the hell happened up there, Thropp?" Weaver was also later called to MacDonald's tent and also questioned. This seems to be the extent of any debriefing or investigations into the mission. No official debriefing was conducted by the 475th FG or Fifth Air Force. Why Weaver and Thropp were never brought together and questioned in detail on the mission remains somewhat of a mystery to this day.

Thropp felt that his tactics during the disastrous dogfight had been correct. "In my opinion, the way I flew the fight and what I did in splitting the element on the very first attack was all according to combat procedures." When asked what he would do differently if he could fly the mission over, he replied:

> The obvious thing to do would have been to drop the tanks. This would have given us much greater maneuverability. My airplane drove like a Mack truck with the tanks on. In my mind the drop tanks were the villain. I would also try and guess why in the hell McGuire stayed in the Lufberry. I have often pondered, *Why in hell did he do that?*

Although McGuire could be severely criticized for ordering his flight to save their drop tanks, the command was perfectly logical to him. The whole purpose of the mission was to allow him to get three kills and pass Bong as the ranking American ace. McGuire wasn't interested in downing one Japanese plane; he wanted three or more. When the Americans encountered the lone Japanese plane they were less than halfway to their destination. McGuire probably reasoned that they could easily dispatch the lone Japanese plane and then fly on to Mindoro. With the drop tanks they could have then flown over the fleet for an hour or two. "McGuire knew," according to Thropp, "that we had to fly over the fleet for a pretty long time to allow the land-based Japanese planes time to come up and challenge us." By dropping the tanks over Negros the fighters would have no chance to spend much time over the Japanese fleet at Mindoro. McGuire wanted three victories, not one; the drop tanks were vital to the success of the mission, as he planned it.

Several authors have implied that McGuire's decision to retain the drop tanks may have been influenced by combat fatigue. Thropp gave the following reasons why he felt McGuire was not affected by combat fatigue: "The wish for victories overcomes fatigue. With combat fatigue you're wor-

Lockheed technical representative Al Nelson and Tom McGuire in front of McGuire's P-38, Pudgy V. 475th Fighter Group Museum

rying about losing your life, you fall apart emotionally. No one ever saw Tom McGuire fall apart emotionally, or shirk from combat."

In his combat report Weaver mentioned ground or antiaircraft fire. Either McGuire or his plane may have been hit by Japanese ground fire and this could have led to the fatal crash. Thropp did not observe any ground fire. "But that doesn't mean it wasn't there," he said. "Ground fire usually has to be intensive and tracers to be seen."

It is also worth noting that the Japanese pilots McGuire's flight encountered over Negros were extremely skilled and aggressive. Charles MacDonald once remarked that "the Japanese didn't tend to press home their attacks, like we did." However, both Japanese pilots encountered over Negros pressed home their attacks with skill and daring, to almost pointblank range. Outnumbered and outgunned, they fought bravely and undoubtedly surprised and confused the Americans with their aggressiveness.

The real villain of this sad affair, however, was the mind-set McGuire brought to the mission. Once committed to passing Bong's record at any cost, McGuire was no longer the cool, calculating, experienced squadron commander but a "Zero-happy" pilot who was ready to throw caution to the wind. Like an alcoholic trapped in denial, McGuire was caught in a mental attitude that committed him to a reckless course of action. The result was an overconfidence that led to disaster.

Major McGuire had been flying a spare P-38 the day he went down, and *Pudgy V*, with its thirty-eight little Japanese flags painted on the nose, sat alone on the runway, a reminder that all people, even aces, are mortal. The war still raged and combat planes were always in short supply, so they scraped all the elaborate paint work off the fighter and sent it to another group.

McGuire was awarded a posthumous Medal of Honor for his conspicuous gallantry in action over Luzon on December 25 and 26, 1944, and McGuire AFB in New Jersey was named in his honor. He probably would have received much satisfaction from all of this, but one suspects that what would have pleased him most would have been to have the squadron painter put the forty-first little Japanese flag on the nose of *Pudgy V*.

Chapter 12

Edward "Butch" O'Hare of the Navy

Lt. Comdr. Edward Henry "Butch" O'Hare was the Navy's first ace and the first Navy fighter pilot to receive the Medal of Honor in World War II. Born in St. Louis, he graduated from the US Naval Academy in 1937. During a Japanese bomber attack in February 1942, he shot down five enemy bombers attacking his career, the Lexington. *His courage in warding off this attack perhaps saved the carrier and won for him the nation's highest military decoration. He returned to sea in 1943 as the commander of an air group on the carrier* Enterprise. *He was lost at sea on November 26, 1943, while on a dangerous night mission. O'Hare International Airport in Chicago is named in his honor.*

As the press corps and photographers entered the White House Oval Office they observed President Franklin D. Roosevelt seated at his desk. Grouped around the president were Secretary of the Navy Frank Knox and Adm. Ernest J. King. Standing at attention in front of the president was Lt. (j.g.) Edward Henry "Butch" O'Hare. At O'Hare's right stood his wife, dressed in a trim, tailored blue suit.

President Roosevelt jovially instructed the young officer to stand a little closer to the desk and noted to the assembled group that really two ceremonies would honor O'Hare. Taking up a sheaf of official papers, the president said that they included the orders for O'Hare's promotion to lieutenant commander. These orders, said the president, were signed by Secretary of the Navy Knox, but at the bottom, he, the president, had written, "approved." All O'Hare had to do, the president jokingly announced, was to tear off the bottom part and he would be a lieutenant commander.

According to an account in the *St. Louis Post Dispatch* of April 21, 1942, President Roosevelt, flashing his famous smile, said he now had other and more important things to do. Reaching for a

single sheet of paper, which bore his own signature, he dramatically read that "the President of the United States takes pleasure in presenting the Medal of Honor to Lieut. Edward O'Hare, U.S.N. for service set forth in the following citation."

> For gallantry and intrepidity in the area of combat, at grave risk of his life above and beyond the call of duty, as section leader and pilot of Fighter Squadron 3, when on February 20, 1942, having lost the assistance of his teammates, he interposed his plane between his ship and an advancing enemy formation of nine attacking twin-engine heavy bombers.
>
> Without hesitation, alone and unaided, he repeatedly attacked the enemy formation at close range in the face of their intense combined machine-gun and cannon fire, and despite the concentrated opposition, he, by his gallant and courageous action, his extremely skillful marksmanship making the most of his limited amount of ammunition shot down five enemy bombers and severely damaged a sixth before they reached the bomb release point.
>
> As a result of his gallant action, one of the most daring, if not the most daring single action in the history of combat aviation, he undoubtedly saved his carrier from serious damage.

After reading the Medal of Honor citation President Roosevelt handed it to O'Hare, telling him to hold it in his left hand. Then the president shook hands with O'Hare while the photographers snapped away.

Roosevelt then removed the Medal of Honor from its case and handed it to Mrs. O'Hare, remarking that she had more skillful fingers. While Mrs. O'Hare placed the medal around her husband's neck the president once again shook hands with O'Hare.

Handing the blue morocco case that had held the Medal of Honor to O'Hare, Roosevelt laughed

Edward "Butch" O'Hare near his plane. O'Hare became an early war hero when he attacked a formation of nine Japanese twin-engine bombers that were bearing down on the aircraft carrier Lexington *near the Japanese bases in New Britain on February 20, 1942. For his heroism in breaking up the Japanese attack and saving the carrier, he was awarded the Medal of Honor.* National Archives

and said "that it had been a swell show," according to the account in the *St. Louis Post Dispatch*.

After the 15 minute ceremony O'Hare left the Oval Office with the Medal of Honor hanging from his neck. At the front door of the White House he and his wife were again stopped by the press and asked to pose for photos. After being photographed many times the nation's newest war hero and his wife were able to escape from the crowds and press to a waiting automobile.

The activities of Edward Henry "Butch" O'Hare had not always warranted the attention of the press. He was born in St. Louis on March 13, 1914. He was the son of Edward J. O'Hare, president of the Sportsman's Park Race Track, who was assassinated in gangland fashion in Chicago on

November 8, 1939. He attended the St. Louis public schools and the Western Military Academy in Missouri. He entered the US Naval Academy from the Eleventh Missouri District on July 24, 1933. He graduated from the Naval Academy and was commissioned an ensign on June 3, 1937. After a tour of sea duty he received his aviation training in Pensacola and San Diego.

The advent of war with Japan on December 7, 1941, found Lieutenant (Junior Grade) O'Hare a member of the US Navy's famous Fighting Squadron 3.

VF-3 had a past history as illustrious as that of any aviation squadron in the Navy. Formed on March 10, 1923, it became the first unit to operate from an aircraft carrier when it began operations

The Grumman F4F-3A Wildcats of VF-3 flown by John Thach, in plane F-1, and Butch O'Hare, in F-13. Thach was a great Navy squadron commander. By early 1942 he had over 3,500 hours flight time and had developed useful ideas on fighter tactics. O'Hare *served with Thach after joining VF-3 in 1940 and together they were on the squadron gunnery team that captured the fleet trophy flying F3Fs. National Archives*

on the *Old Langley* in January 1925. Later, in 1928, the pilots of the unit adopted as their insignia cartoonist Pat Sullivan's Felix the Cat, with the famous feline toting a bomb.

VF-3 was a squadron with high morale, largely because of the leadership exhibited by its commander, John S. Thach. Thach was an outstanding squadron commander and a great fighter pilot. He was also an excellent teacher, able to instill learning and confidence in his students.

Thach stressed gunnery and teamwork while teaching fighter tactics. It was a philosophy shared by O'Hare, who had been with Thach since joining VF-3 in 1940. Thach and O'Hare had been on the squadron gunnery team, which won the fleet trophy flying the F3F, Grumman's last biplane fighter and forerunner of the F4F Wildcat. Thach's rigorous training methods eventually produced a group of sharpshooters.

Thach was also an air tactician of the first order. Long before the outbreak of war he had conceived his famous defensive tactic known later as the Thach weave.

This air tactic was so effective in combat against the nimble Japanese fighters that after 1942 virtually every Navy fighter squadron adopted its use, with USAAF pilots learning it as well. It was still being used as an effective combat technique in jet dogfights over North Vietnam, where American pilots had to "rediscover" the tactic. Essentially, the Thach weave is a means for two or more aircraft to cooperate in mutual lookout and defense against opposing fighters.

After developing his weave Thach was excited and eager to present it to the squadron. John Lundstrom, in his book *The First Team*, gave this account of the first test of the weave in simulated air combat:

He [Thach] arranged for a test, taking four planes with him to act as defenders and assigning four other F4Fs under his protege, Lieut. (jg) Edward H. ("Butch") O'Hare, to play the attackers. To simulate the Zero's supposed superior performance, Thach wired the defenders' throttles so they could not obtain full power, giving O'Hare's four a definite advantage. He told O'Hare to try several types of attacks to see how well his new tactics performed under combat simulation. The results were most encouraging. O'Hare found the maneuvers that Thach's defenders used had both messed up his aim and set up shots by the defenders. He [O'Hare] added that it was disconcerting to line up a shot on target that obviously could not see him screaming in, only to have the quarry swing away at the best moment to avoid his simulated firing! The simplicity of the maneuver lay in the defenders turning to sessor [toward each other] whenever he saw his other section turn toward him. There was no reason to signal or radio each other for bearing or instructions. Likewise O'Hare saw the distinct possibilities for return fire by the defenders,

no matter how the attackers tackled Thach's new formation.

O'Hare and VF-3 were in San Diego making ready to leave for Pearl Harbor on December 8, 1941, as part of the carrier *Saratoga*'s air group. When the *Saratoga* arrived at Pearl Harbor the fires were still burning.

The *Saratoga* sailed from Pearl Harbor, recalled Thach in an August 17, 1942, article he wrote for *Collier's* magazine.

And from then on we cruised around the Pacific hunting Japs. One time we were sixty days at sea without coming into port . . . out between Jap bases south of the equator and west of the dateline, hoping we could run into some of the Jap Navy.

Life on board the *Saratoga* settled down into one of routine. Every day the carrier launched combat patrol fighters while other fighter pilots stood alert in the ready room near the flight deck, ready to take off in a matter of seconds if Japanese aircraft were spotted.

One third of the squadron was usually in the air; another third in the ready room, with planes warmed up on the carrier's deck, ready to go; the last third on short notice anywhere in the ship. Thach in a 1942, *Collier's* magazine article wrote:

When the loudspeakers growled "Fighter pilots, man your planes," men on the alert ran to their planes and scrambled into the air. Other pilots around the ship beat it for the ready room with right-of-way over captains, commanders and admirals. I've seen an admiral jump aside when a young ensign yelled "Gangway for a fighter pilot!"

When not flying or on alert the pilots spent many hours in conferences planning tactics and maneuvers, according to Thach.

We pooled all our knowledge, worked out new methods of attack and tried to invent ways of outsmarting our enemy. We never had any illusions about the courage and skill of the Jap fighters.

On January 27, 1942, VF-3 formally joined the USS *Lexington* Air Group in place of VF-2. US naval carrier air squadrons were autonomous units and could therefore be switched from carrier to carrier swiftly and with a minimum of trouble.

On January 31 the *Lexington* and her escorts set sail from Pearl Harbor. Once settled on the *Lexington* the pilots of VF-3 took the measure of the *Saratoga*'s sister ship. According to John Lundstrom in his book *The First Team*.

There was a different and better spirit aboard the *Lex*. The work on the flight deck went on with less noise and delay. The port holes were opened in the daytime so that fresh air entered the ship, and the evening meal was eaten in whites.

Thach felt the air department of the *Lexington* was first class, wrote Lundstrom in *The First Team*.

"The *Lexington* was a ship administered in every way to enhance the value of the air group. The training of the air group at sea in gunnery and bombing was given high priority."

The *Lexington* left Honolulu as a single-carrier battle force, serving as the flagship and center of a formation of almost a dozen other warships. As soon as it cleared the channel leading out of Pearl Harbor the escorts were far ahead, searching about to be sure the waters were clear of Japanese submarines.

The *Lexington* and her escorts, called Task Force 11, had orders to sail to the South Pacific. Vice Adm. Wilson Brown, who was commanding the strike force, had decided to make a bold attempt to run in within 200 miles of Rabaul, the principal harbor on the island of New Britain. He proposed to deliver a surprise air attack on Japanese shipping concentrations anchored there.

At dawn on February 20 the *Lexington* was within 400 miles of her goal. The task force had not yet reached the point where it would swing to the

Lt. Edward Henry O'Hare, left, and Lt. Comdr. John S. Thach. After his epic air battle to save the Lexington *the national press made O'Hare a war hero and the rest of his squadron members could not resist kidding him about his newfound fame. "We all asked him for his autograph," wrote one of the squadron members. "He took it well and I feel he deserves the publicity he got."* National Archives

southwest for the final approach to the target in order to attack at daybreak the next morning.

Writer Stanley Johnson, who was on board the *Lexington,* described the approach to the target in his book *Queen of the Flat Tops.*

> The whole force was moving in fast, tensed for the effort that was plotted out to the last detail. Everyone in the little fleet knew they were in Japanese waters and every mile was taking them closer to battle and unknown and unforeseeable dangers.
>
> All around the Lexington her long range scouts were scanning the waters, the islands and the skies for enemies.
>
> Over breakfast there was a lot of speculation on the day's outcome. The airmen looked forward to the coming trial with confidence. This was exactly the sort of mission they had been fulfilling in their practices and they were anxious to have an opportunity to carry out the operation with live bombs, real torpedoes and, above all, to have Japanese vessels as their targets.

Nearly 400 nautical miles out of Rabaul the *Lexington*'s radar developed a contact 35 miles to the south. Captain Sherman, skipper of the *Lexington,* ordered Thach's 1st Division to scramble. The *Lexington* swung into the wind to launch the six Grumman fighters.

Once in the air Thach received radio orders to destroy the Japanese snooper. "Lieutenant 'Butch' O'Hare was leader of my second section," wrote Thach. "He and the third section leader started to follow me out but as there was only one enemy plane I motioned them back, much to their disappointment and continued on with my wing man." The Japanese plane was about 20 miles from the task force and on spotting Thach flew into a large bank of cumulus clouds. Thach followed and after a long chase through the clouds shot down the big four-engine bomber, a Kawanishi flying boat.

Less than an hour later another four-engine Kawanishi was discovered on the opposite side of the fleet. The *Lexington*'s fighters found it at 6,000 feet and shot it down in flames, but not before it had notified its base of the presence of the American fleet.

The fighters returned to the *Lexington* and were refueled and rearmed. "As they sat down to lunch it was generally agreed in the wardrooms that there would be a fight that afternoon. The Japs could be expected to make some sort of an effort to attack our ships, probably by aerial assault," wrote Thach in *Collier's.* The pilots had guessed correctly: the assault would come that afternoon and the *Lexington* would be the first major carrier on either side in the Pacific to absorb a major land-based air attack. That the *Lexington* survived was due almost entirely to the bravery of the pilots of VF-3.

The attack began at 1630 as Mitsubishi 64Ms of the Imperial Navy's 4th Air Group approached.

These were the first Bettys encountered by the US carrier pilots. "Then came nine Jap bombers," remembered Thach in *Collier's*, "beautiful, fast, twin-engine jobs looking like B-26s."

The Japanese Betty was powered by a pair of 1,530 hp radial engines. Flown by a crew of seven, it was armed with four 7.7 mm Lewis machine guns—one in the nose, one in the dorsal blister and one in each beam blister—and a 20 mm cannon in the tail. The bomber had a maximum speed of 266 mph. Its range was phenomenal, offering a radius of action with payload of 600 miles. About 2,000 pounds of bombs or one aerial torpedo could serve as the bomb load. Like other Japanese planes it had little armor and no self-sealing fuel tanks. "The crews," wrote John Lundstrom, "themselves christened their bomber with the endearing titles of *hamaki* (Cigar) and Type 1 Lighter."

Unfortunately for the Japanese, no aerial torpedoes were available for the attack on the *Lexington*. The bombers would be forced to make horizontal bombing runs, with a payload of two 250 kilogram bombs per aircraft.

The Japanese bombers approached dangerously close to the *Lexington* before they were intercepted by the carrier's fighter escort. In a running fight three Bettys were shot down before the Japanese formation arrived over the *Lexington*.

Two more were downed during the ensuing air battle, and three of the remaining four were shot down on their retreat.

During the Japanese attack, Butch O'Hare and Lt. Marion Dufilho were kept in reserve. Fourteen of VF-3's sixteen operational fighters were committed to battle and two of these were shot down. Thach observed a direct hit on one F4F's canopy and watched the Grumman dive into the ocean. The other pilot was rescued, wounded.

At 1700, just a half hour after the first radar contact, another threat appeared on the *Lexington's* radar. But this time it was much closer and on the disengaged side of the task force. Nine miles to the east, eight more Bettys were coming in—the second wave from Rabaul, completely unopposed.

The only fighters available to intercept were O'Hare and Dufilho. Seven other F4Fs were to the west pursuing what was left of the Japanese first wave. Five other Wildcats under the command of Don Lovelace circled at low altitude around the *Lexington*, waiting permission to land. These Grummans were almost out of fuel. The carrier's flight deck crew worked frantically to clean the deck to bring them on board.

O'Hare and his wingman first encountered the Japanese bombers only a few miles astern of the *Lexington* and her sister ships. Coming downhill in

Japanese lieutenant Ito's Betty trying to crash into the Lexington *after Butch O'Hare had shot away the bomber's left engine. In only 4 minutes O'Hare made three passes and shot five of the attacking Japanese bombers out of formation.* National Archives

a shallow dive, the eight Japanese bombers were closing fast. Luckily, O'Hare benefited from an altitude advantage of a few thousand feet in which to set up his interception.

In an April 1942 interview with *Life* magazine O'Hare described his initial contact with the Japanese attack force:

> I first contacted them about 12 miles away from the ship. They were flying fast and straight, straight for the carrier which they had apparently been ordered to get at all costs. Counting several machine guns and a cannon on each plane I figured I had to worry about 27 different guns—not all at once of course. I got above them and prepared for the first group to pass.

Making his first firing pass, O'Hare singled out as his target the right trailing bomber in the right V. "I knew my wingman had dived away," recalled O'Hare in Johnson's *Queen of the Flat Tops*, "but there wasn't time to sit and wait for help. Those babies were coming fast and had to be stopped. In the first run I fired into two."

The results of O'Hare's deadly shooting soon began to tell on the Japanese bombers. "Quickly I dropped, pressed the trigger and saw two of them get hit and drop out," wrote O'Hare in a 1942 *Life* magazine article. "They burst into flames and fell."

O'Hare then crossed to the other side of the Japanese bomber formation. After firing into the port engine of a bomber, according to the account in Johnson's *Queen of the Flat Tops*, O'Hare "pulled away slightly while this third plane skidded violently and fell away, then went back in and fired into the trailer of the middle V, still shooting at the engines."

A fourth bomber soon fell victim to O'Hare's marksmanship. As he related in the April 1942 *Life* magazine article:

> It seems as if all you need to do is to put some of these .50 caliber slugs into the Jap engines and they come apart and tear themselves right out of the ships. The engine fell out of this fourth plane, too, and I could see the plane commence to burn.

As O'Hare started into his third firing pass the Japanese planes began their bomb run on the *Lexington*. Soon the sky was filled with black shell bursts as the gunship's 5 inch guns came into action. The Japanese bombers were still in formation as O'Hare selected the lead bomber for his next target. Closing within pointblank range, O'Hare watched as his machine gun bullets tore into the bomber's port nacelle, which flared up and exploded. The bomber's big, twin-banked radial engine actually wrenched loose of its mountings and dropped away. So violent was the blast that Japanese in the other aircraft later reported that the lead bomber had suffered a direct hit by an antiaircraft burst. Trailing thick, black smoke, the lead bomber careened left and fell away.

After watching the fifth bomber leave the formation, wrote Johnson in *Queen of the Flat Tops*, O'Hare "gave the remaining four a general burst until [his] ammunition was exhausted."

> My whole action took only 3 or 4 minutes [recalled O'Hare]. They tell me there were sometimes three falling planes in the air at once. I was still worried, though, because what Jap planes were left got through to the carrier.

While O'Hare was making his firing runs on the Japanese bombers Thach and several of his original group of six had turned and were heading at full speed back toward the Japanese bomber formation.

As Thach and his fellow pilots closed in they could see O'Hare. In Johnson's *Queen of the Flat Tops*, Thach noted that he was making his attacks

> with perfect flight form, exactly the way that we had practiced. His shooting was wonderful—absolutely deadly. At one time as we closed in I could see three blazing Japanese planes falling between the formation and the water—he shot them down so quickly.

Thach marveled, in *Queen of the Flat Tops*, that O'Hare could press his attacks so close to the Japanese planes and still survive. "Each time he came in, the turtle-back guns of the whole group were turned on him. I could see the tracers curling all around him and it looked to us as if he would go at any second. Imagine this little gnat absolutely alone tearing into that formation."

After O'Hare's last attack the four Japanese planes left reached their release point and dropped their bombs toward the *Lexington*.

Captain Sherman was standing on the bridge watching the four-plane formation closely. He saw the bombs fall away from the Japanese bombers and judged their probable course.

"Hard aport," Sherman ordered the helmsman. As the big carrier, traveling at 25 knots or faster, started its swing some bombs landed within 50 yards of it but did no damage.

The Japanese attack over, the *Lexington*'s harried plane handlers rearranged the deck for recovery operations. Soon nine F4Fs were lined up in a landing circle awaiting their turn to land. Upon landing, they would receive a grateful reception. Topside on board the *Lexington* the savage air battle had unfolded before excited officers and crew. According to John Lundstrom's book *The First Team*, Vice Adm. Wilson Brown "later remarked that it was necessary to remind his staff that this was serious business and not a football game, so vociferously did they whoop with every kill."

As O'Hare landed and taxied his F4F to a spot on the deck, the crew of the *Lexington* mobbed him in their wild enthusiasm. O'Hare, wrote Lundstrom in *The First Team*, revealed how nervous he had been during the whole ordeal: "When the fight was over I thought I'd lost my voice. I screamed in the cockpit to see if my voice was O.K. It was. Only the transmitter had gone sour."

After landing, all O'Hare wanted was more bullets and a drink of water; he was ready to go up after the Japanese again. Someone pulled him from the excited crowd of admirers and led him up to the bridge of the *Lexington,* where Vice Admiral Brown and Captain Sherman offered their sincere congratulations.

Although the Japanese had lost eighteen of the twenty planes they sent to attack Task Force 11, the way they pressed home their attacks made a strong impression on Thach, according to Johnson, writing in *Queen of the Flat Tops:*

> Those Japs came in with great determination. The first lot went right for the *Lex.* They never hesitated a second, despite our attack, until their leader was shot down. . . . The second nine never faltered and came right on in to the bitter end, even though O'Hare was eating them up from behind and we were coming in from ahead.
>
> The morale of the Japanese was shown by their ability to hold formation and keep their line headed toward the *Lex* without maneuvering in any way. . . . They held onto their bomb loads until they were shot up or burning or beginning to fall. Another thing: none of them attempted to leave the burning planes by parachute.
>
> O'Hare's firing was a real record. We figured that he used only about sixty rounds to each of the planes he knocked down. That, of course, is deadly shooting.

O'Hare became a national hero for his determination and bravery in protecting the *Lexington* from enemy attack. Newspapers throughout the United States highlighted their front page with accounts of his heroism. The March 4, 1942, front page of the *Chicago Tribune* was probably typical:

> A thrilling account of an attack by 18 Japanese heavy bombers on a United States aircraft carrier and other warships in which 16 of the enemy planes were shot down was told by the Navy tonight.
>
> A lieutenant junior grade, Edward H. O'Hare of St. Louis, 28, shot down six of the planes. The other 10 were accounted for by other fighting planes from the carrier, two of which were lost, and by anti-aircraft fire from the warships.
>
> The carrier and the other ships—cruisers and destroyers—suffered not a scratch.

On March 16 Vice Admiral Brown's Task Force 11 set course for Pearl Harbor. During the homeward voyage, the weather was generally excellent and the carrier planes did little flying, offering the opportunity for rest and a chance to catch up with required reports and paper work. Although Thach was recommended for the Navy Cross for his part in the air battle of February 20, he was more concerned with another award that had been proposed.

Thach and other senior officers felt that O'Hare's action had earned him the Medal of Honor.

Butch O'Hare in his F4F Wildcat. O'Hare was overwhelmed by the publicity he received during his return to the United States. Jeff Ethell

O'Hare soon discovered what Thach was up to, and according to John Lundstrom, writing in *The First Team:*

> Daily Butch begged Thach not to do it. "It'll only mess things up," he insisted. "We've got no use for medals out here. I only did a job. You shot down four Nips yourself that day. I don't want to be recommended for any medal."

On March 26 the *Lexington* launched her air group at 0730 to fly to fields on the island of Oahu. Once in the Hawaiian Islands O'Hare found himself an instant celebrity and faced the ordeal of talking to a multitude of reporters and radio commentators. One such interview held at the Bachelors' Officers' Quarters at Pearl Harbor was probably typical and was recalled by Foster Harley in *Pacific Battle Line:*

> To reporters . . . O'Hare last week told his story. "This is like when I started the attack," he began. "I couldn't talk then either."
>
> "What system of attack did you use?" he was asked.
>
> "Fire till they catch fire," said Butch.
>
> And what did he think about when he found himself up there alone with the nine enemy bombers and his wingman dropping out with jammed guns?
>
> "You really haven't any choice," said O'Hare. "You've got to go in."

O'Hare soon departed the Hawaiian Islands under special orders for Washington, D.C. An April 17, 1942, article in the *St. Louis Post Dispatch* gave the following account of his arrival in Phoenix on his way to the nation's capital:

> 29 year old Lieut. Edward H. O'Hare of St. Louis, the Navy's No. 1 air hero, found many peace time

memories today in the Salt River Valley of Arizona, where he wooed and won his bride of seven months, the former Rita Wooster of Muscatine, Iowa.

"I'm on vacation and, boy does it feel good," said Lieut. O'Hare, after he and his wife embraced at the airport when he arrived by airline from San Francisco last night.

Tears shone in Mrs. O'Hare's eyes as she greeted her husband, whom she had not seen since the war's outbreak.

"Oh, Butch, it's so good to have you here again," she said.

Lieut. O'Hare, [who had downed] six Japanese planes in one afternoon off the Gilbert Islands was anxious for some rest and relaxation.

"Let's not talk about my experiences," he said. "This is a family reunion, you know."

There was much speculation among members of the family, just before O'Hare's arrival, as to his Washington, D.C. mission. Belief was expressed that he might be in line for a high Navy decoration, but O'Hare only laughed when this was suggested to him.

He said he had no idea of why he had been summoned from the Hawaiian Islands to Washington, adding: "In the Navy, you go where you're ordered."

O'Hare flew to Washington, D.C., and on April 21 received the Medal of Honor from President Franklin D. Roosevelt. After the award ceremony O'Hare was scheduled to return home to St. Louis for a parade to be given in his honor.

On April 25 O'Hare and his wife landed at Lambert-St. Louis Field after a flight from Chicago. The April 26, 1942, *St. Louis Post Dispatch* reported that "he was immediately rushed to a mass interview. As he was questioned, he came closer to losing his voice than he did when the nine bombers were shooting at him in the clouds."

After the interview ended, O'Hare and his entourage departed for Sixteenth Street and Washington Avenue where the parade was to form. O'Hare, his wife and his mother were seated in a flag-draped black convertible. Behind came another open car with Mayor William Dee Becker and Lt. Comdr. H. B. Miller of Washington, a public relations officer who accompanied O'Hare to St. Louis. Following were several cars for reporters.

Captured Japanese G4M Betty bomber. In 1942 the Betty was one of the best twin-engine medium bombers in the world. It was nearly as fast cruising at altitude as the F4F flying at maximum speed. The bomber had an enormous range, made possible by *two 600 plus gallon gas tanks located in the wings. The gas tanks were not armored and this was the bomber's major weakness. A hit in either tank would blow up the plane, killing the seven-person crew.* National Archives

The *St. Louis Post Dispatch* gave the following description of the parade:

From a patch of blue sky somewhere south of the equator and west of the dateline in Mid Pacific, Lieut. Comm. Eddie O'Hare, the Navy's No. 1 hero, returned yesterday to his home town to be signally honored....

It was a proud and cordial throng that lined Washington Avenue as the parade got under way from Sixteenth Street a moment before the scheduled start at noon....

Confetti and torn paper streamed from the upper floors of buildings along the parade route.

It was, at Comm. O'Hare's own request, a small parade, but St. Louisans made it a hearty welcome.

Although honored by the St. Louis parade and ceremony, O'Hare was overwhelmed by the intense response accorded him as one of the country's first war heroes. Before returning to duty he took a well-deserved leave.

Late summer of 1943 found O'Hare commanding VF-6, which flew the F6F Hellcat, In *Hellcat*, Barrett Tillman wrote,

O'Hare preached the Bible according to Thach. Teamwork and marksmanship were the virtues O'Hare stressed, and the factors he looked for when selecting a wingman. He settled on Lieutenant (jg) Alexander Vraciu.... The two soon became close friends.

On October 5 and 6, 1943, O'Hare and his Hellcat squadron were part of Task Force 16, which sailed to attack Wake Island. This marked the first time in the war that the Navy was able to put six aircraft carriers together in a single strike force.

During one of the raids on Wake, O'Hare was leading his VF-6 division south of the island when he noticed three Zekes and gave chase. The outnumbered Japanese dove for their airfield, but O'Hare shot one down before they could race to safety. O'Hare's section leader, Alex Vraciu, closed in on a second Zeke and shot it down. The third Japanese fighter landed and lurched to a halt, and the pilot jumped out just in time. The Hellcats were just behind, burning the Zeke and two bombers despite the thick ack-ack fire. On the way back to the carrier O'Hare picked up an airborne Betty below the cloud layer. With his wingman covering him O'Hare pressed home his attack and left the flaming bomber falling toward the sea. It was O'Hare's seventh confirmed victory, and it would be his last.

November 1943 found O'Hare promoted to commander of Air Group 6 on the aircraft carrier *Enterprise*. Once stationed on the *Enterprise* O'Hare had taken a personal interest in flying night flights from carriers.

At this time the Navy was worried about single or small groups of Japanese bombers attacking the carriers at night and hitting them when they were virtually defenseless. To counter this threat O'Hare and other pilots of the air group came up with an innovative idea. Onboard the *Enterprise* was a new radar-equipped Grumman TBF-IC Avenger. At the signal of a Japanese night attack the Avenger would take off and orbit the carrier while two night-qualified Hellcat pilots would form up with it and use its radar to help locate the Japanese planes.

On November 25 and 26 Task Group 50.2 had been subjected to night torpedo attacks by Japanese bombers. On the night of the twenty-fifth the Japanese had apparently been unable to locate the task force, although one of the bombers passed directly over at an altitude of 300 to 500 feet. On the twenty-sixth the Japanese struck again, this time dropping flares. The flares fell too far out to be effective, however. The Japanese started in but withdrew after losing one or two planes to ship antiaircraft fire.

Anticipating a third Japanese attack on the night of November 27, the *Enterprise* launched an Avenger flown by Comdr. John Phillips and Hellcats flown by Lt. Comdr. Butch O'Hare and Ens. Warren Skon.

Once launched, O'Hare and Skon were vectored on a number of courses in search of Japanese planes. They were, however, unable to make any contact. This continued for nearly an hour and by then it had grown so dark that O'Hare realized that they would be ineffective without the help of the radar-equipped Avenger.

O'Hare and Skon spent the next half-hour trying to establish a rendezvous with the TBF, which in the meantime had shot down a Japanese plane. The remainder of the mission was described by Ensign Skon in Charles Cannon's book *Life of O'Hare:*

We saw this plane hit the water and burst into flames while we were still several miles from the TBF. When we had closed on the TBF to about a mile, Lieutenant Commander O'Hare called Lieutenant Commander Phillips and asked him to turn on his red light so that we might join him, and Lieutenant Commander Phillips answered that he was about to shoot down another Betty and didn't like to turn it on. He flashed it on and off, shot down the second Jap plane and then turned it on for us to close on him.... At the time of the join-up Lieutenant Commander O'Hare was about 300 feet and I about 100 feet from the TBF, stepped down slightly below it. We were flying at an altitude of approximately 1,000 to 1,200 feet at the time. I should estimate that Lieutenant Commander O'Hare was about 200 feet from me and on the TBF's starboard stern when the TBF's turret gunner opened up with his .50 caliber. I could still catch Lieutenant Commander O'Hare's position from the turtle-back light, and the tracers seemed to pass between us. Between 5 and 10 seconds after the turret gunner opened up, Lieutenant Commander O'Hare slid out of formation, under and slightly ahead of me.... I could not tell if he was making a run or was out of control and skidding. It could have been the latter. . . . I started to follow him down. He was by this time moving too fast, and his turtle-back light . . . disappeared from sight. . . . It impressed me at the time as unusual that Lieutenant Commander O'Hare should suddenly make a run without calling us to say that he was about to, especially after he and I had spent the last half-hour trying to locate the TBF.

Repeated radio calls failed to elicit a reply from O'Hare, and Skon closed up with Phillips and both began to search for O'Hare. They stayed in the area looking for some sign of O'Hare's plane but all they spotted was a dull yellow light in the water, which Skon felt was a Japanese rendezvous flare that had burned down. Finding no trace of O'Hare the two aircraft returned to the *Enterprise*.

What happened to O'Hare has never been determined. One theory is that an enemy aircraft slipped into the three-plane formation and shot O'Hare down before he could react. Another theory is that Phillip's rear turret gunner fired on O'Hare's Hellcat by mistake or fired on an enemy aircraft and accidently hit O'Hare.

Ensign Skon wrote in Cannon's *Life of O'Hare:*

It never occurred to me that the TBF's gunner had fired at Lt. Comdr. O'Hare's plane, as its tracers at all times seemed to pass between us. I saw no gunfire other than the TBF turret gunner, although nontracer fire might have escaped my notice.

No trace of Lieutenant Commander O'Hare or his plane was ever found. His death was not in vain, however. Admiral Radford, writing in John Aryle's book *The Great Pacific Victory,* believed that during the battle in which O'Hare lost his life the night fighters saved the carriers from "certain torpedo hits."

The United States needed heroes in the dark, early days of World War II. As the Japanese rolled to victory after victory they appeared invincible. O'Hare's heroic defense of his carrier provided a needed lift to home front morale and furnished a likeable hero. O'Hare was not a public relations hero, manufactured to meet the needs of the moment, however. The Navy Cross and the two Distinguished Flying Crosses he was subsequently awarded offer ample proof of his bravery and his dedication to duty and his country.

US Navy personnel in San Diego watch a captured Japanese Zeke being prepared to be testflown in 1942. Butch O'Hare shot down a Zeke during an October 1943 raid on Wake Island. At the time he *was flying an F6F Hellcat. The Zeke had great range and was highly maneuverable but lacked armor plating to protect the pilot and gas tanks.* National Archives

Index